Working-Class Community in the Age of Affluence

It has appeared to many commentators that the most fundamental change in what it meant to be working class in twentieth-century Britain came not as a result of war or of want, but of prosperity. Social investigators documented how the relative affluence of the 1950s and 1960s improved the material conditions of life for working-class Britons whilst eroding their commitment to the shared life of 'traditional' communities.

Utilising an oral history case study of sociability and identity in the Yorkshire town of Beverley between the end of the Second World War and the election of Margaret Thatcher's government, *Working-Class Community in the Age of Affluence* challenges this influential narrative. An introductory essay outlines how sociologists and historians understood the complex social, cultural and economic changes of the post-war decades through the prism of affluence, and traces how these changes came to be seen as deleterious to the 'traditional' working-class community. The book then proceeds thematically, exploring change across areas of social life including family, neighbourhood, workplace and associational life.

This book represents the first sustained historical analysis of change and continuity in working-class community living during the age of affluence. It suggests not only that older social practices persisted, but also that new patterns of sociability could strengthen as much as undermine community. Ultimately, *Working-Class Community in the Age of Affluence* asks us to rethink assumptions about the decline of local solidarities in this pivotal period, and to recognise community as a key feature of working-class life across the twentieth century.

Stefan Ramsden is post-doctoral researcher at University of Hull, UK. After a decade working in the museums sector, he decided to pursue his interest in working-class history through returning to full-time study, and completed a PhD in 2013. Since then he has worked as a history teacher, lecturer and researcher in the University of Hull.

Perspectives in Economic and Social History

Series Editors: Andrew August and Jari Eloranta

For a full list of titles in this series, please visit www.routledge.com/series/PESH

Working-Class Community in the Age of Affluence

Stefan Ramsden

Routledge
Taylor & Francis Group

LONDON AND NEW YORK

First published 2017 by Routledge

2 Park Square, Milton Park, Abingdon, Oxfordshire OX14 4RN
52 Vanderbilt Avenue, New York, NY 10017

Routledge is an imprint of the Taylor & Francis Group, an informa business

First issued in paperback 2019

British Library Cataloguing in Publication Data
A catalogue record for this book is available from the British Library

Library of Congress Cataloging in Publication Data
A catalog record for this book has been requested

ISBN: 978-1-138-20716-5 (hbk)
ISBN: 978-0-367-87479-7 (pbk)

Typeset in Times New Roman
by Taylor & Francis Books

For Amy

Contents

Figures

Acknowledgements

Material from Stefan Ramsden (2016) 'The Role of the Industrial Workplace in Working-class Community, 1945–1980', *Family & Community History*, 19:1, 34–49, copyright © Family and Community Historical Research Society, reprinted by permission of Taylor & Francis Ltd, www.tandfonline.com on behalf of Family and Community Historical Research Society. Original article available from: http://www.tandfonline.com/loi/yfch20.

Material from Stefan Ramsden (2015) 'Remaking Working-Class Community: Sociability, Belonging and "Affluence" in a Small Town, 1930–80', *Contemporary British History*, 29:1, 1–26, reproduced by kind permission of Taylor & Francis Ltd. Original article available from: http://www.tandfonline.com/loi/fcbh20.

The names of all interviewees conducted by the author and quoted in this book have been changed; the author also refers to a small number of interviews conducted and held by the East Riding of Yorkshire Council Museums Service; these interviewees are named, in accordance with the permissions given to East Riding of Yorkshire Council.

Abbreviations

CLB	Church Lads' Brigade
CWG	Cook, Welton and Gemmell, company operating Beverley Shipyard from the early twentieth century until 1963
ERALS	East Riding of Yorkshire Council Archives and Local Studies Service
ERYMS	East Riding of Yorkshire Council Museums Service
HMSO	Her Majesty's Stationery Office

1 Introduction

Vic and Sarah Baker brought up four children during the 1960s and 1970s in the small Yorkshire town of Beverley. Both worked full-time in a local tannery, Vic taking as much overtime as was available. In 2010, the couple recalled what had motivated them to put in these long hours:

> Sarah: If I could have afforded to stay at home, I would have done, but you went for the money. You could put a bit more on the table, maybe put an extra bun on the table. You lived a little bit better. We did it to try and have a better life for ourselves ...
> Vic: Doing what we did, we could afford to run a little car. And of course, we went out all over the place with them [their children] ... that was what you could afford to do. When you got there you might treat them to an ice cream ... . When things really got better, we used to go to Yarmouth every year.

But the payoff for a long week in the tannery was not only better provisioned home and enhanced family leisure – sociability was also an important part of Vic and Sarah's 'better life':

> Vic: You wouldn't have had much of a social life if you didn't [work so hard] ... .
> Sarah: Saturday was your main night out ... we used to meet up with our friends ... .
> Vic: We didn't all work together, so you'd catch up with local gossip ... there'd be eight, maybe nine of us.

The twenty-five years from 1950 to 1975 saw many among the working classes achieve lifestyles that were a definite improvement on what had gone before. Full employment, rising wages, a profusion of consumer products and a vastly expanded welfare state meant that, in Eric Hobsbawm's words, 'for the first time in history, most workers in Britain have been able to live a life worthy of human beings' (1984: 193). Social investigators in 1950s and 1960s Britain were keen to audit the social and cultural impacts of this new prosperity, heralded as an 'age of affluence'. According to many, material abundance brought a new world of choice: casting off the restrictive mores and self-discipline of Victorianism, the working classes adopted an unashamedly consumerist approach not only to material acquisition but also to lifestyle and culture. Workers abandoned their 'traditional' communities in search of improved housing and higher earnings, turning from the communal life of the streets to the private life of the home. The first generation of historians of post-war working-class life did not demur from this basic narrative, but more recently historians have begun to reassess the impacts of 'affluence'. This book contributes to this reassessment by presenting the first sustained historical analysis of change and continuity in working-class community living during the age of affluence.

The book draws on more than 100 oral history interviews with ninety-three residents of Beverley, East Yorkshire, to tell the story of working-class people remaking community-of-place in ways appropriate to changing material conditions across the three post-war decades. Exploring in depth the experiences of those who lived through the age of affluence in one town allows us to see community life in the round, revealing richness, complexity and paradox. Of course, Beverley was no more 'typical' than Bethnal Green, Luton, Featherstone, Brighton, or any of the other towns and cities on which sociologists and historians have based their case studies. Indeed, it is Beverley's differences from many of the sites of well-known studies that make the town particularly interesting as a vantage point for considering the impact of affluence on working-class life: post-war social investigators were fascinated with new patterns of social life on the suburban council estates to which many among the working classes migrated across the post-war decades; however, because Beverley was a small town, the move to new estates had a relatively muted impact on social networks and sociable practices, allowing us a clearer view of the effects of other material changes.

In this introductory chapter I show how contemporary social investigators portrayed post-war affluence as deleterious to what they saw as 'traditional' working-class community, and explore how this portrayal has influenced historians. I argue that specific claims about post-war working-class community should be seen in the context of wider theoretical assumptions about the social impacts of modernity, and outline grounds for resisting narratives of community decline. Finally, I detail the methodological assumptions relating to class, community, oral history and case-study research that underpin the discussions in this book.

Affluence and the working classes

In 1950s and 1960s Britain, practitioners of the emerging discipline of sociology fixed their attention on the everyday life of working-class people.

Struck by the social, economic and cultural changes that seemed to be erupting everywhere around them – the replacing of crumbling Victorian terraced streets with vast new housing estates, the proliferation of consumer goods including cars and televisions, an apparent decline in traditional values – investigators sought to capture, measure and comprehend the changing texture of British life through the methods of social science, including survey, interview and observation. Investigators documented what they saw as the vanishing traces of an old, pre-war world – the ways of life of the 'traditional' working classes – giving way to a new world of expanding material, social and cultural horizons, for which the single noun 'affluence' became shorthand. The designation of the 'age of affluence' as the threshold of a new epoch in the social history of the working classes has had enduring influence.

Few historians dispute that the third quarter of the twentieth century saw significant advances in material wealth for many in the western world, and that along with prosperity came social and cultural change. Following the Second World War, Britain endured several years of 'austerity' as the government sought to address economic problems caused by wartime debt, imposing tight controls on domestic consumption and encouraging industry to manufacture for export. Austerity began to turn to prosperity in the early 1950s, when American Marshall Aid spending in Europe, the devaluing of the pound and global economic buoyancy helped Britain to become more prosperous. Rationing finally ended in 1954 (Bernstein 2004: 50). By the later 1950s, full employment, economic growth, rising wages and increased consumption meant that commentators were beginning to speak of an 'affluent society' (Galbraith 1958; Zweig 1961). However, by the 1970s, a series of economic shocks (including the 1973 oil crisis) and a precipitous decline in British manufacturing brought to an end a period of economic growth that had been more-or-less continuous since 1945 (Black 2000: 236). Many historians would agree with Hobsbawm (1995: 257–8) that the prosperity of the third quarter of the twentieth century 'broke all records'; the two decades from the mid-1950s until the middle of 1970s are often referred to as the 'age of affluence' (Taylor 2005; Hollow 2014).

That the British working classes participated in the gains of this age of affluence seems relatively uncontroversial. Between 1951 and 1974, real wages (that had already been rising in the inter-war period) roughly doubled (Bernstein 2004: 308). Across the 1950s alone, the average British weekly wage increased from £6 8 shillings to £11 2 shillings (Hollow 2014: 4). In contrast to the periods before and since, a political consensus favouring full employment helped to keep jobless percentages 'abnormally low' – below 2 per cent for the first two decades after 1945, rising only to 5 per cent of the workforce in 1976 (Gazeley and Newell 2007: 265). Furthermore, the welfare state that William Beveridge had promised in his 1942 report was largely implemented by the post-war Labour government. This included state payments for the sick, unemployed, elderly and low earners (Bernstein 2004: 308–9). In addition, the launch of a National Health Service in 1948 benefited those who might otherwise have struggled to pay for health care. As a result of these changes, indicators of absolute poverty showed significant decline. For example, Seebohm Rowntree found that only 2.8 per cent of the population of York lived below his calculated poverty line in 1950, down from 31 per cent in 1936 (Bedarida 1991: 212). Such improvements were to continue – between 1945 and 1975 infant mortality rates more than halved (Wilson 2006: 217).

The conditions of the working classes were also ameliorated by improvements in the quality of the national housing stock. The slum clearances of the interwar period continued at an accelerated rate after the war; local authorities built 3,761,239 homes between 1945 and 1970 (Hollow 2014: 2). The private sector provided just as many new houses, and the proportion of homes in owner-occupation rose from one third in England and Wales in 1951 to two thirds in 1991 (Bernstein 2004: 313). By the early 1960s, the scale of construction had significantly altered the topography of many British towns and cities, as Kynaston (2015: 446) notes:

> for all the obvious importance of long-established cities, the fact was that a rapidly increasing number of people – probably at least several million – were now living in a wide variety of new (or newly expanded) towns and housing estates on the periphery of those cities, or even well outside them.

Occupants furnished their new homes with an ever-increasing array of consumer goods. Spending on domestic appliances (vacuum cleaners, washing machines, cookers and a host of new electrical goods including toasters, coffee percolators and hairdryers) increased from £189 million to £1,268 million in the ten years after 1945 (Hollow 2014). Whereas hardly any British households had a television in 1945, by 1960, 82 per cent owned a set (Bernstein 2004: 313; Kynaston 2015: 529).

New spending power was apparently connected to changing behavioural patterns in relation to leisure and work. Car ownership (14 per cent of British households had a car in 1951, rising to 52 per cent in 1970) allowed families to take weekend and evening trips away; higher wages and paid holidays (by the 1960s most workers were given two weeks) allowed many to travel away from home for annual breaks, and by the 1960s an increasing proportion of the population were taking holidays abroad (Bernstein 2004: 308, 313, 317). Similarly, numbers dining in restaurants increased through the 1960s and 1970s (Marwick 1998: 793). On the other side of the balance sheet, there was a decline in cinema attendance during the 1950s and 1960s, and British pubs were closing at the rate of one each day in 1961 (Kynaston 2015: 527). Just as changing leisure patterns can be linked to rising prosperity, so too can working patterns. As Vic and Sarah Baker's testimony quoted at the beginning of this chapter suggested, working-class people won their share of the spoils of affluence through hard work: the post-war decades saw a significant rise in both male overtime and in women's work outside of the home (22 per cent of married women in Britain were in work in 1951, rising to c.51 per cent in 1971) (Todd 2008; Rule 2001; Wilson 2006: 209).

Less measurably, many commentators consider that post-war prosperity helped bring about a culture of choice and individualism that increasingly inflected social life (Bedarida 1991: 257; Offer 2008). A relaxation of traditional restraints was evident, particularly during the 1960s, in the proliferation of youth subcultures, new artistic and musical forms, increasingly liberal social attitudes and challenges to taken-for-granted gender roles (Bernstein 2004: 275–325; Marwick 1990: 141–53). Kenneth Morgan (1992: 255) points out that:

> during the early Wilson years the idea of 'the permissive society', focusing especially on images of 'swinging London' became common currency. Tourists came to London to gaze at an affluent society throwing off the Victorian shackles and the legacy of post-war austerity and puritanism and expressing itself in a startling and revolutionary way.

As the above quote implies, the throwing off of Victorian shackles was perhaps less vigorous in the provinces. However, the loosening of social constraints became legal reality through a series of parliamentary Acts that helped to define the 'permissive society'. These included: the Betting and Gaming Act (1960), the Abortion Act (1967), the National Health Service (Family Planning) Act (1967), the Sexual Offences Act (1967), the Divorce Reform Act of 1969 and the Equal Pay Act of 1970 (Marwick 1990: 141–9). At the same time, British society was becoming more pluralistic in ways that were not domestically driven. Post-war Commonwealth immigration helped to enrich the cultural life of the British Isles, bringing new choice in terms of music, food and youth culture (Bernstein 2004: 293, 427, 520–1; Kushner 1994).

Many British social investigators during the 1950s and 1960s became concerned with documenting and analysing the impact of all of this change on the everyday life of the working classes (Roberts 1999). One count lists twenty-four British studies of British working-class life between 1956 and 1971 (Day 2006: 57, 64). Interest in the working classes seems to have been animated by the sense that this was the class undergoing the most acute change. Initially, however, many post-war investigators of working-class life were struck not by change but by apparent continuity with earlier decades. Young and Willmott's influential 1957 book *Family and Kinship in East London* depicted a lively working-class neighbourhood shaped by a traditional culture with roots in a preindustrial past. These authors had no doubt that this was a 'community', a face-to-face local social and cultural system that shaped the social horizons and allegiances of its residents: 'Bethnal Green … is, it appears, a community which has some sense of being one. There is a sense of community, that is a feeling of solidarity between people who occupy common territory' (Young and Willmott 1962/1957:112–3). The notion that residents of an area of inner-city London were living in settled communities was surprising, since it cut across prevailing sociological wisdom: sociologists had supposed that urban life was inimical to the

dense social networks and cultures of mutual obligation that they largely associated with pre-modern and rural contexts (Day 2006: 91–93; Cohen 1985: 26).

However, community was a theme developed in many other post-war studies.
Of those twenty-four studies of working-class life published between 1956 and
1971 noted above, fifteen dealt in some measure with the subject of community
(Day 2006: 57, 64). Though there were some differences between the accounts,
there was considerable reinforcement of themes also, and in 1965, social psycho-
logist Josephine Klein felt justified in distilling from various studies the key
features of what she and others termed 'traditional working-class communities': close-knit extended families, tightly woven neighbourhood networks,
gender-divided sociability conducted informally in streets, pubs and local
shops, wives' reliance on female relatives living close by (usually mothers) for
social, material and psychological support. She wrote that:

> In these communities, the networks of component families are often so close-
> knit, and the relationships within the local population group so clearly
> distinguished from external relationships, that the local population can
> almost be called an organized group.
>
> (Klein 1965: 128)

Such communities were both setting and guarantor of 'traditional working-class
life', Klein argued, since in places where everyone knew everyone else, and all
shared similar living conditions, the social pressure to conform perpetuated
long-standing cultures.

At the same time as documenting the persistence of 'traditional' working-class
communal living, researchers also suggested that forces of change threatened the
demise of these communities. For Young and Willmott, the key development
was removal of people from old inner-city neighbourhoods to new suburban
housing estates. The first part of their book is given over to a description of
the 'traditional' working-class community in Bethnal Green, where multiple
generations of family members lived close to each other. The second part
depicts life in the new 'Greenleigh' suburban council estate, to which many of
the borough's residents moved (either reluctantly, because their homes were
earmarked for slum clearance, or eagerly, attracted by more salubrious housing).
In Greenleigh, ties with extended family were broken, and the neighbourhood
no longer felt like a community (Young and Willmott 1962/1957: 186–201).
In a similar vein, John Macfarlane Mogey's study of Oxford (1956) emphasised
the effects of movement away from old to new neighbourhoods by contrasting
the communal life of the inner city with the more individualistic life in suburban
estates. Other authors saw rising living standards as the key force eroding
traditional communities, since prosperity freed people from reliance on kin
and neighbours and enabled a refocusing on home and nuclear family. Klein
(1965: 263), for example, quoted Ferdynand Zweig's proposition: "'the higher
the level of prosperity, the higher the fences'". For Richard Hoggart (1958:
340), it was the insidious spread of commodified and Americanised mass

culture – 'full of a corrupt brightness, of improper appeals and moral evasions' – that weakened the grip of the traditional knowledge systems underpinning working-class community.

Though different authors emphasised different forces of change, most saw these as inter-connected. For example, Goldthorpe *et al.* (1969) considered that affluence stimulated choice and new aspirations, therefore encouraging geographical mobility which in turn freed the nuclear family unit from the normative influence of neighbourhood and extended family. Young and Willmott, whilst prioritising the effects of the move to suburban Greenleigh, wrote that such moves simply intensified wider societal changes that were also underway in old Bethnal Green, including a new emphasis on home, 'companionate marriage' and nuclear family (1962/1957: 17–31). Klein agreed, writing that 'the break with tradition which a geographical move entails allows other social forces to make a relatively more forcible impact' (1965: 220). For these writers, affluence, or at least the easing of material want, was integral to the changes they posited: post-war prosperity helped remove the social and economic conditions to which 'traditional working-class community' had been the cultural response, and enabled new attitudes, aspirations and practices relating to the home, family, leisure and sociability. Indeed, for many social investigators of the 1950s and 1960s, it made sense that rising prosperity would result in cultural change since class culture was rooted in economic and material circumstances (Klein 1965: 209–16; Hoggart 1958: 72–101). As post-war affluence seemingly eroded outward differences between the working and middle classes, particularly in terms of consumption patterns, many observers felt that class perceptions of society would disappear (Abrams, Rose and Hinden 1960). For Zweig (1961: 212), the new material conditions of working-class life were already leading workers to adopt middle-class lifestyles and values: 'The acquisitive society has succeeded in expanding its frontiers and converting its natural antagonists to its own creed'. This view became characterised as the 'embourgeoisement thesis'.

The 'embourgeoisement thesis' was tested and convincingly disproved by John Goldthorpe's research team studying affluent car-plant workers in 1960s Luton (Goldthorpe *et al.* 1969). Nevertheless, this team upheld the idea that affluence was shaping working-class culture into new forms. Goldthorpe *et al.* observed that many of the workers in the Vauxhall plant had moved away from 'traditional' communities of the kind described by Klein in order to earn high wages in a non-traditional industry (1969: 86). The researchers argued that these workers had chosen 'privatised' lifestyles:

> Some of the values that sustain the communal, kin-based sociability of the traditional type of working-class community were no longer dominant ... primacy was clearly given to the material well-being, the social cohesiveness and the autonomy of the conjugal family over against the demands or attractions of wider kinship or community ties.
>
> (Goldthorpe *et al.* 1969: 108)

Furthermore, instead of seeing the social world divided along quasi-tribal lines – the 'us' and 'them' of class or community – these 'privatised' workers increasingly conceptualised social distinctions as rooted solely in differential earning power. The Luton team's *Affluent Worker* study, amongst the most respected and influential post-war investigations of working-class life, put empirical and theoretical flesh on the skeleton of the 'new' working classes through elaborating the concept of 'privatism'. However, as we have seen the 'privatised worker' they posited was foreshadowed in earlier accounts: the rise of the 'companionate marriage' and a refocussing of attention away from the broader community and extended family onto the home and the nuclear family was noted (to varying extents) in books by Young and Willmott (1962/ 1957), Zweig (1961), Hannah Gavron (1966) and Ronald Fletcher (1966). In Klein's words: 'The neighbourly tie is weakening as the family tie becomes stronger' (1965: 224).

So, although the body of work produced by social investigators during the post-war period was varied, some common themes emerged. Authors shared a strong sense that post-war change was significant and epoch-changing: new lifestyles associated with 'affluence' appeared abundantly clear, the social and cultural impacts of slum clearance and suburbanisation were undeniable and traditional working-class life as it had long been lived in close-knit, communal neighbourhoods was fading as workers focussed on enjoying home comforts, nuclear-family privacy and their new-found freedom as consumer-citizens.

Historians pick up the baton

Interest in producing empirically rich portraits of everyday working-class life as it was lived in particular communities waned during the 1970s. Theoretical and methodological concerns over the extent to which the many studies of individual communities added up to cumulative knowledge, a crisis in confidence in the concept of 'community', alongside a general sense that true community required a degree of isolation that was no longer possible in an era of mobility and mass communication, led sociologists to move away from the genre (Day 2006: 51–2). Nevertheless, post-war social investigators have furnished us with many detailed and valuable accounts of the everyday life of the working classes, some of which were highly influential both at the time of their publication – Young and Willmott's *Family and Kinship* reached a mass audience when it was serialised in the London paper *The Star* in 1957 (Kynaston 2015: 20) – and subsequently. Not least, this body of work has proved to be a rich evidential base for social historians of twentieth-century Britain.

In addition to mining the monographs of post-war social investigators for empirical source material, social historians of twentieth-century Britain have often been strongly influenced by these authors' interpretations of change. The notion that the communal life of the traditional working classes was replaced by individualistic, consumerist lifestyles surfaces frequently in historical accounts of the period. For Hobsbawm (1995: 16, 305–6), working-class communities from the late nineteenth century until the early 1950s had been based on mutuality and 'collectivity: the domination of "us" over "I"', and an informal sociability lived in the public spaces of neighbourhoods. The affluence of the third quarter of the twentieth century eroded these communal values, replacing them with 'a society consisting of an otherwise unconnected assemblage of self-centred individuals pursuing only their own gratification'. Hobsbawm (1995: 307) utilised the Luton team's terminology, arguing that 'prosperity and privatization broke up what poverty and collectivity in the public place had welded together'. Similarly, Elizabeth Roberts, one of the few historians to use new empirical research to address the subject of working-class community in the latter half of the twentieth century, considered that older forms of neighbourhood sociability declined in the 1950s and 1960s. She too cited Goldthorpe *et al.*'s description of 'privatised', individualistic workers (Roberts 1995: 14, 199–229). Until relatively recently, much the larger part of the historiography of the British working classes was dedicated to periods prior to 1945, but even this work often utilised the post-war investigators' conceptualisation of change. Ross McKibbin (1998: 164–205) takes from the post-war studies the division of the working classes into 'traditional' and 'new' subcultures, and describes how the 'new' working classes could be found living in interwar housing estates. Similarly, Melanie Tebbutt (1995: 151) commented on the 'process of centralization and privatization in family life which started during the inter-war years'.

Recently, historians have begun to focus squarely on the post-war working classes. Monographs on working-class life in the post-war era by historians such as Ben Rogaly and Becky Taylor (2009), Ben Jones (2012), Selina Todd (2014), Mark Clapson (2012) and Tony Blackshaw (2013) utilise new empirical research (most include oral history interviews) rather than relying on research reported by post-war social investigators. However, the notion that the material changes of the post-war affluent era helped to precipitate a decline in the community life of the working classes is often still present. Ben Jones' treatment of working-class community is finely nuanced, but his work contains assumptions that seem to derive from this canonical narrative. Without citing evidence, Jones suggests that the built environment of new housing estates limited 'everyday sociability', leading to a 'magnified domesticity', and that post-war affluence 'heightened the opportunity for individual and family privacy' (2012: 146, 201). Similarly, Selina Todd asserts that 'post-war working-class identity was predicated on, rather than opposed to, individualism' (2008: 514); David Kynaston, in a passage reminscent of Young and Willmott, laments the loss of community in post-war urban reconstruction:

> A contestant on Wilfred Pickles show Sam Ward, a park attendant living in Dagenham, said 'I'd sooner be back in old Poplar; you can't beat the neighbours.' One can perhaps exaggerate the neighbourliness of those neighbours, but (as in the Gorbals and, in due course, many other

rundown inner-city areas) they were about to be cast to the four winds, as their intimate, intensely human world disappeared for ever.

(2015: 12)

So we see how an influential narrative of community decline established by post-war social investigators has informed the way in which this period is represented in the historiography. For the earlier historians, this influence derived from the fact that the monographs of post-war social investigators were their principal source material. Though more recent historians have conducted their own empirical research into the period, or have looked beyond the published works and interrogated the research archives and inter-view notes of post-war investigators, the 'traditional'/new dichotomy remains attractive as a way of characterising changing patterns of community life.

Community and modernity

In fact, the notion that stable community living was undermined by rapid economic, social and cultural change in the post-war period is a particular iteration of a more general theme. Since the nineteenth-century origins of academic sociology, theorists have sought to understand how social cohesion was impacted by 'modernity' – a set of processes that began to gain pace in post-medieval Europe, intensifying with the industrial revolutions of the nineteenth century, and continuing to find new forms today. Modernity is often associated with an intensified pace of change linked to historical processes including rationalisation, globalisation, urbanisation, industrialisation, mass communication, individualisation, economic liberalisation and the rejection of tradition (Giddens 1990: 1–2; Bauman 2001: 21–32; Gilleard and Higgs 2005: 21–37). Theories about the social impacts of modernity have often juxtaposed pre-modern 'community' – natural, sentiment-based, unconscious social bonds – with the more selective, calculated, instrumental affiliation that pro-liferated as societies became more complex, economies more integrated and networks of interdependency more widely cast.

Two of the founding fathers of academic sociology, Ferdinand Tönnies and Émile Durkheim, each sought to understand dramatic upheavals in European societies at the end of nineteenth century by positing a transition between different types of social tie. Ferdinand Tönnies published his influential articulation of this theme in 1887. Tönnies was concerned with the impacts of modernising processes on social cohesion, and contrasted two types of social tie. *Gemeinschaft* (often translated as 'community') referred to the social bonds based on 'natural' affinities that developed between families, people who lived in close proximity to one another and those who were alike because of shared 'calling' or occupation – kin, neighbours, workmates and friends (Tönnies 1955: 17–26). However, individuals needed to enter into rational exchange to satisfy needs that could not be met through these immediate *Gemeinschaft* relationships. Rational, calculative exchange based on mutual benefit (as, for example, in waged labour) was the basis for the social tie known as *Gesellschaft* ('society' or 'association'). Graham Day notes that, though these were 'ideal types' and each was present in any given society, both Tönnies' own writings and subsequent interpretations have associated *Gemeinschaft* with small-scale, rural and pre-modern social groupings and *Gesellschaft* with more complex, urbanised and industrialised societies (Day 2006: 5).

In a work published six years after Tönnies', Émile Durkheim also implied that modernity militated against community – or, at least, against certain kinds of community. Like Tönnies, Durkheim juxtaposed two types of social tie. The first of these was 'mechanical' solidarity, rooted in homogeneity and shared 'collective consciousness'. Such consciousness was strongest in pre-modern societies where specialisation was relatively underdeveloped, and where collective life – including customs, rites, religion, tradition, laws – was extensive. Durkheim contrasted this with 'organic' solidarity, a term implying the interdependence of different organs within a body: in modern complex societies, characterised by advanced division of labour, extensive specialisation and heterogeneity, society was knit together predominantly through ties between interdependent but distinct individuals. Though Durkheim did not consider that 'organic' entirely replaced 'mechanical' solidarities in modern societies, he did suggest that modernity weakened the collective consciousness on which the latter social bond was based (Durkheim 1984: 64, 84–5, 106, 127–30).

Both Tönnies' and Durkheim's ideas about the impact of modernity on forms of social solidarity were echoed in subsequent theoretical formulations. The influential 'Chicago School' of urban sociologists in the 1920s and 1930s posited modern urban life as antithetical to community – true *Gemeinschaft* was impossible because an individual's work, leisure and domestic lives were separated spatially and conducted with different people (Day 2006: 10; Cohen 1985: 26). Similarly, some post-war British sociologists considered that modern society, which was largely urban, militated against ties of the *Gemeinschaft* type. So, Ronald Frankenberg (1966: 16–21) drew a typological continuum of community, from its strongest in rural settings to its most attenuated in urban settings, measured through indices such as 'role complexity' and 'network density' in each type of context; Elizabeth Bott (1971: 216–7) considered that contemporary families were typically situated amidst a constellation of social ties resembling a loose 'network' rather than a close-knit 'group'. In 1974, Norbert Elias proposed a return to long-range 'process' theoretical frameworks of the kind pioneered by Tönnies and Durkheim, arguing that changing community patterns could only be understood through reference to a wider theory of societal change: 'community bonds change when the structure of wider society changes'. Like Durkheim, he emphasised the historical shift towards increasingly complex societies: 'in less differentiated societies many more functions are performed at the community level than in more highly differentiated societies' (Elias 1974: xxi, xxxii).

Recent social theorists also sound variations on the theme that modernity has compromised, if not destroyed, community. These theorists often posit an intensification of modernity in the later twentieth century, when the flows of ideas, information, people and capital eroded solid identities and undermined allegiance to old certainties of class and community. Like Tönnies, Zygmunt Bauman (2001) associates true community with pre-modern times. He argues that the transition to modern capitalism required destruction of communal ties and obligations in order to set capital free to make profit. During the first, 'solid', stage of modernity (from nineteenth-century industrial revolutions until the latter half of the twentieth century), community of sorts was still possible, since social and economic life was based around relatively stable productive forces. But with the shift to our present, 'liquid', stage of modernity, predicated on consumption, individualisation and constant flux, at best we can hope only for fleeting experiences of community (Bauman 2001: 7, 13, 30; Blackshaw 2013: 32–9). Similarly, Anthony Giddens (1990: 100–20) argues that 'late modernity' has radically undermined the importance of local social ties. This has occurred through a process of 'time-space distanciation' – that is to say, the forces and agencies that influence and sustain our lives are no longer local but instead are spread out in time and space. Furthermore, Giddens posits a 'transformation of intimacy' in late modernity, whereby selective, chosen relationships replace the given, institutionalised bonds of family and community. Interestingly, some authors place the transition to this new phase of modernity in the immediate post-war period with which the present book is concerned. So Tony Blackshaw (2013) pinpoints the generation who came of age in the 1940s and 1950s as an 'Inbetweener' generation, with one foot in the 'solid modern' certainties of class and community, and another in the individualistic, uncertain freedoms of 'liquid' modernity. As a result, he argues that working-class 'Inbetweeners' try to recapture elements of the local communities of their youth, but are doomed to failure because the holistic embrace of these communities is no longer either possible or desirable.

There is, of course, much disagreement amongst the social theorists briefly surveyed above, but they share, along with the more empirically minded post-war social investigators and historians, the notion that 'to find true examples of community one needs to look to the past' (Day 2006: 17). Indeed, the narrative of lost community is deeply embedded in the cultural history of the western world. Like the Garden of Eden from which Adam and Eve were expelled, 'community' is a mythic state of grace from which we have fallen, and each generation imagines a 'golden age of community' situated just out of reach in the past (Williams 1973: 35–45; Allan and Crow 1991: 26). Thus, specific claims about declining working-class community during the age of affluence can be seen in the context of these powerful and recurring 'declinist' narratives running not only through the social sciences but through collective imagination more generally.

Critiques

However, this is not to say that sociologists and historians all agree that working-class community was lost during the post-war age of affluence. It is sometimes argued that the two or three decades following the Second World War saw considerable continuation of 'traditional' patterns. Sociologist Peter Willmott (1963: 111) described how residents reestablished 'fundamental regularities' of working-class life after two decades on the Dagenham council estate in the early 1960s. Historian Rosalind Watkiss Singleton (2010: 38–9) contends that in the Black Country 'post-war affluence impacted minimally upon traditional mores of neighbourliness and community cohesion; kinship networks and matrilocality remained central tenets of life'. Similarly, Clapson (2012: 218), surveying social change on a Reading council estate between 1930 and 2010, pointed to continuities in associational life, arguing that whilst 'some social historians are convinced that the community life and neighbourliness of the working class declined after the Second World War ... the Whitley Estate was perhaps at its most stable between the latter 1940s and the 1970s'. Authors such as Daniel Wight (1993) and Tim Strangleman (2001) show that working-class people continued to draw on local social networks and cultures of communality in post-industrial contexts from the 1980s to the 2000s. Deindustrialisation itself can be overstated; Valerie Walkerdine's description of community in a steel-working town in South Wales in the 2000s could have been written in the 1950s:

> The industrial mode of production, with its central works and terraced housing, together with the historical specificities of the family wage, with women at home, produces a specific sense of time and place in which femininity is performed – in which washing is pegged out, people natter and emotional issues get discussed – as well as a particular gendered affective community.
>
> (Walkerdine 2010: 101)

This perspective suggests that deeply ingrained patterns of communal sociability were adapted rather than abandoned as material conditions altered.

A rather different perspective is offered by critics who consider that the 'traditional working-class community' was largely dreamt up by post-war sociologists. Since, they suggest, the communality of 'traditional' working-class neighbourhoods is heavily exaggerated, we should treat with caution any claims about a collapse of community amidst post-war affluence. Joanna Bourke argued that those positing models of 'traditional working-class community' often extrapolated from the fact of spatial immobility an unjustified degree of place attachment and group identity. Bourke pointed out that 'sense of community' is poorly defined in most accounts and, in any case, is almost impossible to prove: evidence suggests that interwar 'traditional communities' were sites of competition as much as cooperation, and most residents could not wait to escape once better housing became available. 'Working-class community' for Bourke was largely a result of wishful thinking on the part of authors informed either by 'backward looking romanticism' or 'forward-looking socialism' (Bourke 1994: 136–169). Whilst few others are quite so trenchant, many authors consider that the received view of 'traditional' working-class culture is overdrawn. Mike Savage argues that construction of a 'traditional' working class was a discursive necessity; post-war British sociologists sought to establish their discipline as one uniquely positioned to interpret change, and were therefore keen to portray post-war affluent society in terms of 'the bursting out of the "new" and the "vital" from the shell of the old and redundant' (Savage 2010: 163). Jon Lawrence (2013: 285) also considers that post-war social investigators and subsequent historians have fetishised the distinction between supposed 'traditional' and 'new' working classes: 'The idea of a transition from an older, homo-social male culture, rooted in work and leisure, to a new, more family-centred culture was ... ahistorical'. Ian Roberts (1999) writes that the construction of a distinction between traditional and new working classes is itself 'classed'. Most post-war writers on working-class life were either from the middle classes (for example, Willmott and Young), or had risen from working-class origins via the grammar schools (for example, Richard Hoggart (1958), Brian Jackson (1968), Jeremy Seabrook (1973)); as such they were ill-equipped to empathise with the contemporary working classes ('unfamiliarity breeds condescension'), but predisposed to find virtue in older iterations.

A third group of authors do not pronounce specifically on the debate about post-war working-class community, but challenge the broader assumption that modernity erodes locally based social ties and sentiments. Many point out that local sentiment and attachment may change in form without necessarily losing salience. Writing in 1978, Albert Hunter contended that 'mass society' required the creation of new kinds of local allegiance based on affective ties rather than mutual dependence; therefore, instances of community in the present should not be seen as a 'persistence' of an old kind of social bond, destined to decline, but as examples of a new type of social formation (Hunter 2004). For Anthony Cohen (1985), the structural changes of modernity had little impact on community, which he saw as an entirely subjective, imaginary construct. Cohen described how community inheres in sets of mutable symbols that people draw on to communicate their similarity and difference – these symbols can be constantly manipulated to take account of structural change. Though a locality's distinctiveness may appear, to the outsider, to be eroded through integration into mass society, there is often 'a symbolic recreation of the distinctive community through myth, ritual and "constructed" tradition' (Cohen 1985: 37). Interestingly, the notion of community as subjective can result in a reversal of prevailing assumptions about declining communality as modernity progresses. For example, Talja Blokland's oral history with working-class residents of the Hillesluis neighbourhood in Rotterdam suggested that community was actually rather weak in the early and mid-twentieth century, since the neighbourhood was riven by multiple status and religious distinctions. However, she observed that white working-class Hillesluis residents during the 1990s were prompted by a recent wave of immigration to create common ground between themselves by sharing memories of a mythical lost working-class community;

in this way they constructed in the present a sense of community that had been lacking in the past (Blokland 2005). Indeed, many recent sociologists and geographers have sought to restate the importance of the local social worlds following a period in which globalisation theorists assumed the eclipse of the local scale. Savage, Bagnall and Longhurst (2005: 3) consider that it has become 'standard fare' to point out that globalised modernity has not eradicated but instead prompted new manifestations of local belonging.

However, despite the many dissenting voices outlined above, the notion that there has been a decline of community in recent times remains pervasive in popular as well as academic discourse. Thus the *Daily Mail* (28 November 2011) reported the results of a survey conducted by a used-car business:

> community spirit has almost vanished in modern Britain with fewer people prepared to look out for their neighbours or ask them for help ... . Gone are the days when people would have homely conversations over the garden fence or nip round to borrow some milk because the local corner shop had shut.

Then Prime Minister David Cameron echoed media representations of contemporary working-class community by painting British council estates as dark, forbidding places where the only forms of association are those between criminals (Cameron 2016). Influential social theorists regard newer incarnations of community thrown up by a globalised world as somehow inauthentic in comparison with older versions (Lash and Urry 1994; Bauman 2001; Castells 2004). Most pertinently for the subject matter of this book, many historians writing about the working classes during the post-war age of affluence support the view that the social, economic and cultural changes associated with the age of affluence undermined the coherence of working-class communities (Bernstein 2004: 318–20; Bedarida 1991: 251–2; Hall 2012: 1–10; Kynaston 2015: 12; Snell 2006: 4). This is, in part, due to the enduring influence of key works of post-war social investigation, including books discussed above by Hoggart, Willmott and Young and Goldthorpe *et al.* The prominence of the declinist narrative may also result from its logical coherence. Developments associated with modernisation – globalisation, individualism, mass communication, centralisation, consumerism and the decline of absolute poverty – appear to have intensified since 1945 and must surely have impacted on working-class communities. Indeed, simple observation of the world around us often seems to confirm this commonsense interpretation.

Class, community and case-study research

This book contributes to a growing historiography of working-class life in post-war Britain by presenting the first sustained historical analysis of the impacts of post-war 'affluence' on working-class community. The book constructs this analysis through reference to extensive historical research in one particular town – Beverley, in the East Riding of Yorkshire. The aim is to provide a detailed description of community life in the three post-war decades in order to intervene in wider debates through a dialectic of comparison and contrast. The selection of this case-study town is important empirically, since it adds information about a type of context largely missing from discussions of working-class community (the small town). It is also important theoretically, since Beverley's industrial and demographic stability across this period offers a distinctive perspective from which to consider the impact of rising living standards – the story of migration from inner-city neighbourhoods to suburban council estates has dominated much of the sociology and historiography of the period. As a preliminary to the substantive chapters, I offer below brief clarification of my approach to the key concepts 'community' and 'class', an outline of methodological assumptions in relation to oral history and case-study investigations and an introduction to the case-study town itself.

The term 'community' has a wide range of meanings. David Lee and Howard Newby (1983: 57–8) reduced the multiplicity of available definitions to three conceptual strands: community as a geographical definition, referring to people living in a particular bounded space; community as a local social system, suggesting links and relationships between residents of a particular area; community as a quality of social relationships, a feeling of belonging and identity that is summed up by the term 'communion' and need not be coterminous with a particular locality. In this book, we will be concerned specifically with 'community' understood in terms of *local* social relationships and identifications – what is sometimes termed 'community-of-place'. This is because I wish to engage with claims, outlined above, that the 'age of affluence' helped to cause a decline in this type of community.

As both Craig Calhoun and Norbert Elias have pointed out, there is something specific about relationships amongst groups of people who live near to each other and who are caught in 'close-knit' networks (those in which there is a good chance that a person's social contacts will also know each other independently of that person). Calhoun (1998: 390) argued that although we may refer to a range of different types of groupings as 'communities', there is a sociological specificity to 'the life people live in dense, multiplex, relatively autonomous networks of social relationships'. Similarly, Norbert Elias and John Scotson (1965: 101) considered that the 'network of relationships between people organised as a residential unit' was sociologically distinctive. According to Elias (1994), when a group of people live amongst each other for a long time, group norms develop, along with a sense of belonging and identification – a 'we image' becomes part of the 'I image'. My intention here is to take these two dimensions of community-of-place – social relationships and identity – and to consider how the changes associated with the age of affluence may have affected their patterning. However, this book is not about community-of-place in general, but about *working-class* community-of-place. The focus on working-class community arises from the fact that, as we have seen, sociologists and historians have often presented this class as the last refuge of community-of-place in modernity. According to this view, whereas the expanding, mobile middle classes had long based their sociality around more geographically attenuated 'networks', working-class social life remained concentrated at the local scale until post-war affluence began to dissolve their community orientation.

Most authors writing about working-class community have tended to define 'working class' through reference to occupation – citing, for example, the Registrar General's scheme of classification. This scheme, used by the Office for National Statistics between 1911 and 1998, divided society into six groupings of occupations deemed broadly similar in terms of economic and social status, with groups I, II and IIIa containing the middle classes – professionals, managers and white collar workers – and the working classes represented by groups IIIb, IV and V (the skilled, semi-skilled and unskilled manual grades) (Roberts 2001: 23–24). There are undoubtedly problems with defining class in this way; it is difficult to assign a class position to those who move between occupational groupings, and the patriarchal assumptions that underpin classification schemes lead to the misclassifying of many women (Skeggs 1997: 80–81). Furthermore, class would have little resonance if it were no more than a sociological category. Indeed, the concept of class usually also implies subjectivity and identity – which is to say that class operates through social distinctions people perceive and feel. And, as Andrew August (2007: 2) highlights, most researchers no longer presume that identities are directly and unambiguously rooted in socio-economic position. It has often been observed that people avoid class terminology in narrating their own understandings of the social world, instead applying other kinds of social distinctions – referring, for example, to a broad group of 'ordinary' people in contrast to a small elite of the super-wealthy (Klein 1965: 278–81; Skeggs 1997: 74–97; Savage 2005). Neither should *culture* be simply read off economic position, as Jon Lawrence (2000: 315) points out:

> In what sense, we should ask, were cultural practices such as football, music hall, the pools or the fish and chip supper 'working-class'? Such practices were neither universally popular among people conventionally termed 'working-class', nor were they exclusively enjoyed by people in 'working-class' (i.e. 'manual') occupations.

Despite its problems and complexities, class for many authors retains considerable power as an explanatory framework. Sociologists inspired by Pierre Bourdieu contend that class works on a deep level to condition individual subjectivity, informing the plethora of commonsense and commonplace choices that accumulate to reinforce cultural, social and economic distinctions; thus those who reject class labels may still find themselves 'positioned' within classed society (Atkinson 2010: 1–7; Lawler 2008: 125–8; Skeggs 1997: 8–12; Devine and Savage 2005).

My approach to class has been to take a socio-economic definition for the sake of the empirical research. It is difficult to select source material on the basis of subjective understandings of class, since most people most of the time do not make such understandings apparent (Jones 2012: 35). I also consider that, for the period of the study, the heuristic of socio-economic class does not do too much violence to the reality. This is because in the mid-twentieth century the terms 'working class' and 'middle class' were common currency, social mobility was low and it is probable that, in Arthur McIvor's words, 'most people had a deep sense of their class identity' (McIvor 2013:16–17). The model of a social world divided into classes is only one of a number of competing 'images of society', but for many people in the early and mid-twentieth century it was the one that seemed the best fit with their own experience (August 2007: 2–3). At the same time, I do not treat the connection between socio-economic position, class identity and culture during the period of the study as a given – rather than assuming the salience of class, I placed this among the topics for empirical enquiry. Throughout the book I will use the noun 'working classes' rather than 'working class', to indicate my sensitivity to the diversity of working-class positions and identities.

Although records of everyday working-class life do exist (diaries, trade union and associational records, working-class journalism, autobiography), these are unlikely to be present in sufficient quantity and quality to make possible the detailed reconstruction of informal sociability in a given locality. Therefore, this book, like other recent studies, relies extensively on oral history interviews conducted with those whom, during the post-war decades, could have been designated 'working class' using conventional socio-economic criteria. But there are problems associated with using oral history for recovering aspects of historical experience. Many academic oral historians now consider that the subjective dimension that makes oral testimony peerless as a technique for exploring how people interpret and come to terms with their own historical experience renders the method far less effective for recovering 'objective' details about the past (Abrams 2010: 6–7; Thomson 2006). I have sympathy with this viewpoint: There is no doubt that individuals compose memory narratives for particular present-day psychological and social purposes; that these narratives can include 'false memories'; that oral accounts are often deeply influenced by 'cultural scripts' – taken, for example, from the media, popular culture and educational contexts; that the power dynamics of the interview situation shape the testimony in significant ways (James 2006; Abrams 2010: 66–70; Portelli 1991; Popular Memory Group 2006).

Nevertheless, I reject the view that oral history is of little use for recovering historical data. Anna Green (2004) argues that, rather than memory narratives being simply overdetermined by ready-made cultural scripts, individuals creatively select and synthesise elements from diverse and often competing discourses in order to reflect their experiences. She notes a certain hypocrisy in the fact that, while many historians respect the oral testimony of elites – routinely using the reminiscences of artists and politicians as source material – the profession is apparently suspicious of the ability of ordinary people to present useful accounts of their past. Paul Thompson (2000: 137–44, 158–60) counters the notion that memory is inevitably fallible by citing studies that demonstrate how oral narratives can convey details about the past with remarkable accuracy, especially if an event or practice was considered important at the time it was encoded into memory. Thompson goes on to suggest that the specific problems presented by oral testimony can be mitigated through the critical principles historians apply to *all* evidence: 'look for internal consistency ... seek confirmation in other sources ... be aware of potential bias' (Thompson 2000: 119). Neither should the subjectivity of oral history be seen as an advantage only for those researchers investigating contemporary attitudes to the past; like Alessandro Portelli (1998: 38), I found that some interviewees were willing to reflect on how their own assumptions, identifications and beliefs had changed over a lifetime.

So, in conducting the research for this book I assumed that oral history can be used for recovering historical details about the past, but that the data it produces need to be treated with caution. I attempted to counter the distortions inherent in reminiscence narratives in a number of ways. First, I interviewed a large number of people – more than 90 individuals – helping to reduce the impact of any individual misremembering and making it possible to check for consistency across the interviews. Furthermore, I attempted to counterbalance the use of oral history by reviewing qualitative material from newspapers, official records and the archives of clubs and societies. Reading different kinds of sources against each other in this way can prevent an account being too heavily inflected with the sources of bias prevalent in any one type of source material (see, for example, Williamson 2009).

Oral history is aligned with qualitative social research paradigms, meaning that practitioners tend to adopt an exploratory, 'inductive' approach, starting with open rather than closed research questions, and building hypotheses through the data collection process (Yow 2005: 1–15; Ragin 1994: 85). Although neither qualitative research nor oral history methodology require that research interviews are collected from a single locality, a concern with exploring social life in context has led many researchers working within these paradigms to select a case-study approach. As David Sabean observed, 'once we center our attention on relationships, we are forced into research strategies which favour the local and the particular' (quoted in Reay 1996: 260). Through narrowing the focus to one particular locality it is possible to consider the complex inter-action of a broad range of contextual factors and to consider the influence of processes at both local and wider scales on social action (Reay 1996: 257–62). For this reason, much of the research for the present book is taken from a case study of the social history of a working-class population living in one town.

Although case-study research presents many possibilities in terms of exam-ining the multifaceted texture of social worlds, the extent to which findings have broader applicability is always open to question. No single town can ever be deemed 'typical' of the national experience; despite some authors' portrayal of a homogenous 'traditional working-class culture' persisting into the mid-twentieth century, it seems that working-class life varied quite considerably across the economically, geographically and historically diverse terrain of the British Isles (Clarke 1979: 240; Massey 1995; Howarth 2011: 92). However, this does not mean that there is nothing of wider significance to be learned from the individual case study. Just as no town can be adjudged typical of a nation, it would also be wrong to assume that situations and events found in a particular locality do not have parallels elsewhere. A small northern town in the post-war decades, though unique in many respects, was part of a Britain ever more integrated and centralised, and was therefore subject to cultural, economic, political and social influences that were more general (Birch 1959). The challenge for the case-study researcher (indeed, perhaps, for any researcher) is, as Liz Spencer and Ray Pahl (2006: 6) noted, to present 'detailed description of concepts and cases' in order for readers to judge the extent to which findings may be applied to other social milieux. I will attempt to aid the reader in this assessment by using the wider literature to draw points of comparison and contrast.

The town selected for the case study is Beverley, the county town of the East Riding of Yorkshire. Beverley is a small town – its population rose across the period of our study from c.16,000 to c.20,000 (HMSO 1964, 1973, 1984). Beverley sits close to the River Hull, which drains southwards from low chalk hills in the north of the county towards the Humber estuary. Although geographically the town is situated in the north of England, it was never the northern industrial town of popular imagination. Unlike the more rugged upland terrain of western and northern Britain, the East Riding is low-lying, with neither fast-running streams to drive mills nor mineral resources. Therefore, the East Riding economy was dominated by arable farming into the twentieth century, and its towns served as small market centres processing agricultural produce (Caunce 1991: 7–8). But Beverley did have an industrial sector, featuring the kinds of traditional industries (shipbuilding, tanning, engineering) that enjoyed an Indian summer in Britain during the twenty years or so after the Second World War. Indeed, one researcher reported in the mid-1970s that the proportions of Beverley's labour force working in different sectors – primary and secondary industries, construction, services – closely matched national averages (Dodd 1978: 5–6). Just as in many other towns and cities across Britain, Beverley's industrial sector helped underpin a period of full employment from 1945 until the mid-1970s, but declined rapidly in the later 1970s and 1980s.

Beverley is an interesting and worthwhile choice for a case study of community change during the age of affluence for two reasons. First, there is a need to broaden the empirical basis on which our knowledge of working-class social life rests. Existing sociological and historical case studies of working-class populations concentrate on a few settlement types – urban populations in the throes of relocation to suburban estates, locales dominated by a single, emblematic industry such as coalmining, shipbuilding or fishing. The texture of everyday life for working-class populations of small towns with mixed economies has rarely been considered, even though this was a time when just under 30 per cent of the urban population of England and Wales lived in towns with between

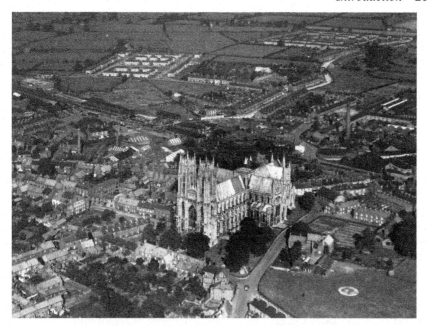

Figure 1.1 Beverley in 1937, looking east: showing Armstrong Patents' factory, Hodgson's tannery and inter-war council housing estates.

10,000 and 50,000 residents (Wood and Carter 2000: 417). Furthermore, whilst there are strong traditions of regional history research focusing on the experiences of working-class populations in industrialised Lancashire (Roberts 1984, 1995; Davies 1992; Glucksmann 2000) and North-East England (Williamson 1982; Colls and Lancaster 2005; Tabili 2011), the East Riding of Yorkshire has received little academic attention. Second, the town offers an opportunity to consider how factors *other* than urban reconstruction may have impacted on working-class community life. The migration of populations from crumbling inner-city neighbourhoods to distant suburban council estates has been central to most sociological and historical accounts of social change across the period; as a result it can be difficult to discern whether the proposed changes to patterns of community life resulted from this dislocation, or from other background factors including rising living standards. In Beverley, although the council participated in the house building that was so marked across the country in the post-war decades, social disruption caused by the move to council estates was much less than in larger towns and cities, since the distance between old and new neighbourhoods was often less than a mile. The fact that the town's working-class population was relatively undisturbed by urban reconstruction allows a greater appreciation of the extent to which other changes associated with the age of affluence impacted on community life.

In order to situate the findings from Beverley amidst wider currents in the literature of post-war working-class life, this book will adopt a thematic approach. Chapter 2, 'Families', takes sociological descriptions of the 'privatisation' of family change during the age of affluence as its starting point, arguing that in fact two distinct models of behaviour in relation to sociability and the family – on the one hand, 'family centredness' and on the other, a separate conjugal sociability with peers and extended family – had long been available to the working classes and continued to be so through our period. Chapter 3, 'Neighbours' notes that, as living standards rose in the post-war period, there was some decline in the extent to which neighbours relied on each other for the provision of essential services and material assistance. But the chapter shows that there were also new ways in which neighbours might cooperate and socialise together. Chapter 4, 'Friends' considers that argument that the age of affluence brought a new emphasis on 'chosen' friends, reducing the social importance of neighbours, family and workmates and therefore weakening the ties of community. The chapter argues instead that friends were part of the constellation of local ties that made place feel socially familiar and helped to create a valued sense of ontological security. Chapter 5, 'Workplaces' points out that the historiography of working-class life in the age of affluence has tended to underplay the role of industrial workplaces, and argues that this is a significant omission: industrial employment reached a peak after the Second World War, and local industry was vital component of social and cultural continuity in many towns. Chapter 6, 'Civil Society and Associational Life', argues that post-war affluence did not lead to any net diminution in participation in local clubs, societies and associations. Through involvement in associational life and local politics, the working classes rubbed shoulders with middle classes, contributing to a local civil society that to some extent transcended class. The final substantive chapter, 'Identity and Place', turns to consider the creation of a subjective sense of community through discourse, ritual and symbol, refuting suggestions that working-class attachment to place in the mid-twentieth century was 'functional'.

The evidence presented in this book offers strong grounds to reject the received narrative that improved material conditions during the post-war 'age of affluence' resulted in a decline in community and a rise in individualistic, 'privatised' lifestyles – that, in Hobsbawm's words 'prosperity and privatization broke up what poverty and collectivity in the public place had welded together' (Hobsbawm 1994: 307). I will argue that such 'epochal' conceptions of change, positing unbridgeable discontinuities between working-class pasts and presents, distract us from recognising important continuities in the ways that class structures social experience. Not least of these continuities is the centrality of community-of-place in working-class life.

References

Abrams, Lynn (2010) *Oral History Theory*, London: Routledge.
Abrams, Mark, Richard Rose and Rita Hinden (1960) *Must Labour Lose?* Harmondsworth: Penguin.

Allan, Graham and Graham Crow (1991) 'Privatisation, Home-centredness and Leisure', *Leisure Studies*, 10:1, 19–32.

Atkinson, Will (2010) *Class, Individualization and Late Modernity*, Basingstoke: Palgrave Macmillan.

August, Andrew (2007) *The British Working Class. 1832–1940*, Harlow: Pearson.

Bauman, Zygmunt (2001) *Community: Seeking Safety in an Insecure World*, Cambridge: Polity Press.

Bedarida, Francois (1991) *A Social History of England 1851–1990*, 2nd edition, London: Routledge.

Bernstein, George L. (2004) *The Myth of Decline. The Rise of Britain Since 1945*, London: Pimlico.

Birch, Anthony Harold (1959). *Small-Town Politics: A Study of Political Life in Glossop*, London: Oxford University Press.

Black, Jeremy (2000) *Modern British History Since 1900*, Basingstoke: Macmillan.

Blackshaw, Tony (2013) *Working-class Life in Northern England, 1945–2010*, Basingstoke: Palgrave Macmillan.

Blokland, Talja (2005) 'Memory Magic: How a Working-Class Neighbourhood Became an Imagined Community and Class Started to Matter When it Lost its Base', in Fiona Devine, Mike Savage, John Scott and Rosemary Crompton (eds), *Rethinking Class. Culture, Identities and Lifestyle*, Basingstoke: Palgrave Macmillan, 123–138.

Bott, Elizabeth (1971) *Family and Social Network: Roles Norms and External Relationships in Ordinary Urban Families*, 2nd edition, Thetford: Tavistock.

Bourke, Joanna (1994) *Working Class Cultures in Britain 1890–1960: Gender, Class, and Ethnicity*, London: Routledge.

Brown, L. (1989) 'Modern Beverley: Beverley After 1945', in K.J. Allison (ed.), *A History of the County of York. East Riding: Volume 6: The Borough and Liberties of Beverley*, London: Oxford University Press, 136–160.

Calhoun, Craig (1998) 'Community Without Propinquity Revisited: Communications Technology and the Transformation of the Urban Public Sphere', *Sociological Inquiry*, 68:3, 373–397.

Cameron, David (2016) 'Estate Regeneration', *Sunday Times*, 10 January 2016.

Castells, Manuel (2004) *The Power of Identity*, 2nd edition, Oxford: Blackwell.

Caunce, Stephen (1991) *Amongst Farm Horses. The Horselads of East Yorkshire*, Stroud: Alan Sutton.

Clapson, Mark (2012) *Working-Class Suburb: Social Change on an English Council Estate, 1930–2010*, Manchester: Manchester University Press.

Clarke, Peter (2004), *Hope and Glory. Britain 1900–2000*, 2nd edition, London: Penguin.

Cohen, Anthony P. (1985) *The Symbolic Construction of Community*, London: Routledge.

Colls, Robert and Bill Lancaster (eds) (2005) *Geordies. Roots of Regionalism*, 2nd edition, Newcastle: Northumberland University Press.

Cooper, Rob (2011) 'Love Thy Neighbour No More' *Daily Mail*, 28 November 2011, (downloaded 1 May 2016 from http://www.dailymail.co.uk/news/article-2067048/ Community-spirit-disappeared-70-admitting-dont-know-neighbours-name.html).

Davies, Andrew (1992) *Leisure, Gender and Poverty. Working-class Culture in Salford and Manchester, 1900–1939*, Buckingham: Open University Press.

Day, Graham (2006) *Community and Everyday Life*, London: Routledge.

Devine, Fiona and Mike Savage (2005) 'The Cultural Turn, Sociology and Class Analysis', in Fiona Devine, Mike Savage, John Scott and Rosemary Crompton (eds), *Rethinking Class. Culture, Identities and Lifestyle*, Basingstoke: Palgrave Macmillan, 1–23.

Dodd, R.M.J. (1978) 'The Changing Structure of Industry in Beverley, North Humberside 1801–1978', BA thesis, University of Durham.

Durkheim, Émile (1984) *Division of Labour in Society*, Basingstoke: Macmillan.

Elias, Norbert and John L. Scotson (1965) *The Established and the Outsiders: A Sociological Enquiry into Community Problems*, London: Frank Cass.

Elias, Norbert (1974) 'Foreword – Towards a Theory of Communities', in Colin Bell and Howard Newby (eds), *The Sociology of Community*, London: Frank Cass, ix–xlii.

Elias, Norbert (1994) 'Introduction. A Theoretical Essay on Established and Outsider Relations', in Norbert Elias and John Scotson, *The Established and the Outsiders. A Sociological Enquiry into Community Problems*, 2nd edition, London: Sage, xv–lii.

Fletcher, Ronald (1966) *The Family and Marriage in Britain*, Harmondsworth: Penguin.

Frankenburg, Ronald (1966) *Communities in Britain*, Harmondsworth: Penguin.

Galbraith, John Kenneth (1958) *The Affluent Society*, London: Hamish Hamilton.

Gavron, Hannah (1966) *The Captive Wife: Conflicts of Housebound Mothers*, London: Routledge & Kegan Paul.

Gazeley, Ian and Andrew Newell (2007) 'Unemployment', in Nicholas Crafts, Ian Gazeley and Andrew Newell (eds), *Work and Pay in 20th Century Britain*, Oxford: Oxford University Press, 225–263.

Giddens, Anthony (1990) *The Consequences of Modernity*, Cambridge: Polity.

Gilleard, Chris and Paul Higgs (2005) *Contexts of Ageing. Class, Cohort and Community*, Cambridge: Polity.

Glucksmann, Miriam (2000) *Cottons and Casuals: The Gendered Organisation of Labour in Time and Space*, Durham: Sociologypress.

Goldthorpe, John Harry, David Lockwood, Frank Bechhofer and Jennifer Platt (1969) *The Affluent Worker in the Class Structure*, London: Cambridge University Press.

Green, Anna (2004) 'Individual Remembering and "Collective Memory": Theoretical Presuppositions and Contemporary Debates', *Oral History*, 32:2, 35–44.

Hall, David (2012) *Working Lives. The Forgotten Voices of Britain's Post-war Working Class*, London: Transworld.

Hobsbawm, Eric (1984) 'The Formation of British Working-Class Culture', in Eric Hobsbawm, *Worlds of Labour*, London: Weidenfeld & Nicolson, 176–193.

Hobsbawm, Eric (1995) *The Age of Extremes 1914–1991*, London: Abacus.

Hoggart, Richard (1958) *The Uses of Literacy*, Harmondsworth: Penguin.

HMSO (1964) *Census 1961 England and Wales. County Report. Yorkshire, East Riding*, London: HMSO.

HMSO (1973) *Census 1971 England and Wales County Report. Yorkshire East Riding. Part 1*, London: HMSO.

HMSO (1984) *Census 1981: Key Statistics for Urban Areas: The North: Cities and Towns*, London: HMSO.

Hollow, Matthew (2014) 'The Age of Affluence Revisited: Council Estates and Consumer Society in Britain 1950–1970', *Journal of Consumer Culture* (downloaded 3 February 2016 from http://joc.sagepub.com/content/early/2014/02/05/1469540514 521083.full.pdf)

Howarth, Janet (2011) 'Classes and Cultures in England After 1951: The Case of Working-class Women', in Clare V.J. Griffiths, James J. Nott and William Whyte (eds), *Classes, Cultures and Politics: Essays on British History for Ross McKibbin*, Oxford: Oxford University Press, 85–101.

Hunter, Albert (2004) 'Persistence of Local Sentiments in Mass Society', in W. Allen Martin (ed.), *The Urban Community*, Upper Saddle River, NJ: Pearson Education, 72–88.

Jackson, Brian (1968) *Working Class Community. Some General Notions Raised by a Series of Studies in Northern England*, London: Routledge & Kegan Paul.

James, Daniel (2006) 'Listening in the Cold: The Practice of Oral History in an Argentine Meatpacking Community', in Robert Perks and Alistair Thomson (eds), *The Oral History Reader*, 2nd edition, London: Routledge, 83–101.

Jones, Ben (2012) *The Working Class in Mid Twentieth-Century England: Community, Identity and Social Memory*, Manchester: Manchester University Press.

Klein, Josephine (1965) *Samples from English Cultures (Volume 1)*, London: Routledge & Kegan Paul.

Kushner, Tony (1994) 'Immigration and "Race Relations" in Postwar British Society', in Paul Johnson (ed.), *Twentieth Century Britain. Economic, Social and Cultural Change*, London: Longman, 411–426.

Kynaston, David (2015) *Modernity Britain. 1957–1962*, London: Bloomsbury.

Lash, Scott and John Urry (1994) *Economies of Signs and Space*, London: Sage.

Lawler, Steph (2008) *Identity: Sociological Perspectives*, Cambridge: Polity.

Lawrence, Jon (2000) 'Review Article: *The British Sense of Class. Class in Britain* by David Cannadine; *Classes and Cultures: England, 1918–1951* by Ross McKibbin; *A Treatise on Social Theory: Volume III, Applied Social Theory* by W. G. Runciman', *Journal of Contemporary History*, 35:2, 307–318.

Lawrence, Jon (2013) 'Class, "Affluence" and the Study of Everyday Life in Britain, c.1930–1964', *Cultural and Social History*, 10, 273–299.

Lee, David and Howard Newby (1983) *The Problem of Sociology*, London: Hutchinson.

Marwick, Arthur (1990) *British Society Since 1945*, 2nd edition, London: Penguin.

Marwick, Arthur (1998) *The Sixties: Cultural Revolution in Britain, France, Italy, and the United States, c.1958–c.1974*, Oxford: Oxford University Press.

Massey, Doreen (1995) *Spatial Divisions of Labour. Social Structures and the Geography of Production*, 2nd edition, Basingstoke: Macmillan.

McIvor, Arthur (2013) *Working Lives. Work in Britain Since 1945*, Basingstoke: Palgrave Macmillan.

McKibbin, Ross (1998) *Classes and Cultures: England, 1918–1951*, Oxford: Oxford University Press.

Mogey, John Macfarlane (1956) *Family and Neighbourhood. Two Studies in Oxford*, London: Oxford University Press.

Morgan, Kenneth O. (1992) *The People's Peace. British History 1945–1990*, Oxford: Oxford University Press.

Offer, Avner (2008) 'British Manual Workers: From Producers to Consumers, c. 1950–2000', *Contemporary British History*, 22:4, 538–571.

Popular Memory Group (2006) 'Popular Memory. Theory, Politics, Method', in Robert Perks and Alistair Thomson (eds), *The Oral History Reader*, 2nd edition, London: Routledge, 43–54.

Portelli, Alessandro (1991) *The Death of Luigi Trastulli and Other Stories. Form and Meaning in Oral History*, Albany, NY: State University of New York Press.

Portelli, Alessandro (2006) 'What Makes Oral History Different?', in Alistair Thomson and Rob Perks (eds), *The Oral History Reader*, 2nd edition, New York: Routledge.

Ragin, Charles (1994) *Constructing Social Research. The Unity and Diversity of Method*, London: Pine Forge Press.

Reay, Barry (1996) *Microhistories: Demography, Society and Culture in Rural England, 1800–1930*, Cambridge: Cambridge University Press.

Roberts, Elizabeth (1984) *A Woman's Place: An Oral History of Working-class Women 1890–1940*, Oxford: Blackwell.

Roberts, Elizabeth (1995) *Women and Families: An Oral History, 1940–1970*, Oxford: Blackwell.

Roberts, Ian (1999) 'A Historical Construction of the Working Class', in Huw Beynon and Pandeli Glavanis (eds), *Patterns of Social Inequality. Essays for Richard Brown*, London: Longman, 147–160.

Roberts, Kenneth (2001) *Class in Modern Britain*, Basingstoke: Palgrave.

Rogaly, Ben and Becky Taylor (2009) *Moving Histories of Class and Community. Identity, Place and Belonging in Contemporary England*, Basingstoke: Palgrave Macmillan.

Rule, John (2001) 'Time, Affluence and Private Leisure: The British Working Class in the 1950s and 1960s', *Labour History Review*, 66:2, 223–242.

Savage, Mike (2005) 'Working-Class Identities in the 1960s: Revisiting the Affluent Worker Study', *Sociology*, 39:5, 929–946.

Savage, Mike (2010) *Identities and Social Change in Britain Since 1940. The Politics of Method*, Oxford: Oxford University Press.

Savage, Mike, Gaynor Bagnall and Brian Longhurst (2005) *Globalization and Belonging*, London: Sage.

Seabrook, Jeremy (1973) *The Unprivileged. A Hundred Years of Family Life and Tradition in a Working-class Street*, Harmondsworth: Penguin.

Singleton, Rosalind Watkiss (2010) '"Old Habits Persist" Change and Continuity in Black Country Communities: Pensnett, Sedgley and Tipton, 1945–c.1970', unpublished PhD thesis, University of Wolverhampton.

Skeggs, Beverley (1997) *Formations of Class and Gender*, London: Sage.

Snell, Keith (2006) *Parish and Belonging, Community, Identity and Welfare in England and Wales, 1700–1950*, Cambridge: Cambridge University Press.

Spencer, Liz and Ray Pahl (2006) *Rethinking Friendship. Hidden Solidarities Today*, Princeton, NJ: Princeton University Press.

Strangleman, Tim (2001) 'Networks, Place and Identities in Post-Industrial Mining Communities', *International Journal of Urban and Regional Research*, 25, 253–267.

Tabili, Laura (2011) *Global Migrants, Local Culture: Natives and Newcomers in Provincial England, 1841–1939*, Basingstoke: Palgrave Macmillan.

Taylor, Robert (2005) 'The Rise and Disintegration of the Working Classes', in Paul Addison and Harriet Jones (eds), *A Companion to Contemporary Britain*, Oxford: Blackwell, 371–388.

Tebbutt, Melanie (1995) *Women's Talk? A Social History of 'Gossip' in Working-Class Neighbourhoods, 1880–1960*, Aldershot: Scolar Press.

Thompson, Paul (2000) *Voice of the Past. Oral History*, 3rd edition, Oxford: Oxford University Press.

Thomson, Alistair (2006) 'Anzac Memories: Putting Popular Memory Theory into Practice in Australia', in Robert Perks and Alistair Thomson (eds), *The Oral History Reader*, 2nd edition, London: Routledge, 244–254.

Todd, Selina (2008) 'Affluence, Class and Crown Street: Reinvestigating the Post-War Working Class', *Contemporary British History*, 22, 501–518.

Todd, Selina (2014) *The People. The Rise and Fall of the Working Class 1910–2010*, London: John Murray.

Tönnies, Ferdinand (1955) *Community and Association (Gemeinschaft Und Gesellschaft)*, London: Routledge & Kegan Paul.

Walkerdine, Valerie (2010) 'Communal Beingness and Affect: An Exploration of Trauma in an Ex-Industrial Community', *Body and Society*, 16, 91–116.

Wight, Daniel (1993) *Workers Not Wasters: Masculine Respectability, Consumption and Unemployment in Central Scotland: A Community Study*, Edinburgh: Edinburgh University Press.

Williams, Raymond (1973) *The Country and the City*, London: Chatto & Windus.

Williamson, Bill (1982) *Class, Culture and Community. A Biographical Study of Social Change in Mining*, London: Routledge & Kegan Paul.

Williamson, Margaret (2009) 'Gender, Leisure and Marriage in a Working-class Community, 1939–1960', *Labour History Review*, 74:2, 185–198.

Willmott, Peter (1963) *The Evolution of a Community: A Study of Dagenham After Forty Years*, London: Routledge & Kegan Paul.

Wilson, Dolly Smith (2006) 'A New Look at the Affluent Worker: The Good Working Mother in Post-War Britain', *Twentieth Century British History*, 17, 206–229.

Wood, Bruce and Jackie Carter (2000) 'Towns, Urban Change and Local Government', in A. H. Halsey and Josephine Webb (eds), *Twentieth Century British Social Trends*, Basingstoke: Macmillan, 412–433.

Young, Michael and Peter Willmott (1962) *Family and Kinship in East London*, Harmondsworth: Pelican.

Yow, Valerie (2005) *Recording Oral History: A Guide for the Humanities and Social Sciences*, 2nd edition, Walnut Creek, CA: AltaMira.

Zweig, Ferdynand (1961) *The Worker in an Affluent Society. Family Life and Industry*, London: Heinemann.

2 Families

Ellen Ingleton, born in 1936, grew up in a street of small terraced houses in Beverley. Ellen's maternal aunt lived in the same street, and her grandma lived just around the corner. The boundaries between the households were often blurred: 'when the air raid went off we used to run down to my aunty's ... she had ten children ... . We were pretty close – we more or less all grew up as brothers and sisters really, always in and out of each other's houses' (Ellen Ingleton, interview, 20 April 2010). This closeness, physical and emotional, between extended family members was central to the model of 'traditional working-class community' proposed by some post-war social investigators. These authors considered that a post-war decline in the solidarity of extended families was part of the unravelling of cohesive working-class communities.

Post-war sociological portraits of the 'traditional working-class community' often depicted residents enmeshed in local networks of which extended family members were crucial nodes. As Michael Young and Peter Willmott (1962/ 1957: 104) wrote:

> When a person has relatives in the borough, as most people do, each of these relatives is a go-between with other people in the district. His brother's friends are his acquaintances, if not his friends; his grandmother's neighbours are so well known almost to be his own. The kindred are, if we understand their function aright, a bridge between the individual and the community.

In 'traditional' working-class communities, high rates of endogamy (marriage between individuals living within a particular locality) and the propinquity of multiple generations of families helped to create localities in which most people were known to one another (Young and Willmott 1962/1957: 116). Furthermore, it was family members living close by who provided much of the mutual assistance that was key to the 'neighbourliness' often attributed to 'traditional' working-class community (Klein 1965: 134). Young and Willmott (1962/1957: 44–62) showed how, in Bethnal Green, married women usually sought to live near to their mothers so that they could take advantage of their assistance, advice and support whilst bringing up their own children. A corollary of the central role played by extended family in this model of 'traditional' working-class life was the social distance between many husbands and wives. The presence of relatives living close by militated against a close conjugal bond – wives socialised with their families, and husbands with their mates (Klein 1965: 139).

However, some authors suggested that this situation was reversed during the age of affluence: the working classes were now prioritising marriage and children over communal relationships with extended family. This was partly a result of structural changes beyond workers' immediate control: with the acceleration of slum demolition in the 1950s and 1960s, many were obliged to move to new council estates at some distance from their old communities (Young and Willmott 1962/1957: 121–47). As a result, old neighbourhoods became more thinly populated and the density of family ties was diluted; those who moved away from their natal communities were separated from the support networks of extended family. In their new environment, husbands and wives needed to rely on each other for support and sociability and thus could forge closer bonds than had often been the case in the traditional communities (Bott 1971: 219). But it also appeared that many among the working classes embraced the opportunity to leave the auspices of the extended family for improved housing and higher wages (Goldthorpe *et al.* 1969: 96–7, 158–9). Authors in the later 1950s and 1960s pointed to the rise of the 'companionate' marriage – more equal, sharing and caring than previously – general to working-class life in old neighbourhoods as well as new (Young and Willmott 1962/1957: 17–31; Fletcher 1966: 144–5). At the same time, it was thought that married couples were placing new emphasis on their children, on whom they lavished time, money, attention and perhaps, most importantly, their hopes and aspirations (Goldthorpe *et al.* 1969: 105–8, 129–32; Klein 1965: 300–2). Ferdynand Zweig (1961: 209) observed that the workers he interviewed in the late 1960s had a 'romanticised idea of the family', and that fathers were becoming 'big brothers' to their children rather than the 'feared and distant' characters of the past. For authors such as Zweig (1961: 207) and Josephine Klein (1965: 211–2), the new cultural priority afforded to family life was enabled by the propitious post-war economic climate – improved housing and new forms of leisure made time spent in and around home and family more appealing. Young and Willmott (1973: 28–9) also connected changes in family life to the 'affluence'. For them, the new position of the nuclear family in working-class life represented a shift to the next stage in the development of the family in modernity – whereas previously the demands of production had separated the nuclear family (husbands in the productive sphere, wives in the reproductive), in conditions of post-war plenty it was brought back together as a 'unit of consumption'.

Since the three-generation extended family had been central to 'traditional' patterns of community – in which sociability faced outwards through the extended family rather than inwards towards home and nuclear family – its replacement with the more 'privatised' family (Goldthorpe *et al.* 1969: 96–7) appeared to diminish community vitality. Klein (1965: 186, 193) argued that, since extended families had provided most of the mutual assistance in 'traditional' communities (the day to day loan of foodstuffs and assistance with babysitting, for example), those who moved away from these communities were forced to seek assistance from neighbours. Whilst this assistance was sometimes given, many, fearing their neighbours might make onerous demands, limited their liability by reducing contact. There was also the simple fact that many working-class people chose to focus on the life of the home and nuclear family to the detriment of engagement in wider sociability. On the one hand this was about allocation of leisure time – so Zweig (1961: 207–9) argued that the modern worker was 'domesticated', spending leisure time at home with his family watching television for example, rather than in the pub with workmates. On the other, it was about priorities. John Goldthorpe *et al.* (1969: 96–108) pointed to the fact that a new desire to provide materially for the family often meant overtime for men and long hours working outside the home for women, and neither parent was left with much time or energy for sociability beyond the home. Klein (1965: 222–223) argued that the move to new housing that many families undertook to provide a better start in life for their children implied financial and temporal costs: rents were higher, and new housing was often many miles on the bus from both workplaces and sociable haunts such as pubs. The natural response was to spend leisure time at home, immersed in emotionally satisfying family life.

In the retrospective view of historians and today's sociologists, the post-war age of affluence still frequently appears as a period in which the typical working-class family assumed a more streamlined 'nuclear' form, jettisoning wider communal entanglements. Certainly, the statistics show this as a period in which marriage was popular. The marriage rate had been rising since the First World War and reached a peak during the 1960s when 80 women out of every 100 aged between 20 and 40 years of age was married (Bedarida 1991: 267). Claire Langhamer (2005, 2012) fuses cultural and economic explanations for the popularity of domestic life in this period, arguing that post-war affluence enabled 'dreams of domesticity' to become reality for many; furthermore, she considers this a period in which ideals of romantic love were elevated above all other considerations. Similarly, Selina Todd (2008, 2014: 203–12; Todd and Young 2012) places working-class aspirations in relation to home and family central to her interpretation of post-war change, arguing that these aspirations drove working-class men and women to put in the long hours at work that underpinned the economic buoyancy of the period. Dolly Smith Wilson (2006: 217) suggests that the movement of married women into the workplace in the post-war decades was motivated by 'a desire for a different family life-style'. Recent authors have seen the 'dedomesticisation' of married women through their movement in large numbers into the workplace that took place in the post-war decades as an important part of the remaking the nuclear family as a more self-contained unit (Charles 2012; Moran 2012: 182).

This purported 'privatisation' of the working-class nuclear family during the age of affluence was integral to many claims about the demise of community-of-place (Goldthorpe *et al.* 1969: 96–102; Cronin 1984: 165–207; Roberts 1995: 238; McKibbin 1998: 164–205). But the extent to which 'traditional' extended family groups fractured into 'privatised' nuclear-family units as a result of rising living standards has been questioned. Studies depicting 'new' patterns of isolated, privatised family life focussed on particular contexts – new council estates (Young and Willmott 1962/1957; Mogey 1956) or populations that had recently migrated for work (Goldthorpe *et al.* 1969). Willmott (1963) himself found that after a number of years, extended family often followed one another to live on council estates and that patterns of three-generation family life familiar from the old East End were reproduced. Fiona Devine (1992) in her restudy of Luton Vauxhall workers, the context for Goldthorpe *et al.*'s influential 1960s study, pointed out that the 'privatism' the sociologists discovered there may have been a function of the pioneer nature of the population they studied. Many of the Luton workers had only recently moved to the town at the time Goldthorpe *et al.* interviewed them; by the 1980s, when Devine conducted her restudy, extended family members had often followed the original pioneer generation to the town. Even where extended family still lived at some remove, this did not prevent frequent contact and support between members. Neither were these workers' social lives confined to home and family – they frequently socialised with local friends including workmates and neighbours. An alternative critique of the notion of post-war decline of the 'traditional' patterns of working-class family life points out that working-class people had long prioritised their nuclear family and the privacy of the home above extended family and community (Franklin 1989; Pahl 1984: 325–6; Lawrence 2013).

This chapter uses detailed evidence from the Beverley oral histories to examine the claim that the working classes became 'privatised' (to use Goldthorpe *et al.*'s term) during the post-war decades of 'affluence', replacing wider sociability and extended family support with an increasing emphasis on spouse and children. I will compare the patterns revealed in the oral history from the 'pre-affluence' period (approximately 1935–1954) with the 'affluent era' (approximately 1955–1975) as a way of assessing change and continuity. The evidence presented here supports those authors who consider that the notion of a lurch towards the privatised nuclear family during the 'age of affluence' is misleading. Instead, it appears that two distinct models of behaviour in relation to sociability and the family – on the one hand, 'family centredness' and, on the other, a separate conjugal sociability with peers and extended family – had long been available to the working classes and continued to be so through the three post-war decades.

The conjugal relationship

Models of the 'traditional working-class community' elaborated by post-war authors such as Klein (1965: 158–60) and Mogey (1971: 151) suggested that married couples occupied separate social spheres. Because of high endogamy rates (the extent to which local people married each other), both spouses had pre-existing social and family networks to hand that tended to militate against their spending significant time together and bonding as a couple (Bott 1971: 92–5, 218–9). Indeed, the divide between male and female worlds was fundamental to 'traditional working-class community', impelling husband and wife into alliances with others beyond the home. Men spent most of their day at work, and in the evenings and weekends saw male friends and workmates away from the home – watching and playing sports, absorbed in hobbies, drinking in pubs and working men's clubs. Women had to fit their sociability around their daily domestic tasks, talking with female neighbours in the street and shops, or making regular visits to female relatives (mother and sisters) living close by (Klein 1965: 171–2). In their study of a small Yorkshire coal-mining town, Norman Dennis, Fernando Henriques and Clifford Slaughter (1969 – first published in 1956) presented an iconic account of a traditional working-class community with the highly segregated marriage at its very core. For these authors, marital relationships were shaped by the demands of coal production. The vast majority of employment in 'Ashton' (Featherstone) was men's work in the coal industry; wives stayed at home bringing up their children. This economic divide was reflected culturally and socially in highly gender-divided identities and leisure. Coal-mining helped to create men with a tough self-image who spent their leisure time spent with other men drinking and gambling, and whose masculinity required that they were obeyed at home; the book illustrates this with a much-quoted vignette of a miner throwing his tea onto the fire because his wife had not prepared it to his liking.

Social investigators found examples of the 'traditional' working-class marriage alive and well in the post-war decades (Dennis, Henriques and Slaughter 1969). Nevertheless, it seemed to many that the traditional-type marriage was destined to decline as husbands and wives came to occupy ever more equal, or at least 'symmetrical', roles (Young and Willmott 1973). Young and Willmott (1962/1957: 59) considered that 'a new kind of companionship between man and woman ... is one of the great transformations of our time'; their own survey suggested that men helped with housework to a greater extent than in the past, that husbands and wives took important decisions about family life together, and that, rather than going to the pub several times a week, the modern man was just as likely to bring a bottle of beer home and watch television with his wife and family. Young and Willmott (1962/1957: 17–30) discerned this tendency towards more loving and equal marriages in the old neighbourhoods as well as the new, and connected this trend to social changes including smaller average family sizes and improved housing. Elizabeth Bott (1971: 219) suggested that the shift to 'companionate' marriage was given significant impetus when married couples left their natal communities, for example to move into new housing estates. Cut off from their pre-existing networks, they were compelled to rely on each other for companionship. With married couples' attention now focused on each other and on the home, there was less likelihood that the kinds of communities purported to have flourished in the old neighbourhoods would be re-established in the new.

Pre-affluence – 1935–1954

Endogamy rates among the working-class population of Beverley in the 1940s and early 1950s were high. A sample of marriage registers for St Nicholas Church, which ministered to the working-class eastern part of Beverley, for the five years up to 1955 shows that of a total of eighty-four weddings, 53 per cent were between two people with Beverley addresses (St Nicholas Church Marriage Registers). The oral evidence suggests that almost all young people were married from their parents' homes, and therefore in over half the marriages in this church, each spouse would have had parents and a pre-existing social network in the town. From the thirty-four oral history interviewees born up to 1940, many of whom married in the 1950s, 94 per cent were born and bred in the town, and 73 per cent indicated that they had at least one parent who was also born and bred in the town. Although not all were asked where their spouse was from, it was possible to deduce that at least 32 per cent married another Beverley person, whilst at least 26 per cent had married non-Beverlonians. This statistical information alone suggests that a high proportion – perhaps close to half – of working-class marriages in late 1940s and early 1950s Beverley were between two people from the town. Many of the partners in these marriages were at least second generation Beverlonians and so had family and social networks locally. We might therefore expect, as Klein (1965: 160, 171) suggested of traditional working-class communities, that marriages would have been imposed on pre-existing networks and that the couples would seek sociable fulfilment outside the marriage.

Despite Beverley providing the kind of stable setting that authors such as Klein and Bott considered favourable for the 'traditional'-type marriage, the extent to which pre-affluent-era marriages in the town fit this model was mixed. Some interviewees did indeed describe marriages in which couples' sociability rarely overlapped. Some told how, in the 1940s and 1950s, their father spent much of his time in the pub, and their mother had a few regular companions perhaps from amongst family and neighbours. Joan Gibson's account of her father's priorities in the 1940s was typical:

> Of course, Dad went to the pub, Beehive, when he was at home. It's what men did. Dick's dad was the same. Come home from work and go to the pub …
>
> I know my mum used to say he'd rather spend his money on pints for his friends than on us … most of the men were like that then, a bit like Andy Capp in the paper you know, they do what they want.
>
> (Joan Gibson, interview, 17 March 2010)

Perhaps a quarter of the conjugal relationships described in the 1930s through to the mid-1950s were highly separate in this sense. But there were also married men who did not seek the pleasures of the pub in the 1930s, 1940s and early 1950s, and who were described as home-centred (interviews: Hilda Little 19 March 2010; Ellen Ingleton, 20 April 2010). Some interviewees emphasised their fathers' involvement with hobbies, such as keeping birds, gardening or allotments. These hobbies could involve husband and wife socialising together, as Marianne Woolly (interview, 22 February 2010) remembered in the 1930s and 1940s:

> [Dad's] life was the birds. I mean he was president, chairman, of the Caged Bird Society, he kept budgerigars, canaries and stuff, that was his big hobby. So, and in a way that was my mum's social thing, you know, being with him, one of the tea ladies, you know like the women in the background of all these local clubs.

Perhaps the typical pattern of conjugal sociability for couples with children in the pre-affluent period was mixed. Husbands would spend some sociable leisure away from the home with mates in the pub or engaged in another form of associational activity, and their wives spent a greater proportion of their time in or around the home, but might accompany their husbands to the pub or cinema on a designated evening each week. For example, Peter Stephenson (interview, 27 May 2010) remembered that his father:

> went on his way from work, maybe had a couple of pints ... they [mum and dad] used to come here [the Humber Keel pub, early 1950s] ... Saturday night, concert night you know ... someone playing piano and drums and then volunteers singing and that ... they was all neighbours that lived round us, and they brought their wives and that, and that bar through there, the men used to play dominoes, and the women used to sit through here and have a few drinks and that, and then the men used to come through and have a sing.

This pattern, in which married men reserved the Saturday night to take their wife to the pub or club, was recalled by other Beverley interviewees (interviews: Hannah Witham 26 April 2010; Anna Mason 12 July 2010; Dick Gibson 11 March 2010; Fred and May Peters 24 June 2010). It appears to have been widespread in 'traditional' working-class contexts, for example in the pit-mining village of Trimdon near Hartlepool where one former miner recalled "'Saturday night was the night out with the wife. Friday night was the lads' night out'" (Hall 2012: 45). Married couple's sociability together need not, of course, revolve around drinking. Although Jack Blakeston's depiction of his tannery worker father was very much in terms of a 'traditional' working-class male, who liked 'pub, and dominoes and darts', Jack also recalled that his father and mother went together one night each week to their neighbours' house to listen to *The Man in Black* on the radio. These neighbours visited the Blakestons in turn (Jack Blakeston, interview, 10 August 2010).

Margaret Lane (2014: 450) reports that in her oral history research focusing on working-class marriage in Hull in the 1920s to the 1940s, most interviewees recalled affection, shared decision-making and considerable leisure time spent together (usually in the home): 'the stereotype of men spending excessive time and money at the pub – whilst women enjoyed their leisure exclusively with other women – was not commonly reflected in my Hull evidence.' My evidence did not allow quite such a definitive rejection of the 'traditional' model of marriage, but it did confirm that working-class marriages in the early-to-middle decades of the twentieth century could be more supportive and 'companionate' than has sometimes been portrayed.

Affluent era – 1955–1975

The dynamics of marital relationships in the earlier period were nevertheless guided by prevailing material and cultural conditions. Until at least the 1960s, there were strong social presumptions about which leisure pursuits were appropriate for each gender. For example, married women's leisure, shaped by ideologies of femininity and motherhood, tended to take second place to the demands of domestic work and childcare (Langhamer 2000: 25–6; Moss 2011); lack of money might prevent husbands and wives socialising outside of the home together (Lane 2014: 450). In practice, therefore, working-class married couples' opportunities for shared leisure tended to be fairly limited – as Lane contends: 'most leisure time – for men and women – was spent in the home across the whole of this period [1900–1970]' However, the post-war age of affluence brought economic, social and cultural change favourable to a more expansive shared sociability for some working-class couples: the rigidity of gender roles arguably eased, especially as more married women went out to work (Brooke 2001; Lawrence 2013), and trends towards smaller family sizes, growth in real wages, the provision of statutory holidays and improved housing meant that many married couples had the time and money to engage in a social life together. As Bernstein (2004: 317) states, 'people had more money to spend on what they wanted, and more leisure time to do a greater variety of things'.

The Beverley evidence suggested changes in patterns of conjugal sociability appearing across the 1960s and 1970s. A large proportion of the interviewees born after 1940, who married in the 1960s and later, described an outward looking sociability conducted *with* one's spouse, rather than separately. These interviewees stressed that whereas their fathers typically took their mothers out only once a week, often to pub or club on a Saturday night, they themselves socialised much more extensively as couples. John and Margaret Day (interview, 23 November 2009) did not have their first child until nine years after they married in the early 1960s, describing this time as 'our real socialising years'. Dennis Duke (interview, 14 July 2010), a former barge skipper, married in the early 1970s, recalled that he and his wife occasionally went out separately but usually socialised together, and that they had a group of friends whom they saw regularly. Gerald Ibbotson (interview, 7 July 2010), a tradesman printer during the 1970s, often went out with his wife and friends for meals. Jim Fisher (interview, 16 December 2009) and his wife married in their early twenties in 1971, but waited until they were in their thirties to have children, spending the intervening years socialising together. Starting a family initially curtailed joint conjugal sociability for some, but the availability of babysitting services from family members living locally meant that as children grew up couples were able to continue socialising (interviews: Janet Thompson 23 November 2009; Ellen and Harry Malster 21 May 2010). However, the home was the principal setting of married life, and changes in housing during this period could bring new ways for husbands and wives to spend time together. Few interviewees who grew up before the Second World War lived in homes that their parents owned, but at least 60 per cent of the interviewees born after 1940 had eventually bought their own homes. For many young married couples, buying and working on a property was a shared project that appeared to have strengthened the conjugal bond (interviews: George Little, 12 March 2010; Ellen Ingleton 20 April 2010; Fred Reid 26 January 2010). Furthermore, improved housing enabled couples to entertain friends at home (as will be discussed further in Chapter 4, 'Friends').

But despite new opportunities for marital togetherness, some marriages continued to look like the 'traditional' model. 'Affluence' should not be exaggerated – as in the earlier period, some interviewees suggested that there were times when they could rarely afford to go out and socialise, particularly when children were young (interviews: Bill and Jane Holland 11 November 2009; Peter Lawson 4 May 2010). Furthermore, the norms that underpinned gendered conjugal roles and differential access to leisure persisted across the age of affluence, and indeed for much longer (Roberts 1995: 22, 43, 113; Williamson 2009; Hunt and Satterlee 1987; Walkerdine 2010). The Beverley evidence shows that many men spent a large amount of time in the company of their mates at the pub or in sports teams in the 1960s and 1970s and that there was a male drinking culture that some men indulged in as often as finances and their wives allowed. Bob Garbutt and David Hughes were friends who told stories of hedonistic drinking exploits in Beverley pubs across the period, a habit that marriage and the advent of family life did not seem to have disrupted unduly (interviews: Bob Garbutt 28 June 2010; David Hughes 24 June 2010). Their stories of the time they spent in the pubs away from their families were ruefully corroborated by their wives. Other interviewees remembered that despite marriage there was still plenty of time for friends and male-only drinking in the 1960s and 1970s (interviews: Mick Underwood 21 July 2010; Derek Saltmer 25 January 2010; Les White 29 October 2010; Michael Hudson 17 December 2010). Although most of his spare time was spent with his wife and family, Gerald Ibbotson (interview, 7 July 2010) remembered that he and two neighbours spent Thursday night visiting local pubs for many years. The practice of taking wives out on a set specified night of the week and seeing male friends on other evenings, familiar from older generations, was still continued by at least some from the generation who married in the 1960s (Les White, interview, 29 October 2010). Similarly, their involvement in sports and hobbies continued to take some men away from their families and wives – sometimes excessively so (interviews: Michael Hudson 17 December 2010; Neil Cooper 14 April 2010; Sally Adams 21 June 2010). Even men who were otherwise family-centred spent time alone or with mates in pursuits including fishing and playing sports (interviews: Dick Gibson, 11 March 2010; George Little 12 March 2010; Margaret Day 23 November 2009). Neither the radio nor the television ended participation in sports or destroyed the trade of pubs as Jack Binnington (interview, 13 July 2010) remembered:

> Tellies came late into our house at Beckside because we had a brewery to keep you see … . Father saw it as an irrelevance, he could spend that money in pub … . He became addicted to it [*television*], but his pub life still went on.

It must also be noted that across our period many working-class wives had occasional nights out away from both home and husband. Williamson (2009) reports that many of her interviewees from the mining community of Cleveland in the North East remembered going out dancing with female friends in the 1940s and 1950s. Although my interviewees rarely recalled that wives went dancing without their husbands (interviews: Iris Brown 21 May 2010; Ivy Shipton 17 May 2010), there were other occasions for female company and a change from the home. Whist nights were popular, organised by churches or other voluntary groups (*Beverley Guardian*, 12 January 1957; John Day, interview, 10 November 2009). Some women, often groups of neighbours joined by assorted friends and relatives, organised clubs who met regularly in each other's homes or in the function rooms of pubs; sociability was probably the most important function of these groups but they could also be structured around activities such as whist and even amateur dramatics (interviews: Lynne Norton 9 November 2009; Jack Blakeston 10 August 2010) (similar clubs have been noted by Hall (2012: 46) in working-class communities in mid-century South Wales). As more married women went out to work in the post-war decades, many enjoyed the companionship of the factory floor and organised nights out with workmates, including weekly dates playing bingo or darts (interviews: Jean Benson 4 January 2010; Doris Daniels 13 November 2009). The trend across the twentieth century towards reduced birth rates no doubt freed leisure time – whereas at the end of the nineteenth century, working-class women on average spent more than fifteen years pregnant or caring for small children, by the mid-century this figure had fallen to four years (Bedarida 1991: 272).

Historians have been influenced by the idea that traditional marriages were losing ground to new, more companionate partnerships in the post-war decades. Certainly, the rise of companionate marriage observed by Young and Willmott (1962/1957), Bott (1971) and Fletcher (1966) echoes in accounts positing a 'transformation of intimacy' in which marriage became the central social bond across the second half of the twentieth century (Giddens 1990; Phillipson *et al.* 2001: 118–132). Claire Langhamer (2012: 292) argues that this development gained significant impetus in the post-war age of affluence: 'the specific post-1945 context of rising living standards provided the material conditions within which love could eclipse pragmatism in the making of everyday marriages.' However, the evidence from the Beverley study and others (for example, Lane 2014) does not support the notion of a clear-cut movement from 'traditional', gender-divided marriage to a more companionate, loving marriage in the post-war decades. Rather, marriages varied widely in the extent to which they might be characterised as 'traditional' or 'companionate' all across our period. Many working-class couples formed mutually supportive partnerships long before the supposed post-war rise of more companionable marital relationships. Furthermore, many husbands and wives led largely separate social lives during the age of affluence, and as Williamson (2009) has argued, long-standing gender norms underpinning husbands' greater access to sociable leisure were slow to disappear. It may be that the 'companionate marriage' was a product of sociological discourse rather than a reflection of real change in marital relations: Davis (2009) considers that sociologists writing in the conditions of rising affluence in the later 1950s and 1960s shared in the wider optimism of the time and thus tended to concentrate on the positive, 'companionate' aspects of marriage rather than gender division and inequality. These were features that later authors discovered were still all too present.

Child-centred attitudes

Alongside the separation of male and female social worlds in 'traditional working-class communities', post-war social investigators also noted husbands' limited involvement in bringing up their children. Klein (1965: 177) summarised: 'in the more traditional areas, children are more or less exclusively the wife's domain'. A number of social investigators commented on the reduction of this paternal aloofness during the post-war age of affluence. Children, it seemed, were becoming a shared concern of husband and wife, and the central focus of family life in ways that had not always been the case. Young and Willmott's (1962/1957: 301) Bethnal Green informants suggested:

> We're different with our boy, we make more of a mate of him. When I was a kid, Dad always had the best of everything. Now it's the children who get the best of it.

It is probable that this narrative overemphasises the degree to which men in 'traditional' working-class families were absent from the life of the home. The low visibility of male parenting in some working-class historical contexts may have reflected predominant cultural scripts about appropriate male and female behaviour rather than actual practices – behind closed doors fathers in 'traditional' settings could be just as caring as the new family men described by Young and Willmott (Abrams 1999). Indeed, the family-centred working-class father was documented as far back as the nineteenth century (Pahl 1984; Lawrence 2013). The Beverley evidence examined below broadly supports this critique; however, just as we need to be careful about the stereotype of the traditional working-class father standing aloof from his family, it also seems unlikely that most parents ever shared completely equal responsibility for childcare, either before or during the advent of the age of affluence.

Pre-affluence – 1935–1954

There is no doubting that some Beverlonian men described in the testimony resembled the 'traditional' working-class father. Many interviewees emphasised an aloofness on the part of fathers. Ivy Shipton's (interview, 17 May 2010) account of family life in the late 1940s and early 1950s was typical:

> My dad was a man with his own interests. He liked the horses, and he liked the greyhounds, and he liked his garden. I would say probably a typical working man's interests really … he did gamble. And even up to just before he died … I think he had left the family quite short of funds from time to time … . But, I suppose that was the way it was then … . He went to the races … in August, he always went … I suppose sometimes at the expense of family holidays really. I don't remember ever going away on holiday as a child … . We went to the cinema quite often me and my mother, and then my dad would often meet us afterwards, or we would go to the cinema then we would go down to [cousin] Ken's mum's, Aunt Cora, and then my dad would come from the pub or the club and meet us and walk home.

In the 1930s through to the mid-1950s it was usually mothers who took children away for a day on the bus, paid into a 'diddlum' for a summer coach trip or took them for a week away with a relative somewhere (interviews: Betty Carr 19 March 2010; Joan Gibson 17 March 2010; Jack Binnington 22 June 2010). Most children spent a large amount of time independent of parents altogether, playing in the streets and surrounding countryside (interviews: Jack Blakeston 10 August 2010; Jack Binnington 22 June 2010; Betty Carr 19 March 2010).

Dennis, Henriques and Slaughter (1969: 171–226), a classic account of 'traditional' working-class life, described how miners in the post-war Yorkshire mining town of 'Ashton' spent much of their leisure time in the pubs, clubs and hobbies, away from their wives and children. This degree of aloofness was not so clear in Beverley. Interviewees who grew up in the 1930s and 1940s recalled that fathers took an interest in their children and that the nuclear family did spend leisure time together. Numerous interviewees told how, in the 1930s and 1940s, their fathers took them on walks through the town and surrounding countryside;

this was often a weekly ritual whilst mothers prepared Sunday dinner (interviews: Joan Gibson 17 March 2010; Ellen Ingleton 20 April 2010). Others recalled that both of their parents went on these walks, and some remembered family day-trips and holidays (interviews: Hannah Witham 26 April 2010; Ken Ingleton 23 March 2010; Marianne Woolly 22 February 2010). Even Ivy Shipton, quoted above describing a childhood from which her father was often detached, recalled weekend walks with her father. Some interviewees' fathers had taken them to watch rugby, football or cricket matches (interviews: George Little 12 March 2010; Dick Gibson 11 March 2010). Lorry drivers and barge skippers sometimes took their children with them on trips away (interviews: Joan Gibson 17 March 2010; Jack Blakeston 10 August 2010). Fathers might take children to visit relatives (interviews: Bob Garbutt 25 June 2010; Matthew Walton 22 July 2010; George Wigton 15 February 2010). Fathers and children ate together, played games together, undertook domestic chores and worked together on gardens, allotments and small holdings (interviews: Matthew Walton 22 July 2010; Fred Reid 26 January 2010; Neil Cooper 14 April 2010; Jack Blakeston 10 August 2010). Though television in the 1950s is often thought to have brought families together and discouraged broader sociability, it was preceded by the radio, which in many ways had the same function in providing nuclear families with a shared activity at home (for example, John and Margaret Day, interview, 8 December 2009).

Affluent era – 1955–1975

It seems likely that as living standards improved, not just in the post-war period but also more broadly across the twentieth century, new kinds of relationship between material considerations and family life came increasingly to the fore. Certainly, family size became more and more a matter of choice for working-class couples across the twentieth century (Fletcher 1966 112–8; Bernstein 2004: 275–325); parents with fewer children could focus more of their time and money on each child. Family-oriented attitudes preceded the age of affluence, as we have seen above, and may have helped fuel 'affluence', since parents who worked hard to provide materially for their children powered both economic production and consumption (Todd 2014: 199–212). Improved homes and new consumer goods raised the benchmark in terms of the material lifestyle parents should provide for their children (Devine 1992: 207).

As with those East End parents interviewed by Young and Willmott (1962/1957) and quoted above, many Beverley interviewees who raised families from 1950s onwards stressed that they had a different approach to parenting to that they had experienced during their own upbringing. They frequently recounted striving to give their children the things their own parents had not been able to give them. Sarah Baker (interview, 29 May 2010), who along with her tannery worker husband Vic brought their family up in the 1960s and 1970s, spoke for many other interviewees:

I've always said I would like to give our children as much as we can afford, what we knew our parents couldn't give us. And of course our Jan's [Sarah's daughter] admitted since, they do, their generation does the same as what we've said ... each generation tries to do a bit better. My mother, she used to say, 'Oh, I can't afford to give you this, I can't afford to give you that,' but they used to smoke and drink ... if I couldn't afford to give our bains sommat, I wouldn't smoke. We used to go out on a Saturday night ... but we never went out during the week, I mean we couldn't afford it ... ... I've always said if it affected putting food on the table I would have stopped, but our parents wouldn't have done that.

Jack Binnington (interview, 13 July 2010), a barge skipper, recalled that during the 1970s:

I wanted my family to have things and look smart and go to school clean and tidy ... and be happy at school, not worrying 'what am I going home to?'... pub and things like that didn't enter my mind.

As well as the perceived duty to provide materially for children at a time when the minimum expected level of material comfort was moving upwards, many interviewees recalled the pleasure they had taken in their parental role. Dennis Duke (interview, 14 July 2010), a barge skipper and later a lorry driver, brought up a family in the 1970s and expressed a common attitude of parents from his generation towards their children: 'We wanted to spend as much time with them as we could when they was growing up.'

Prioritising and spending time with children was undoubtedly made easier by improvements in the kinds of home to which working people could aspire. The older among the Beverley interviewees often grew up in poorly maintained, rented terraced housing, without electricity or running water; none brought their own children up in such conditions. As in many other towns and cities across Britain, the local council undertook a huge building programme after the war – 800 houses were built on the Swinemoor estate alone between 1945 and 1964 (Brown 1989: 156). Keith Barrett (interview, 2 September 2010) recalled that as a small boy in the late 1950s he was moved with his family to a council house from a condemned property:

It was a big improvement from the other place ... it was, like, full of insects, cockroaches, and there was no heating in there except, like, the fire in the front room, no hot water ... I can remember the tin bath ... [the house] had gas lighting.

Surveys and oral history research in numerous British contexts reveal that for tenants of poor quality private housing, council accommodation in this period represented 'almost unbelievable luxury' and a much better environment in which to bring up children (Todd 2014: 179–80). As well as the expansion of council housing stock, private house-building also boomed after the war. This and the provision of affordable mortgages meant that at least 60 per cent of those born after 1940 had been able to buy their own homes. As the quality of housing increased, it became more practical and desirable to use homes as a site for leisure time and a context for nuclear-family sociability. Private and council houses with gardens and driveways meant that DIY and gardening became necessary tasks; homes with gardens also enabled men to undertake pigeon keeping, motor mechanics and craft hobbies that required at least a small amount of land. Sometimes children were involved with these activities, but even where they were not, time spent in these kinds of activities kept fathers close at hand (interviews: Lynne Norton 9 November 2009; Patrick Mateer 13 January 2010; Ellen Watton 8 March 2010; Keith Barrett 2 September 2010).

However, the notion that it was the move to council estates that *created* this kind of family-centredness (Bott 1971) needs to be treated with caution, since there is significant evidence that the motivation that propelled many married couples to swap old communities for new estates was deep concern for their children's quality of life. Todd (2014: 178) reports that in a 1955 survey that asked 600 people in inner city Liverpool where they would like to live 'those with young children wanted to move to the suburbs. They wanted their children to grow up in a "healthy" environment, "with clean air, and a park to play in".' Similarly, the aspiration to own a house could mean voluntarily sacrificing some of the benefits of community. Ellen Ingleton remembered how she and her husband, an electrician at Armstrong's Patents in Beverley, curtailed their social life for several years in order to save the money to buy their first house in the later 1950s (interviews: Ellen Ingleton 20 April 2010; Jim Fisher 16 December 2009).

Other innovations of the affluent era enabled families to spend more time together. The number of domestic households in Britain with use of a car doubled between 1955 and 1965 (Gunn 2011). In the small town of Beverley, where workplaces were usually within easy walking or cycling distance, the purchase of a car was often motivated by the prospect of family days out (interviews: Jack Binnington 13 July 2010; Ed Byrne 24 May 2010; Ivy Shipton 17 May 2010; John and Margaret Day 8 December 2009). The outings that interviewees recalled from childhoods in the 1930s and 1940s had frequently been with their mothers on the bus; by the 1960s mothers and fathers together regularly took their children on weekend and evening trips to the coast and countryside by car. Jack Binnington (interview, 13 July 2010) recalled his first family car in the 1960s: 'We had a little red Mini for our first car, and we loved that little red Mini, four people fit into it lovely and so you'd go off for days.' Ellen and Harry Malster (interview, 21 May 2010) bought a car in the early 1960s when their children were small and their weekend family excursions to local countryside and seaside sites were fairly typical:

Harry: We used to go to Brid a lot at weekends.
Ellen: Yes, early on a Sunday morning we used to go.

Harry: Rides round Rosedale [in the North York Moors National Park] and round there.

In this way, ownership of cars provided a shared weekend activity for many nuclear families. In contrast, those interviewees whose parents had not had a car in the 1960s often recalled less time spent with their family: 'Most of the time I just played with all local kids and your mums was at home … maybe people would come round or she'd maybe go gossiping at someone else's house … we didn't do a real lot as families' (Keith Barrett, interview, 2 September 2010).

When asked about what they had done together as families, interviewees usually discussed holidays. Rising living standards and car ownership in the 1950s through to the 1970s provided opportunities for many more to spend a week away with mother, father and siblings. Even in the relatively poor inner-city areas of Liverpool, a quarter of residents had a holiday away from home in 1955 (Todd 2014: 201). Whereas 15 per cent of the Beverley interviewees mentioned holidays with parents in the 1930s and 1940s, at least 36 per cent of interviewees went on holidays with the whole nuclear family in the 1960s and 1970s. Elaine Mateer (interview, 29 March 2010) recalled only day trips until the family got a three-wheeled car in the late 1960s, from which point in time they began to have annual trips, camping in Scotland and the Lake District amongst other places. Likewise George Little (interview, 12 March 2010) recalled how he was given a van by his father-in-law in the 1960s, which made family holidays viable:

> It was ideal for us with the kids. We went for miles in it … and then we progressed to going every year for a week to Scarborough, and we used to go in this van … . Because it had a good luggage space in the back.

Although package holidays to Spain were within the reach of some British working-class families as early as the mid-1950s (Todd 2014: 201), family holidays abroad were only recalled by one Beverley couple, June and Dave Ireland (interview, 15 July 2010), who took their family on a coach trip to Italy in the 1970s; this couple had achieved social mobility through grammar school into lower white-collar positions.

The fruits of affluence – improved homes, cars, holidays, televisions – provided enhanced possibilities for spending time as a family. For many parents, the intrinsic satisfactions of family life could eclipse the appeal of wider sociability. Jack Binnington (interview, 13 July 2010) recalled the precious time spent with his young family during the 1970s:

> Having a big group of friends? No we never … it was us four that I lived for and worked for … . We didn't say to people: 'I'll see you Saturday night in the pub.'

It must also be noted that spending more time at home was not always a positive choice. Just as in the earlier period, lack of money and time could preclude wider sociability. The expense of bringing up children and striving to provide materially for families in times of rising expectations about living standards was one of the factors that helped push more British women out into full-time work and men into accepting more overtime during the post-war decades (Todd 2008: 506); thus, there might be little time for socialising with friends during the early years of marriage and child rearing (Bill and Jane Holland, interview, 11 November 2009). Children, mortgages, holidays and cars were expensive and could soon soak up the small rises in family incomes and leave little money over for sociability (interviews: Vic Baker 29 May 2010; Hilda Little 19 March 2010).

In some respects, this evidence of increasing emphasis on time spent as a family unit appears to lend some credence to the privatism thesis, which posited a broader withdrawal from communal sociability. However, such home-and-family focus was at its height whilst children were young, and other parts of the lifecycle were much more sociable, as will be seen in Chapter 4. Furthermore, an orientation towards the nuclear family did not necessarily preclude wider sociability – there was evidence of socialising with others as a family unit. Interviewees spoke of family trips and holidays with friends' families in the late 1950s through to the 1970s:

> [In the early 1960s] We did have friends nearby who had a car ... they had a big Vanguard estate ... we'd all pile into there for the day, and zoom off to Hornsea, spend the day on the beach ... talk about over-crowding a vehicle.
>
> (William Vincent, interview, 25 May 2010)

> [In the later 1970s] When the kids were little we all went on holiday together ... the Yorkshire Dales, we used to rent a cottage there ... a big house, slept ten, we used to go, us four, Pat and Bruce with their two girls, and two of the chaps that I've just been talking about.
>
> (Janet Thompson, interview, 23 November 2009)

> We went to Cornwall quite a lot with friends didn't we? In various cars, sometimes we used to take a couple of days to get there.
>
> (Ellen Malster, interview, 21 May 2010)

Post-war developments also meant that families could exchange visits with friends who had moved away. The improvement in housing standards for many meant that they could entertain friends and their families at home, and cars facilitated such visits. Hilda and George worked in Beverley and brought their family up in the town, whereas Hilda's friends' husbands' jobs in the RAF took them to other parts of the country. During the 1970s the couple would visit these friends in Lincoln and York, using the car to take their children with them. As their children grew up, the couples arranged an annual weekend together, meeting at one or the others' homes (interviews: Hilda Little 19 March 2010; George Little 12 March 2010). Bernard Hunt (interview, 12 January 2010) recalled that whilst bringing up his family in the 1960s and 1970s he was able to maintain links with a family in Holland. As a child Bernard had become friends with the Dutch family who had a market gardening business near Beverley. Bernard, a groundsman at Hodgson's sports club, took his wife and children for four trips to Holland a year: 'Even when I couldn't afford it I took the boys, the boys were brought up there really.' These Dutch friends visited the Hunts in their Beverley home in return.

So, rather than seeing the nuclear family during this period simply as an isolated and privatised 'unit of consumption' (Young and Willmott 1973: 28–9; Goldthorpe *et al.* 1969: 96–7, 117), we might be tempted to characterise it as a unit of sociability. However, we should not imagine that 'homo-social' (Lawrence 2013) behaviour associated the 'traditional' working-class male disappeared in this period. Masculine sociable cultures continued throughout the period covered by this book, and meant that some husbands frequently left their wives looking after the children whilst they spent time with their mates (Abrams 1999: 227; McIvor 2013: 113–114). Michael Hudson (interview, 17 December 2010), who grew up on Beverley's Model Farm estate of privately owned houses in the 1970s, remembered:

> With it being an estate pub, you had all your mates ... and I think he [father] was in darts team ... . If we went out on a summer's evening, you know, the women would literally sit in the car park, in the beer garden, and the glasses of lemonade for the kids would be passed out of the window, with a bag of crisps, and you would be expected to stay there for two hours with a bag of crisps and a glass of lemonade, while all the men were in the bar getting tanked up ... . It was all blokes, I mean the only women there were the ones behind the bar.

As noted above, otherwise family-centred fathers often spent time away from the home engaging in male-dominated pastimes such as fishing, football, rugby, darts and golf. Sally Adams (interview, 21 June 2010) described how, in the 1960s, her father was in many respects a 'family man' but was nevertheless devoted to his hobby of racing whippets on a Sunday: 'my mum would be tearing her hair out, she'd have plans to do other things, but if my dad had a race on, that'd be it.'

Relations with extended family

For the post-war social investigators, the corollary to a purported new emphasis on spouse and children during the age of affluence was the decline of the extended family, thought to have been the bedrock of 'traditional' working-class community (Zweig 1961: 194, Goldthorpe *et al.* 1969: 104–8;

Young and Willmott 1962/1957: 186–201). These authors argued that in the traditional communities, families formed much less distinct household units. In particular, women were thought to maintain a close filial bond with their mothers even after marriage, and to involve them heavily in the upbringing of their own children. Young and Willmott (1962/1957: 47–8) considered that in 1950s Bethnal Green the extent of contact between extended family living close-by, particularly that between mothers and daughters, justified terming the extended family a 'group':

> The daily lives of many women are not confined to the places where they sleep; they are spread over two or more households, in each of which they regularly spend part of their time ... [the 'family group'] commonly consists of a small cluster of families, that is, the families of marriage of the daughters and their common family of origin, and it is made up in the main of the three generations of grandparents, parents, and grandchildren. When people talk about 'the family', it is very often this combination of the two sorts of family which they have in mind.

In a later book (Young and Willmott 1973), the authors argued that the post-war working-class family was entering the latest of at least three stages in the history of the family in western modernity. Before the industrial revolution, the nuclear family had worked together as a unit of production, perhaps on the land or in household industries. The industrial revolution split working-class families into individual producers – husbands, wives and children were contracted individually to work for wages in large factories. This was the stage in which extended families were especially important as a source of support and assistance, particularly for those women whose work was in the home bringing up the next generation of workers. This second stage continued up until the post-war age of affluence, at which point the nuclear family was becoming united again as a unit of consumption and the importance of the extended family dwindled (Young and Willmott 1973: 28–9). The Bethnal Green residents whom Young and Willmott interviewed in the 1950s were therefore representatives of an older, vanishing working-class culture.

Other observers concurred with Young and Willmott that the extended family was losing its centrality in working-class life during the affluent decades as workers became more focussed on the home and nuclear family. Most connected this trend to the increasing ability and willingness of working-class people to strive for improved material conditions. Goldthorpe *et al.* (1969: 104–8) suggested that many of the workers they interviewed in Luton had been tempted away from their natal communities by the lure of high wages in the Vauxhall plant; they were often grateful for the privacy their new 'individuated' home-centred lives afforded, and relieved that they were no longer obliged to keep up relations with assorted local relatives. More recently, Harris (1994: 54) argued that it was the choices that women in particular made about work in this period that led to the diminution of the filial bond and downgrading of the extended family as group. Middle-aged mothers who went out to work could no longer provide the level of support and assistance to their daughters that had been a feature of the traditional community. Others posit a gradual trend across the later twentieth century towards the replacement of kinship with friendship as the key emotional anchor in modern life (Peel, Reed and Walter 2009; Spencer and Pahl 2006). The Beverley evidence, however, shows continuity in the importance of kinship – locally resident extended family could be as important for support and sociability in the 1970s as in the 1930s, though often in different ways.

Pre-affluence – 1935–1954

Beverley interviewees often recalled that they had kin living near at hand who were part of their everyday lives in the ways reminiscent of the 'traditional' model. The high proportion of interviewees born before 1940 whose parents were also born and bred in Beverley (almost three quarters) compares with Young and Willmott's Bethnal Green, where fifty percent of married residents had parents also living in the borough (Young and Willmott 1962/1957: 36). Many Beverley would have had relatives living in the town, and interviewees often mentioned parents, grandparents and other relatives living nearby in the 1940s and 1950s.

In fact, several interviewees described two or more generations of families living on the same street in the 1940s and 1950s. Approximately one-fifth reported that they had relatives in other houses in the street in which they grew up (though not every interviewee was asked about this). The example of one street of small two-up, two-down rented terraced housing is illustrative: three (unrelated) interviewees grew up in St Andrew's Street in the 1940s, and each remembered that extended family occupied other houses in the same street. Betty Carr (interview, 19 March 2010) lived in a house opposite her paternal grandmother. Carl Bowser (ERYMS interview) lived in the house next door to Betty Carr, and remembered that although his mother's parents had died: 'There was all my relations down there – either there or just into Keldgate ... my uncles and aunts, and my mother's uncles and aunts as well.' Ellen Ingleton (interview, 20 April 2010) grew up in a house on St Andrew's Street in the 1940s with her mother's sister living three doors down and her mother's mother living on Lurk Lane, immediately adjacent to St Andrew's Street. She recalled that such physical proximity led to inter-household support:

> I don't know about neighbours – my Aunty used to borrow sometimes off my mother. Because mother only had us two ... she had a lot of children, and my Uncle Cliff worked away but it wasn't a very big wage ... cup of sugar, things like that, 'can you lend me a shilling 'til the weekend?', things like that.

Betty Carr (interview, 19 March 2010) recalled how, as her parents' house became too small for her and three siblings, she began sleeping in her grandmother's house, also on St Andrew's Street. Other streets also had multiple households of relatives: Ellen Malster (interview, 21 May 2010) recalled that:

> My mother's sister lived next door but one to us for donkeys' years, so they were always together. And my cousin was only a year younger than me so it was like having a sister, so we were always just all mingled in.

Brenda Newby (interview,12 January 2010) described how she saw her own mother, who lived on the same street as her, almost every day whilst bringing up children in the 1950s.

Most did not have extended family living on the same street but nevertheless relied on relatives in the town for mutual support and sociability. Doris Daniels (interview, 13 November 2009) was married in 1951 at the age of 19 and recalled how her mother and her sister were frequent companions when she was bringing up her family, and would help with loans and housework:

> Mam would come, or I went to Mam's, she only lived round the corner in a flat, cup of tea with me Mam when I'd got all finished, and Mam would come here … . Lynne was a good girl, always helped with the children … sometimes when I went to my mother's I used to put a bit of butter, or a bit of sugar [to return an earlier loan] and when I came back it was still under the cover. There was no way she would take this bit of butter or this bit of sugar.

Similarly, many interviewees recalled how families living locally shared garden produce, coupons and other windfalls during rationing, for instance:

> My mum's father he had a smallholding, and so they made their own butter and things like that … . My other grandma [whose husband was a joiner and undertaker], if ever she was lucky enough to get anything, she would always share it with the whole family … whenever they had a funeral and they had to pack any of the bodies in ice, she used to make us ice-cream … she'd come round with it specially.
>
> (May Peters, interview, 24 June 2010)

Sociability with family members living in the town was casual. Families rarely visited as a whole group; more commonly, mothers and fathers took their children on separate visits to their respective parents. For example, Les White (interview, 21 October 2010) recalled how he and his sisters and mother were 'always' round at his maternal grandmother's house, but that 'the only time I went to my dad's side was with my dad'. Often, though not always, the emphasis was on the mothers' relatives (given the already noted tendency for mothers in this period to spend more time with their children than fathers), as Anna Mason (interview, 12 July 2010) recalled of the 1940s: 'My mother had a sister she was particularly close to ... we used to see a lot of her and her family ... . My dad's family, we had very little contact with them.'

Of course, the intensity of this casual sociability with family members living locally varied considerably and most people exercised choice, keeping close contact with one or two relatives but ignoring others. Some interviewees who grew up in the 1940s and 1950s would agree with Les White (interview, 21 October 2010) or Ivy Shipton (interview, 17 May 2010) whose parents socialised with a range of local relatives, and said they were 'always' at a relative's house. For others, sociability with extended family was less frequent. Men in particular often failed to keep in touch with their siblings in adulthood. Some interviewees also recalled that their mothers had spent a lot of time with a favoured sister but little time visiting other relatives (Ellen Watton, interview, 8 March 2010). In the 1940s, Anna Mason's mother, despite having fourteen siblings living in the town – 'eight from the first marriage ... and then five, six from the other marriage' – regularly socialised with only one sister (Anna Mason, interview, 12 July 2010). The finding that sociability with extended family could be quite constrained is consonant with John Macfarlane Mogey's study of a working-class district of Oxford in the 1950s. Mogey (1956: 78–9) wrote that, despite the presence of many local residents who were related to each other, adults' interest in extended family concentrated on the parents firstly and siblings secondly. This selectivity belies suggestions (for example, Phillipson *et al.* 2001: 251–65; Harris 1994) that the extended family was more of a 'group' in traditional working-class settings that it later became.

Affluent era – 1955–1975

In the years of rising affluence from the mid-1950s until the 1970s working-class nuclear families in Beverley did not separate from the extended family in the way some sociologists depicted. Most still had relatives living locally with whom they were involved to varying degrees. Across the latter half of the 1970s, the St Nicholas Parish registers show a slightly reduced but still very high percentage of people from Beverley addresses marrying one another (49 per cent), suggestive of a high proportion of couples both of whom had family living in the town (Beverley St Nicholas Register of Marriages). Amongst the interviewees born between 1941 and 1965, most of whom started families of their own in the 1960s and 1970s, 80 per cent had at least one parent who was born and bred in Beverley.

The demolition of some older homes and the building of post-war private and council housing estates seems to have contributed to a decline in the extent to which relatives lived in the same street. Whereas almost a quarter of the interviewees mentioned family living in the streets where they grew up in the 1940s and early 1950s, only a tiny proportion (around three per cent) of those setting up home for themselves in the 1950s and 1960s mentioned relatives living on the same street. Nevertheless, as in the 1940s and early 1950s, in the period of rising affluence from the mid-1950s onwards, family ties were often important in keeping people in the town. Peter Lawson (interview, 4 May 2010) married a Beverley girl in the late 1960s and said they had never considered leaving Beverley because both liked being close to their mothers. Ellen Malster's desire to remain close to her family led her and her husband to turn down the opportunity to emigrate in the 1960s, although some other family members had done so (Ellen and Harry Malster, interview, 21 May 2010). James and Peggy Alexander (interview, 18 February 2010) considered emigrating to Australia in the 1960s for their daughter's health, but gave family as the reason for staying in the town. Louise Christopher (interview, 25 November 2009) recalled that it was her close relationship with her parents that lay behind her decision not to move south to join her husband in the 1970s.

Whether or not interviewees consciously chose to remain living near to their parents, what sociologists termed the 'propinquity' of extended family remained important and useful to most during the 1960s and 1970s. In some respects, reliance on relatives living locally increased as more mothers with school-aged children went out to work. The rise in married women's work outside of the home was a significant post-war economic and social trend, with 26 per cent of married British women (aged 15–59) going out to work in 1951, rising to 49 per cent in 1971 and 62 per cent in 1981 (Thane 1994: 393). Beverley census statistics suggest a similar expansion locally (HMSO 1956: 439; 1984). Amongst interviewees' own families, a conservative interpretation of the data suggests that at least one third of mothers of small children (up to the age of ten) went out to work in the 1960s and 1970s, as opposed to about 10 per cent of mothers before the Second World War. Some of the services that middle-aged women provided for their married daughters in Young and Willmott's (1962/1957) depiction of traditional working-class life, and that Chris Harris (1994) considers became more difficult in the face of competing demands of female employment in the post-war era, appear to have persisted until the 1970s. This may reflect the fact that the mothers of interviewees were from older generations who were not entering the workforce in significant numbers in the post-war decades. Whilst some interviewees remembered that their parents were not willing to babysit, most had parents who obliged, and this service in particular could be invaluable if a woman wanted to return to work while her children were still young – nurseries were not widely available in the 1950s through to the 1970s. Childcare was required at the beginning or end of the day, and might involve children going to their grandparents' home. Some paid their mothers for this kind of regular childcare, reasoning that the money was better spent within the family than outside (Vic Baker, interview, 29 May 2010). Other grandparents provided this service for free. For single mothers, having parents living nearby was perhaps even more important, as Elaine Mateer (interview, 29 March 2010) found when her marriage broke down in the 1970s. Sally Adams (interview, 21 June 2010) discovered that having her mother at hand was extremely useful when she had to juggle the demands of a severely disabled child with the need to go back to work in the 1970s. Even those who did not work found their mothers could be an everyday source of help and support. Parents were by far the most usual providers of babysitting services for couples who wanted to go out and socialise.

Help from extended family was not restricted to babysitting. Parents and siblings helped in other ways, most notably at the time when a couple were setting up home. Collecting for the 'bottom drawer' was mentioned by some interviewees. This was the tradition by which relatives collected and bought household items (for example, bedsheets, towels and other small items) for a couple who were awaiting the move into their own house (interviews: Jack Binnington 13 July 2010; June and Dave Ireland 15 July 2010). Other gifts and loans from parents to couples setting up home included help with purchasing items of furniture and even the gift of a second-hand car (interviews: Jack Binnington 13 July 2010; George Little 12 March 2010). In this era of rising home ownership, parents and siblings helped with decorating, gardening and DIY tasks (interviews: Lynne Norton 9 November 2009; Dick Gibson 11 March 2010). There were many more examples given of practical help and assistance from family members than from neighbours, and it seems that family were the first port of call for serious material help (whether with substantial babysitting, loans of money or help with tasks). This reflects Klein's (1965: 134) observation that most neighbourhood mutual assistance in the 'traditional' community was supplied by relatives living locally. Jim Fisher (interview, 16 December 2009) recalled that when he and his wife had children:

> If you wanted an hour, Mary [the next door neighbour] said, 'leave the kids for an hour,' or sommat like that, she was there like, but when it came down to serious babysitting it would be my mother-in-law or father-in-law.

Although the parent–child bond continued to be important for certain kinds of support for most across the period, the extent to which regular contact was maintained with adult siblings was highly variable in the affluent period as previously. Sisters were often close. Lynne Norton (interview, 9 November 2009) and Doris Daniels (interview, 13 November 2009) lived on the same council estate throughout most of their adult life and there were periods during which they saw each other every day. Other siblings might have little contact over the course of everyday life, but still considered that brothers and sisters living locally were useful for emergencies, and that the family would all pull together when necessary. The idea that you should not 'live in each other's pockets' was stressed by these interviewees (interviews: Gerald Ibbotson 7 July 2010; Iris Brown 21 May 2010).

Most of the interviewees had grown up in Beverley and remained in the town throughout their adult life. In addition to facilitating the day-to-day mutual assistance that would have been more difficult at a greater distance, propinquity of kin made possible some of the continuation of frequent, casual, extended-family sociability that Young and Willmott (1962/1957) highlighted as a feature of 'traditional' working-class life. Irregular but frequent calling in to parents' houses continued to be commonplace across the age of affluence, and for many families appeared unaltered from the 1930s to the 1970s (interviews: Fred and May Peters 24 June 2010; Elaine Mateer 29 March 2010). So Keith Barrett (interview, 2 September 2010) described his mother's sociability with her sisters in in the 1960s: 'They [mum's sisters] were only round the corner ... so they was always to and fro'; Lynne Norton (interview, 9 November 2009) remembered that her sister and mother both lived nearby and were her most regular companions when she was bringing up her own family in the 1970s, shopping together and helping with domestic work when necessary (in case of illness, for example); Elaine Mateer (interview, 29 March 2010) recalled that in the 1960s her mother was particularly close to an aunt who lived around the corner, and that both gave daily assistance to their aging mother who also lived locally, helping with shopping, housework and building her a fire each day. Rosalind Watkiss Singleton (2010: 114) found a similar degree of continuity across the period 1930–1970 in the Black Country: 'the role played by mothers and grandmothers survived despite the apparent transformation of postwar society.'

In fact, post-war social and economic change could strengthen relationships between extended family members rather than loosening these ties. As Klein (1965: 175) acknowledged, rising living standards could promote easy sociability in the place of material mutual assistance with family. There was some suggestion in the Beverley interviews that a shift in male leisure towards the nuclear family could bring husbands into the ambit of their wives' extended family sociability. James and Peggy Alexander (interview, 18 February 2010), married in the 1960s, recalled:

> We used to visit my mother and father, your aunt and uncle at the shop ... we did spend quite a lot of time visiting ... . We would go round to my parents for tea on a Sunday, and stay just a bit of the evening.

Rising living standards brought new ways for extended families to spend time together. From the 1960s, some went on holiday as a whole nuclear-family unit with other members of the extended family, a phenomenon that was not reported in the previous decades. Julie Davies (interview, 27 November 2009), born in 1965, recalled annual holidays, with several members of the extended family staying in a number of caravans together. Sally Adams (interview, 21 June 2010) remembered similar holidays with her parents and her father's sisters and their children at a local beach resort in the 1960s. When Sally was married she took her own husband and family on holidays with her sister and parents. Ivy Shipton (interview, 17 May 2010), born in 1963, said she had done very little as a family unit with both her parents when she was small, but that:

We did more with them when our children were small ... they went on holiday with us a couple of times, just up to Scarborough ... my mother enjoyed it ... my Dad did too ... but it was a new experience for them really, going in a unit.

The rise in working-class car ownership in the 1950s and 1960s not only provided a new way for husband, wife and children to spend leisure time together, but could also facilitate time spent with other relatives. Jim Fisher (interview, 16 December 2009) remembered Sunday afternoons visiting Hornsea with his parents and grandparents in their car during the 1960s. Ellen and Harry Malster (interview, 21 May 2010) remembered that in the same decade:

Harry: We used to go to Continental in Hull ... .
Ellen: I suppose you'd call it a club nowadays, it was like a variety thing, they had acts on the stage, but the novelty was, you got food. It was the days they started doing what you called scampi in baskets ... there was a bit of dancing ... the whole family used to go there ... there must have been about twenty of us sometimes ... various cars and things, you didn't have to worry about drink driving.

Car ownership also helped people maintain regular contact with family members who lived at a greater distance. Unlike the more casual sociability with family living in Beverley, visits to extended family living in different towns or villages required more organisation, but again were a way in which the nuclear family socialised as a whole unit with others. Peter Lawson (interview, 4 May 2010) recalled that when growing up in the 1960s the main weekend family activity was going out in the car with his parents and paternal grandmother who lived in Hull. Ron Matthews (interview, 2 December 2010) remembered how he and his wife and child would often drive to Ullswater in Cumbria to see his wife's sister for the weekend in the 1970s.

So it seems that, alongside some strands of continuity in extended family relationships, these relationships were partly reshaped and realigned to reflect changing conditions across the age of affluence. However, if there was a shift from extended family as 'group' to 'network', this was rather subtle and was not obvious in the oral evidence I collected. Rather than supporting those who argue for the replacement of extended with nuclear family across this period, then, the research reported here supports those who trace the continuation of the extended family as a central anchor in many working-class lives. As late as the early 2000s, when sociologists conducted a restudy of community life in Swansea 40 years after Harris and Rosser's original investigation, one of the researchers (Charles 2012: 447) was able to write:

Patterns of residence and contact have changed rather less than we had expected. Rather than increases in women's employment and geographical mobility leading to a reduction in the provision of support within extended family networks, we found that such support was widespread and precisely what defined someone as being 'family' and this was the case no matter how near or far families lived from each other.

Conclusion

The extent to which the working-class 'traditional' gender-divided family model was ever predominant in any particular locality was subject to variation, dependant on factors including size of settlement and the nature of local industry. In the small West Yorkshire town of Featherstone during the 1950s, an almost total absence of female employment and the socio-economic dominance of coal-mining led to strongly gender-separated marriages (Dennis, Henriques and Slaughter 1969); however, two decades earlier in the relatively large city of Bristol, high wages and the ability for married couples to move away from their natal communities meant that many working-class marriages appeared to be of the 'companionate', home-centred type (Franklin 1989). Beverley, it appears, did not represent either of these extremes – a variety of approaches to marital togetherness and home-centred behaviour were possible all across our period. The Beverley evidence therefore supports authors who argue that 'the idea of a transition from an older, homo-social male culture, rooted in work and leisure, to a new, more family-centred, culture was ... ahistorical' (Lawrence 2013: 285; see also: Abrams 1999; Roberts 1999; Singleton 2010). We have also seen how rising living standards during the post-war age of affluence could afford opportunities for a new expansiveness in nuclear-family sociability, belying depictions of the family as a 'privatised' unit of consumption.

References

Abrams, Lynn (1999) '"There Was Nobody Like my Daddy": Fathers, the Family and the Marginalisation of Men in Modern Scotland', *The Scottish Historical Review*, 78, 219–242.

Bedarida, Francois (1991) *A Social History of England 1851–1990*, 2nd edition, London: Routledge.

Bernstein, George L. (2004) *The Myth of Decline: The Rise of Britain Since 1945*, London: Pimlico.

Bott, Elizabeth (1971) *Family and Social Network: Roles Norms and External Relationships in Ordinary Urban Families*, 2nd edition, Thetford: Tavistock.

Brooke, Stephen (2001) 'Gender and Working Class Identity in Britain during the 1950s', *Journal of Social History*, 34:4, 773–795.

Brown, Lucy (1989) 'Modern Beverley: Beverley After 1945', in K.J. Allison (ed.), *A History of the County of York. East Riding: Volume 6: The Borough and Liberties of Beverley*, London: Oxford University Press, 154–160.

Charles, Nickie (2012) 'Families, Communities and Social Change: Then and Now', *The Sociological Review*, 60, 438–456.

Cronin, James (1984) *Labour and Society in Britain 1918–1979*, Guildford: Batsford.

Davis, Angela (2009) 'A Critical Perspective on British Social Surveys and Community Studies and Their Accounts of Married Life', *Cultural and Social History*, 6:1, 47–64.

Dennis, Norman, Fernando Henriques and Clifford Slaughter (1969) *Coal is Our Life: An Analysis of a Yorkshire Mining Community*, 2nd edition, London: Tavistock.

Devine, Fiona (1992) *The Affluent Workers Revisited. Privatism and the Working Class*, Edinburgh: Edinburgh University Press.

Fletcher, Ronald (1966) *The Family and Marriage in Britain*, Harmondsworth: Penguin.

Franklin, Adrian (1989) 'Working-Class Privatism: An Historical Case Study of Bedminster, Bristol', *Environment and Planning D: Society and Space*, 7, 93–113.

Goldthorpe, John Harry, David Lockwood, Frank Bechhofer and Jennifer Platt (1969) *The Affluent Worker in the Class Structure*, London: Cambridge University Press.

Gunn, Simon (2011) 'The Buchanan Report, Environment and the Problem of Traffic in 1960s Britain', *Twentieth Century British History*, 22, 521–542.

Hall, David (2012) *Working Lives. The Forgotten Voices of Britain's Post-war Working Class*, London: Transworld.

Harris, Chris (1994) 'The Family in Post-war Britain', in J. Obelkevich and P. Catterall (eds), *Understanding Post-war British Society*, London: Routledge, 45–57.

HMSO (1956) *Census 1951, England and Wales: Occupation Tables*, London: HMSO.

HMSO (1984) *Census 1981: Key Statistics for Urban Areas: The North: Cities and Towns*, London: HMSO.

Hunt, Geoffrey and Saundra Satterlee (1987) 'Darts, Drinks and the Pub: The Culture of Female Drinking', *Sociological Review*, 35:3, 575–601.

Klein, Josephine (1965) *Samples from English Cultures (Volume 1)*, London: Routledge & Kegan Paul.

Lane, Margaret (2014) 'Not the Boss of One Another. A Reinterpretation of Working-Class Marriage in England, 1900–1970', *Cultural and Social History*, 11:3, 441–458.

Langhamer, Claire (2005) 'The Meanings of Home in Postwar Britain', *Journal of Contemporary History*, 40:2, 341–362.

Langhamer, Claire (2000) *Women's Leisure in England, 1920–1960*, Manchester: Manchester University Press.

Langhamer, Claire (2012) 'Love, Selfhood and Authenticity in Post-war Britain', *Cultural and Social History*, 9:2, 277–297.

Lawrence, Jon (2013) 'Class, "Affluence" and the Study of Everyday Life in Britain, c.1930–1964', *Cultural and Social History*, 10, 273–299.

McIvor, Arthur (2013) *Working Lives. Work in Britain Since 1945*, Basingstoke: Palgrave Macmillan.

McKibbin, Ross (1998) *Classes and Cultures: England, 1918–1951*, Oxford: Oxford University Press.

Mogey, John Macfarlane (1956) *Family and Neighbourhood. Two Studies in Oxford*, London: Oxford University Press.

Moran, Joe (2012) 'Imagining the Street in Post-war Britain', *Urban History*, 39:1, 166–186.

Moss, Stella (2011) '"She is Everywhere in Publand". Older Women Drinkers and the English Public House in the Mid-Twentieth Century', unpublished conference paper, Urban History Group Annual Conference, Robinson College, University of Cambridge, UK, 31 March–1 April 2011.

Pahl, Ray (1984) *Divisions of Labour*, London: Blackwell.

Peel, Mark with Liz Reed and James Walter (2009) 'The Importance of Friends: The Most Recent Past', in Barbara Caine (ed.), *Friendship. A History*, London: Equinox, 317–356.

Phillipson, Chris, Miriam Bernard, Judith Phillips and Jim Ogg (2001) *The Family and Community Life of Older People. Social Networks and Social Support in Three Urban Areas*, London: Routledge.

Roberts, Elizabeth (1995) *Women and Families: An Oral History, 1940–1970*, Oxford: Blackwell.

Roberts, Ian (1999) 'A Historical Construction of the Working Class', in Huw Beynon and Pandeli Glavanis (eds), *Patterns of Social Inequality. Essays for Richard Brown*, London: Longman, 147–160.

Rosser, Colin and Chris Harris (1965) *The Family and Social Change: A Study of Family and Kinship in a South Wales Town*, London: Routledge & Kegan Paul.

Singleton, Rosalind Watkiss (2010) '"Old Habits Persist". Change and Continuity in Black Country Communities: Pensnett, Sedgley and Tipton, 1945–c.1970', unpublished PhD thesis, University of Wolverhampton.

Spencer, Liz and Ray Pahl (2006) *Rethinking Friendship: Hidden Solidarities Today*, Oxford: Princeton University Press.

Thane, Pat (1994) 'Women Since 1945', in Paul Johnson (ed.), *Twentieth Century Britain: Economic, Social and Cultural Change*, London: Longman, 392–411.

Todd, Selina (2008) 'Affluence, Class and Crown Street: Reinvestigating the Post-War Working Class', *Contemporary British History*, 22, 501–518.

Todd, Selina (2014) *The People: The Rise and Fall of the Working Class 1910–2010*, London: John Murray.

Todd, Selina and Hillary Young (2012) 'From Baby Boomers to Beanstalkers. Making the Modern Teenager in Postwar Britain', *Cultural and Social History*, 9:3, 451–467.

Walkerdine, Valerie (2010) 'Communal Beingness and Affect: An Exploration of Trauma in an Ex-Industrial Community', *Body and Society*, 16, 91–116.

Williamson, Margaret (2009) 'Gender, Leisure and Marriage in a Working-class Community, 1939–1960', *Labour History Review*, 74:2, 185–198.

Willmott, Peter (1963) *The Evolution of a Community: A Study of Dagenham After Forty Years*, London: Routledge & Kegan Paul.

Wilson, Dolly Smith (2006) 'A New Look at the Affluent Worker: The Good Working Mother in Post-War Britain', *Twentieth Century British History*, 17, 206–229.

Young, Michael and Peter Willmott (1962/1957) *Family and Kinship in East London*, Harmondsworth: Pelican.

Young, Michael, and Peter Willmott (1973) *The Symmetrical Family. A Study of Work and Leisure in the London Region*, London: Routledge & Kegan Paul.

Zweig, Ferdynand (1961) *The Worker in an Affluent Society. Family Life and Industry*, London: Heinemann.

Primary sources

Beverley Guardian, 12 January 1957.

St Nicholas Church Marriage Registers, ERALS, PE 193/7; PE 193/8.

Carl Bowser (ERYMS interview).

Beverley St Nicholas Register of Marriages. No 6, 6 Sept 1969–28 July 1979, ERALS: PE 193/10/1.

3 Neighbours

In 2008, Tom Potter gave me an account of life on Beverley's Cherry Tree council estate during his childhood in the 1940s. He emphasised the ways in which neighbours looked after each other:

> The community looked after itself. Mrs Fisher, next door to us was the local midwife. She wasn't trained to be a midwife, she wasn't qualified to be a midwife ... but the woman had been doing it for years. She knew more about the bloody job than the midwives did. She also laid out the dead. If someone died in the street, 'send for Mrs Fisher'. She knew what holes to plug in and, y'know, what to tie and all the rest of it ... . And then anybody in the street, my job on a Saturday morning was to shop for them, if they were not too able to do it for themselves ... . My dad was a shipyard worker ... a bit of boozer ... like most people who worked at the yard ... . When he came in for his lunch at lunch-time, or his dinner as he called it, and his tea at tea-time, there had to be a pint pot of tea on the table for him, and if there weren't there was a barney. So my mum would be a bit worried if she had no tea, so she would – I would nip next door to Mrs Fisher or Mrs Leighton: 'can you lend my mum a mashing of tea?' and they'd put two teaspoons in a little bag and you'd take it. And that mashing of tea would be for the old fella, no-one else got it.
>
> (Tom Potter, interview, 24 October 2008)

Neighbourliness is also at the heart of many academic portraits of the 'traditional working-class community'. When sociologists and historians refer to 'neighbours' and 'neighbouring' they usually mean the social world of the residential street, the interaction between people living in immediate proximity. According to oral historian Elizabeth Roberts, for many working-class people in the mid-century 'what was of primary importance in practical terms was the street in which you lived and your immediate neighbours' (Roberts 1995: 200). Jeremy Seabrook (1973: 64) described the importance of proximity in his memoir of working-class life in mid-century Northampton:

The closest links were generally established with immediate neighbours. Those a few doors distant were treated with cordiality which diminished progressively as their dwelling-place became farther removed, until those at the end of the street had to be content with a cursory nod and the briefest glance of recognition.

In Tom Potter's account of neighbourhood life in 1940s Beverley, there is a clear gender divide – his father is largely absent (either at work or in the pub), and his mother is at home, plugged into neighbourly networks that she utilises in the day-to-day struggle to make ends meet. Academic accounts also depict the mutuality and sociability of the residential street as a feminine response to relative material austerity (Klein 1965; Roberts 1971; Meacham 1977; Roberts 1984; Tebbutt 1995). Such has been the prominence of women's neighbourly relations within the literature on working-class community that Trevor Lummis (1985: 76) considered that much of what is often called 'community' is in fact the 'class experience of women'.

For Tom, the close neighbourliness he remembered from his youth is a thing of the past: 'people don't look after each other anymore. As simple as that – people have become self-seeking. They want what's good for them.' According to some post-war social investigators and recent historians, the traditional neighbouring practices of working-class women were disrupted after the Second World War by social, economic and cultural change including the rehousing of many of the working classes on council estates, married women going out to work and rising living standards and welfare state safety net that made mutual exchange and assistance unnecessary. So Josephine Klein (1965: 128–33), in her summary of post-war social investigations into working-class culture, contrasted the old streets of terraced housing where everyone knew everyone else, and the frequency of neighbourly contact created shared norms and feelings of solidarity, with new council estates, where there was far less communal sociability. Klein (1965: 224, 263) was clear, however, that the decline in neighbourliness was not only to be found on new estates – estate life intensified a wider trend, arising from the profound social changes felt to be underway in an increasingly affluent society. Oral historian Elizabeth Roberts (1995: 199) utilised Klein's designation of some neighbourhoods as 'traditional ... characterised by the provision of mutual practical help and social support', and considered that as the period (1940–1970) progressed 'we see these experiences becoming increasingly less common ... because the social relationships between those within working-class neighbourhoods underwent significant change'.

In this chapter, I will use the Beverley oral histories to draw different conclusions about the effects of post-war social, economic and cultural shifts on working-class neighbourly practices. In the first two sections, I subject models of 'traditional' working-class neighbourliness to empirical scrutiny, comparing these with the Beverley evidence for neighbouring practices during the years 1935–1954. I argue that though the model of 'traditional' working-class neighbourliness that emerges from the writings of Roberts and others finds some support in the detailed oral testimony, it can easily overstate the degree of homogeneity, helpfulness and interaction amongst residents of working-class streets. The final two sections utilise the Beverley evidence to assess the case for more restricted neighbourly relations in the affluent era, c.1955–1975. I found strong evidence of continuity in social practices, with interviewees describing patterns of neighbourly interaction in the 1970s that often resembled those from the 1940s – particularly on council estates, which, in contrast to some accounts, were not in the vanguard of social change during this period. The changes in patterns of neighbouring that did take place were neither clear-cut nor pointing in a single direction. Affluence reduced the need for some forms of material exchange, but post-war social, economic and cultural developments could prompt new forms of sociability and mutuality between neighbours.

Neighbourly sociability and mutuality, 1935–1954

'Neighbouring' has been a central plank in models of the 'traditional' working-class community. Empirical historiography has often detailed social networks, informal sociability and mutuality in working-class neighbourhoods in the decades between the late Victorian period and 1950. Ellen Ross (1983) described how, in early twentieth-century London slums, women on the edge of poverty used neighbourhood networks of female mutuality as a crucial survival strategy. They gave assistance to neighbours in need – loaning foodstuffs and clothing, minding each other's children, exchanging information and services – as if paying into an insurance scheme. This help was given in the expectation that the favour might one day need to be returned. Although concerned philanthropists, as well as their husbands, often viewed the resources that women paid into these mutual networks as an impediment to saving and therefore to escaping poverty, the women themselves knew the worth of their systems of mutuality and were reluctant to abandon them. Robert Roberts (1971: 26) described a similar degree of instrumentality (leavened at times with sentiment) in the mutuality of the Salford slum where he grew up in the early twentieth century. A number of authors have testified to the persistence of feminine neighbourly cultures in diverse British working-class districts across the early and mid-twentieth century (Tebbutt 1995; Colls 2004; Roberts 1984); Robert Colls (2004: 284), for example, remembered that matriarchs ruled the streets in early 1960s South Shields: 'a hard knot of older women stood at the corner shop, talking calmly, all arms-folded except for one who, arm out straight, gently rocked a pram. Mothers like these held the streets from first morning message to last evening call'. Some authors suggest that the mutuality of working-class neighbours could incorporate men too (Lane 2011: 146; Hall 2012: 43). The Beverley evidence supported the proposition that in some working-class streets during the first half of the twentieth century a culture of sociability and mutuality could prevail. Much of the evidence discussed below relates to a particular street, Beckside, though testimony from other streets is also incorporated.

Settled residence of neighbourhoods

According to Klein (1965: 133–4), cultures of mutuality were most likely to develop in places with a stable population – a core of residents who had long knowledge of each other, who knew what could and could not be expected from neighbours and who might transmit the culture of the street to new residents. Beckside in Beverley in the period 1935–1954 was such a place, a street of rented terraced housing clustered around the head of a centuries-old canal. Jack Binnington (interview, 3 August 2010) recalled that on Beckside there was long continuity of residence of particular families, including different generations of the same family, and that this meant everybody knew everybody else: 'If I looked at Beckside I could tell you everybody who lived from corner of Hull Road, where the fountain is, all the way down up to Potter Hill.' In the 1950s, a number of barge workers living on Beckside descended from several generations who had plied the same trade in the area; these families had often inter-married, giving the profession of 'bargee' an almost caste-like quality (Schofield 1988: 120–9). Jack's own father and grandfather had been barge skippers living in or around Beckside; other Beckside names associated for several generations with the barge trade included Gillyon, Tattersall, Scaife, Verity and Peck (Jack Binnington, interview, 3 August 2010). Jack recalled that during the 1950s another Binnington family lived opposite him on Beckside, and that there were several Lascelles households, two Peck households and several Gillyon households. Some of these families were well known across Beverley for their connection both with Beckside and the barge industry (interviews: Jean Benson 14 January 2010; Dennis Duke 14 June 2010). As described in the previous chapter, many other working-class streets at this time also contained multiple households of extended family.

However, it was not necessary to have families of several generations living on the same street for a sense of familiarity to exist. Streets were remembered as neighbourly when interviewees recalled knowing every resident and where residential turnover was low:

> People tended to stay put on the estate [an inter-war council estate] and we were a close community. I can still remember most of our neighbours [in the 1930s and 1940s], starting with the Smiths at number one, then there were the Cherries, Hiltons, Robinsons, Spinks, Walkers, Kendrews, Marsdens, Hunts, Greys, Rustons, Galbraiths, Buntings.
>
> (Joan Binns, ERYMS written reminiscence)

Such streets, in which everyone was known to everyone else, were the contexts for neighbourly traditions such as collecting for a wreath for a deceased resident. At the time of the interviews John Day (interview, 10 November 2009) still had a list of those who had donated to a collection for his maternal grandfather's funeral in the 1950s. The list was a long one, containing his grandfather's neighbours on Grovehill Road, all of whom John remembered.

Neighbourhood as the social world of women

As noted above, 'traditional' forms of neighbourliness have been seen as part of a working-class culture that was the product of a particular historic period in which husbands were the wage earners and wives kept the home and brought up the children (Garrioch and Peel 2006: 665). There was certainly evidence from the Beverley interviews to support this idea of residential streets as the social domain of women. Judy Whittles (interview, 10 May 2010) grew up in Beckside in the 1940s and recalled how women of her mother's generation were rooted in their streets:

> The women, I won't say they was housebound, but they didn't move off Beckside. They weren't going to bingo, or going to the pub, or, they'd maybe go to pictures occasionally … but most of them, like Mrs Hancock and all them, they never moved, you could have knocked on their door any time of day and they'd be in.

Mothers socialised in the public spaces of their neighbourhoods. Jobs undertaken outside – washing the windows, sweeping the space outside of the house, hanging out clothes – were all occasions for talking to neighbours. Mavis Martin (ERYMS interview) remembered that her mother would brush the street outside their house in the 1940s:

> And she'd say to me dad 'I'll only be two minutes.' 'Oh,' he said, 'There's an hour gone by,' … no sweeping was done, she'd stand talking.

Jack Blakeston's mother put time aside each evening to talk over the fence to her next door neighbour: 'She used to spend an hour every night propped over this fence … supping this tea and having a natter' (Jack Blakeston, interview, 10 September 2010). Doris Daniels (interview, 13 November 2009) brought up a family of her own on the Swinemoor Council estate in the 1950s. With a large family she claimed there wasn't really the time for a lot of sociability in the home, although she did sometimes have neighbours in for cups of tea during the day. She remembered conversation with female neighbours on an evening outside in front of houses:

> After tea you would get the youngsters to bed, and Mrs Keddy would come to gate … and suddenly Bet across the road would come across to her, then they'd maybe see me … by the time we'd finish there'd be five of us … . And when it was cold … well they'd wrap their arms in the pinnies, you see, and stand talking.

Many other interviews recalled that their mothers would stand talking in shared yards, over garden fences or in the street outside the house with neighbours. On warmer summer evenings, Jack Binnington (interview, 22

June 2010) recalled that mothers on Beckside would sit outside with other women and children, sometimes listening to the radio. Klein (1965: 141) noted that women living in the same neighbourhood might meet and interact on a daily basis in local shops. There were approximately twelve shops in or very close to Beckside in the 1940s and 1950s, including a post office, a grocer's, a wet fish shop, and a butcher's shop, as well as small businesses selling fruit and vegetables, ice cream or soft drinks from the front rooms of houses (interviews: Jack Binnington 13 July 2010; Jean Benson 14 January 2010). Peggy Alexander (interview, 18 February 2010) recalled that in the 1940s and 1950s every shop on Beckside had a chair for old people to sit on while they talked to other customers, and that when she took over a shop near Beckside in the early 1960s the extent to which local women used the shop for talking became something of a nuisance.

Most interviewees corroborated the suggestion that homes were little used for sociability by the 'traditional' working classes (Klein 1965: 141). However, neighbouring women who became particularly friendly would visit each other when their husbands were out at work or in the pub. Ivy Shipton (interview, 17 May 2010) recalled her mother visiting and being visited by other neighbours for cups of tea in the 1950s, as did Patrick Mateer (interview, 13 January 2010). On the Cherry Tree council estate in the 1940s, George Hunter (interview, 14 January 2010) recalled that his mother had neighbours around for tarot card readings. Jack Binnington's mother exchanged visits with neighbours, and they would knit and darn together (Jack Binnington, interview, 22 June 2010).

A complex of factors connected to their role as housewives meant that women sometimes required the help and cooperation of those around them. The period 1935 to 1954 contains significant variation in national employment rates – from high unemployment in the 1930s to 'full' employment during wartime and post-war years, but throughout these years there were reasons why borrowing of foodstuffs might be necessary. From the outbreak of the Second World War until 1954, rationing of a variety of foodstuffs and consumables such as coal could make household management difficult (Tom Potter, interview, 24 October 2008). Across the period, the absence of fridges for storing perishable foodstuffs and the lack of shops open on Sundays presented further challenges to household management that meant that provisions could easily run out (Peter Cooper, ERYMS interview). Wages were not high for many workers, and if they had several children it could be a challenge to ensure that wages lasted the week (Betty Carr, interview, 19 March 2010). No banks offered credit for working-class people and so cash-flow problems could develop (Keith Barrett, interview, 2 September 2010). In the households where men gave their wives a proportion of their wages for housekeeping, the problem of budgeting was sometimes seen as solely the mother's (interviews: Betty Carr 19 March 2010; Sally Adams 21 June 2010; Jack Binnington 22 June 2010). While credit was available through 'club men', used to buy more expensive items such as children's clothes, contingent borrowing from neighbours of consumables and sometimes small amounts of money could still be required (interviews: Keith Barrett 2 September 2010; Ellen Ingleton 20 April 2010; Patrick Mateer 13 January 2010).

Most interviewees who grew up, or had their own families, in the 1940s and 1950s could remember loans of small items between women in neighbouring households. Interviewees mentioned that foodstuffs such as milk, eggs, flour, margarine, gravy powder and sugar were all borrowed by neighbours. Households also loaned and borrowed coal. Post-war rationing encouraged the swapping of coupons. This kind of small-scale exchange took place in both the older terraced housing and on the inter-war and post-war council estates. Loans were occasional, often sought by mothers who had run out of something they needed that day.

In addition to these kinds of material exchange, neighbouring women exchanged services. Some women assisted with laying out those who had died at home. Betty Carr (interview, 19 March 2010) remembered that when she was a child in the 1940s her grandma was sometimes called on to perform this task, and Keith Barrett (interview, 2 September 2010) remembered that his mother helped neighbours in this way during the 1950s. Some neighbours assisted each other with babysitting. William Vincent (interview, 25 May 2010) recalled staying with neighbouring families while his parents went out for evenings in the 1950s. Neighbours could also provide childcare for mothers who worked – Iris Brown (interview, 21 May 2010) remembered a female neighbour looking after her after school until her mother or older sister returned from work. Interviewees recalled shopping for elderly neighbours (interviews: Tom Potter 24 October 2008; Ellen Ingleton 20 April 2010; Betty Carr 19 March 2010).

A sad 1945 court case reported in the *Beverley Guardian* (21, 28 April 1945) illustrated how neighbourhood networks could be used to obtain covert and sensitive assistance not readily available otherwise. Mary Harrison of Hull was charged with causing the death of Bessie Lawson, of Schofield Avenue on Beverley's Grovehill council estate, through a botched abortion. Bessie's neighbours Edith Gillyon and Mrs Wright had approached another Schofield Avenue resident, Mrs Boddy, on Bessie's behalf to ask for her assistance. Mrs Boddy's sister, Mary Harrison, was known to perform illegal abortions. Shortly after Mary Harrison performed the abortion operation, Bessie was discovered by her son in a stricken state; knowing that their neighbour Mrs Wright was reputed to be a nurse, it was her he ran to for help.

Rather than simply giving assistance in expectation of the favour one day being returned, a charitable impulse apparently motivated the help many women offered to their neighbours. Hannah Witham (interview, 26 April 2010) described how her mother gave coal to a poorer neighbour who had three children and whose husband was an invalid, even though it was not returned and Hannah's father was strongly opposed to this practice. Fred and May Peters (interview, 24 June 2010) each recalled that in the streets in which they had grown up in the 1940s, their mothers checked on older people and did shopping for them, and that older clothes were passed on to poorer families. May remembered her grandmother gave fruit to a neighbour whose husband had died in the war. Others reported how clothes were passed onto large families in working-class streets in the 1940s (Ken Ingleton, interview, 23 March 2010).

In addition to neighbourhood shops' social function as meeting places, noted above, they were often tied into the street's networks of mutual support (see also Ross 1983; Roberts 1971). The difficulty of managing weekly budgets in a time before widespread bank credit underpinned reliance on the institution of 'tick' in neighbourhood shops. Enid Bolton (interview, 10 March 2010) ran a shop on Grovehill Road in the 1950s and remembered running weekly bills for customers. Furthermore, during rationing, shopkeepers on Beckside ensured that each family got its fair share of any restricted items that became available – sweets, oranges or bananas – and did not mark ration cards (John and Judy Whittles, interview, 10 May 2010).

The close relationship between sociability and mutual assistance amongst women living in the same street is illustrated by the ways in which they combined to provide social activities for themselves and their children. Two women who each kept small shops in Beckside in the 1940s and 1950s, Nelly Hancock and Madge Jackson, organised summer coach trips to the seaside for mothers and children (it was remembered that fathers occasionally came along). Mothers paid in to a weekly 'diddlum' at the shops for these trips (interviews: James and Peggy Alexander 18 February 2010; John and Judy Whittles 10 May 2010; Joyce Sumner 13 August 2010). 'Diddlums' were neighbourhood savings clubs, in which one woman (these were usually female) would agree to hold the savings on behalf of the others and pay out at an agreed time; they were commonplace in working-class settings across England at least until the 1970s (Singleton 2010: 307). Mrs Blakeston ran a weekly whist drive in a room above the Mariner's pub for Beckside women, funds from which were used for an annual coach trip for the street's families (interviews: Joyce Sumner 13 August 2010; Jack Blakeston 10 August 2010). Trips were to the Yorkshire seaside towns of Bridlington or Scarborough, and were popular because neither children nor their mothers often left Beverley:

> And for us to go to Brid [Bridlington]! And all the mothers went, there'd be just from Beckside about three busloads … . If it was a nice day … they'd all get their deckchairs and all sit together and they maybe did that six times a year.
>
> (John and Judy Whittles, interview, 10 May 2010)

Women sometimes cooperated to organise social activities independent of their children. In the 1940s the landlady of the Foresters pub organised a club for women living locally who met upstairs and rehearsed small performances that were held in the pub; annual women's trips were also organised from this pub (interviews: Doris Daniels 16 December 2009; Lynne Norton 9

November 2009). Some women during the 1940s and 1950s organised social clubs in their homes (see Chapter 6: 'Civil Society').

However, we should not see the sociability of the street solely as a feminine realm. Interviewees recalled childhoods in the 1940s and 1950s in which most time outside of school was spent playing locally with other children from their streets. With little traffic to disturb them, children colonised the streets on evenings, weekends and school holidays. The children of Beckside and Flemingate met on a large area at the junction of three streets known as Potter Hill to play games including football, cricket and 'revalio', a hide-and-seek game that could incorporate large numbers (John and Judy Whittles, interview, 10 May 2010). Bill Cooper (ERYMS interview) remembered that in the later 1940s, despite recent slum clearance in the neighbourhood, around forty children from Beckside might congregate at Potter Hill. Older boys organised their own football teams; Bill Cooper remembered two teams from Beckside playing on a makeshift pitch on Figham, a common pasture nearby. Children living on the council estates at this time also had streets and green spaces as their play areas (interviews: Janet Thompson 23 November 2009; Judy and Dave Ireland 15 July 2010). Territoriality was important to children, and many interviewees recalled fights with those from different neighbourhoods in this period (interviews: Matthew Walton 22 July 2010; William Vincent 25 May 2010).

Children were incorporated into their mothers' neighbourly activity. Like Tom Potter in the quotation opening this chapter, some interviewees remembered being asked to shop or collect cinders for neighbours (interviews: Ellen Ingleton 20 April 2010; Betty Carr 19 March 2010; George Hunter 14 January 2010). Socialisation through schools (all primary schools were denominational), home and Sunday School as well as children's organisations with a connection to the Church (Scouts and Guides, Church Lads' Brigade and Girls' Friendly Society) exposed children to the message that it was correct to help one's neighbour. Iris Brown (interview, 21 June 2010) remembered:

> At Sunday school and things like that they always used to be the same: help the neighbour ... . We use to go and knock on the door and say would you like anything brought from shop Mrs Ought? ... . It was always knocked into us ... .
>
> Me mother was funny like that ... you know, you do things for people you don't expect anything in return. 'A thank you is good enough,' she used to say.

It is generally thought that men during this period were less committed to the sociability of residential streets than were women and children (for example, Singleton 2010: 99–100). A husband's daily work usually took him away from the street and into contact with people from a wider area. The male fellowship of pubs, clubs, sports teams and hobby societies was not usually delimited by streets. However, there were ways in which men became involved in the mutuality of their home neighbourhood. Two interviewees who had grown up on Beckside in the 1930s and 1940s recalled that their fathers kept pigs and collected leftover food from neighbours every day, repaying these neighbours with pieces of pig's fry (interviews: Jack Blakeston 10 August 2010; John and Judy Whittles 10 May 2010). Judy Whittles (interview, 10 May 2010) recalled that a neighbouring market gardener on Beckside in the 1940s would leave apples, a swede or a cabbage on neighbours' doorsteps after harvest. Men with allotments handed surplus produce around the neighbourhood, and one interviewee remembered that the barge worker who lived next door would bring 'peanuts off the barges' for her and her sister. John Day (interview, 8 December 2009) remembered in the 1940s his father giving away chrysanthemums and tomatoes grown in the garden of his council house. He would not take payment, although John said his mother might have liked him to. Men also involved themselves in the tradition of collecting for the family of a deceased neighbour (interviews: Janet Hill 3 March 2010; Bernard Hunt 12 January 2010). Although they might not be present in the street as much as women, men also used the outdoor spaces of their neighbourhoods for social interaction. Keith Barrett (interview, 2 September 2010) during this period recalled that neighbouring men on a Beverley council estate would talk over the fence whilst working on their gardens.

So, there is no doubt that Beverley's working classes constituted a relatively settled population during this period, and that norms of neighbourliness, including mutual assistance in times of need, pertained in many of the town's working-class streets. However, we cannot assume that population stability was the prevailing condition in British working-class neighbourhoods in the first half of the century. The working classes have frequently been forced into migration and movement, and many neighbourhoods in the first half of the twentieth century were no more stable than those in the second half (Franklin 1989: 94). Whereas Michael Young and Peter Willmott (1962/1957) considered that population stability in Bethnal Green during the post-war years was the tail end of a longer 'traditional' period of occupational and geographical immobility, Baines and Johnson (1999: 704) instead discovered a high degree of geographical and social mobility in interwar Bethnal Green: 'working-class occupational stability had been significantly attenuated in London by the 1930s … . It is ironic that this is exactly the period identified by many scholars as the apogee of the "traditional" working-class community.' Instead of the first half of the twentieth century envisaged as a long period of stability in working-class neighbourhood life, we should therefore remain alert to the contingency and instability always inherent to working-class life. Settled street communities could soon be broken up as circumstances changed, for example in periods of unemployment, prosperity or slum clearance. Furthermore, as we will now consider, even residents of relatively stable working-class streets were not equally committed to norms of neighbouring, and neighbourliness was often secondary to concerns with status and privacy.

Privacy and competition in 'traditional' neighbourhoods, 1935–54

Post-war social investigators such as Klein (1965) and Young and Willmott (1962/1957; Willmott and Young 1967) did not paint neighbourly relations in traditional working-class communities as always happy and harmonious, but they did imply that status competition was relatively muted, and that cultural norms were the basis of mutual understanding and some degree of sympathy. Willmott and Young (1967: 113) claimed that in long-standing working-class neighbourhoods during the 1950s, familiarity reduced the need to impress or compete with neighbours and resulted in 'a sort of bantering warmth in public'; any claims to superior status would be quickly slapped down: 'it is impossible to "put on airs" or to claim any kind of superiority'. Other authors have detected nostalgic romanticism in this and in other portrayals of 'traditional' working-class settings (Bourke 1994; Moran 2012). Robert Roberts (1971: 30) wrote in his memoire of life in early twentieth-century Salford that 'close propinquity, together with cultural poverty, led as much to enmity as it did to friendship'. Historians including Joanna Bourke (1994: 161) and Melanie Tebbutt (1995: 86–97) argue that close knowledge of each other's business amongst neighbouring women could result in intense status competition, as well as harsh policing of group norms relating to cleanliness and sexual respectability. As a result of the potential for conflict, Bourke (1994:142–3) argues that many working-class people developed 'distancing mechanisms', of which 'keeping "oneself to oneself"' was most effective. Other authors have noted this working-class preference for the privacy of the home in the first half of the twentieth century (Franklin 1989: 101–3; McKibbin 1998: 164–205; Lawrence 2013: 285). Even those authors whose work set the tone for the post-war positive reappraisal of working-class communal values, considered that the working classes 'prized' their homes (Young and Willmott 1967: 113) and their privacy 'You can shut the front door, "live yer own life", "keep y'self to y'self" – that is, to the immediate members of the household ... you want good neighbours but a good neighbour is not always "coming in and out"' (Hoggart 1957: 34). Ironically, this 'traditional' cultural trait of privacy and cordial distance with neighbours can seem little different to the 'privatism' that some authors thought was a consequence of post-war affluence.

Certainly, any notion that working-class neighbourhoods were perceived as socially homogenous by their residents is belied by the Beverley evidence. Interviewees recalled that streets had their 'rough' families. Patrick Mateer (interview, 13 January 2010) grew up in a council house on King's Square in the 1950s and thought that: 'Everybody was in the same boat 'cause nobody had nowt. Nobody had any money.' Nevertheless, he remembered that there were rougher families on the Square: 'Even amongst the working class there was the working, working class, even lower down the scale.' Peggy Alexander (interview, 18 February 2010) grew up on Beckside and recalled that her mother was 'snobby' about some of the neighbours and didn't want her to mix with them. Derek Mitchell (ERYMS interview) recalled that his mother, whose husband owned a plumbing business and who lived in the working-class neighbourhood of Holme Church Lane in the 1940s, 'thought she was a cut above everybody you see being the boss's wife, she was a bit of a snob and she was always dressed up, you never saw her untidy'.

Melanie Tebbutt (1995: 86–97) argued that 'gossip' helped constitute peer judgements about who was 'respectable' or 'rough', with respectability assessed in relation to criteria of sexual propriety and cleanliness that were widespread in working-class populations across the country in this period. Beverley interviewees recalled neighbourhood gossip in similar terms. Peggy Alexander (interview, 18 February 2010) remembered that a topic of disapproving conversation for her mother and a group who met around the yard to the rear of their houses was a neighbour who visited the pub with an American soldier while her husband was away serving in the war. Marianne Woolly's neighbours on the council estate in the 1940s would laugh together about a couple on their square who had lots of public arguments (Marianne Woolly, interview, 22 February 2010). Ellen Ingleton (interview, 20 April 2010) remembered that on her street during the 1940s Mrs Clark's washing was not as scrupulously clean as the others', and that neighbours noted this. As a result of the accumulation of such daily discourse, some families became stigmatised with a reputation for 'roughness' (William Vincent, interview, 25 May 2010). Cleanliness was an important category of distinction – 'rough' homes were those that were unkempt and dirty. Ellen Ingleton (interview, 20 April 2010) remembered: 'I know my mother always said she wouldn't drink any tea out of Mrs Clark's house, cause she said I don't trust her to wash the things out properly.' Obvious poverty or lack of ability to manage (that in the harsh court of local opinion might be judged to amount to the same thing) was revealed through the standards of children's clothing (interviews: Betty Carr 19 March 2010; Ken Ingleton 23 March 2010). Those who did not themselves need to borrow from neighbours looked down on those where were frequently 'on the borrow' (interviews: Jean Benson 14 January 2010; Marianne Woolly 22 February 2010). However, the expression of too much judgemental interest in others' lives could also result in group censure. '"Mother Goose-Gob" or "Old Mother Murphy" with their "thin pointed nose between the aspidistra and the nets" were familiar, despised characters', wrote Bourke (1994:142), quoting from autobiographical literature about working-class life in the first half of the twentieth century. Similarly, in Beverley, those who were thought to pay too much attention to others' business were resented. One former resident of Beckside recalled that Nelly Hancock, the keeper of a small shop and who helped organise children's summer trips, was well known for her nosey concern with her neighbours' business (Beverley Day Club, field notes).

The desire to protect privacy and keep oneself to oneself that many authors have noted as a feature of 'traditional' working-class life was therefore, in part, a response to the pressures of peer judgement. Many Beverley interviewees recalled the strong presumption against inviting neighbours into the home during the 1930s, 1940s and early 1950s. Fred Reid (interview, 26 January 2010) commented that:

> You sort of kept yourself to yourself in the house. My mother used to say to me: 'Don't you go in people's houses, and don't be nosy.'

Only so much privacy was possible, however, and the concern with what neighbours thought and might say led to a fetish for outward displays of respectability. Hoggart (1957: 34–5) wrote that in the working-class terraced streets of inter-war Leeds 'the window ledges and doorsteps scrubbed and yellowed with scouring-stone ... establish that you are a "decent" family'. Jack Binnington (interview, 3 August 2010) recalled similar rituals undertaken by his mother and other women on Beckside in the 1950s:

> Everything had to be spotlessly clean ... certainly kids had to be looking smart, boots polished ... houses had to be smart ... . They'd do their full day's washing on a Monday, Tuesday morning they'd be out doing step-stoning. People used to remark, 'She hasn't done her step-stoning this morning' ... 'Look at them bloody curtains, she's had them curtains up for weeks' ... . Mother is 93 now and on her last legs but she still remarks about cleanliness.

Other testimony suggested the importance of keeping homes externally clean, and of high standards in the washing of clothes and sheets – these were available for public inspection when hung out to dry (see also Tebbutt 1995: 84). Because of the connection of frequent borrowing with 'roughness', there was for many a strong presumption against borrowing items (interviews: Hannah Witham 26 April 2010; Ellen Ingleton 20 April 2010; Judy and David Ireland 15 July 2010; Marianne Woolly 22 February 2010). Some interviewees recalled that husbands strongly discouraged their wives from either lending or borrowing. If borrowing was necessary, most preferred to go to people they had a close relationship with. These could be relatives, close friends or preferred neighbours. Ellen Ingleton (interview, 20 April 2010) remembered that her aunt who lived down her street and had a large family would borrow from Ellen's mother. Iris Brown (interview, 21 May 2010) recalled that her mother was left alone after her father's death in 1946 and occasionally needed to borrow small food items, but would only do so from friends and relatives: 'Aunty Maggie used to say ... "if you want help, you come to me, right, you don't go to anybody else ... you know what folk are like".'

In extreme cases, a concern to maintain social status and resist the judgement of others, reinforced by poverty, could lead to social isolation. Betty Carr (interview, 19 March 2010) recalled how, during the early 1940s, her mother would not allow neighbours into the house and indeed had little to do with them socially. Betty attributed this to her mother's intense concern with status as well as her nervous personality. Betty's mother had been acutely aware of households of higher and lower status on St Andrew's Street where they lived, a street of small two-up, two-down terraced housing noted elsewhere for its close-knit community (Ellen Ingleton, interview, 20 April 2010; Birchall 1988: 135). With four children and a husband who spent some of his modest wage in the pub, she deeply resented her predicament:

> My mother was very proud, she didn't bother a lot with neighbours ... some of the neighbours weren't very choice ... the one reason why she wouldn't bother with neighbours was she didn't want them to know how poor she was ... . At one side of us was a big poor family ... . On the other side of us was a family who had only one child and the husband worked at Hodgson's ...and he was a foreman, so he had a good job. And so they were better off than us. And so my mother was in the middle you see, and so she wouldn't let them know she had no money ... my mother never went out for fourteen years, because she had no clothes to wear ... she was on the verge of a nervous breakdown on more than one occasion.

The wholesale rejection of neighbours because of status concerns was also noted by Judy Whittles (interview, 10 May 2010). Judy's father's income as a coal merchant enabled a slightly higher standard of life than that of some of the neighbours. Although Judy liked living on Beckside, 'my eldest sister hated it ... 'cause she was a bit of a snob I think, she was more ladylike.' Even Jack Binnington (interview, 22 June 2010), who gave one of the most positive accounts of street community in the 1940s and 1950s, acknowledged that some people kept themselves apart.

As well as distinctions relating to economic status and categories of 'roughness', a further distinction in the old neighbourhood of Beckside could exist between the established families and more recent incomers. Jane Holland (interview, 19 November 2009) recalled her awareness of 'established' families after marrying a 'Becksider' in the 1950s:

> Jane: All the people in Beckside, they had all lived together ... they were very clannish ... you'd got the Gillyons, the Hancocks ... Binningtons, and they were all inter-related ... . You knew that if you hit one of them, they'd all shout 'ouch' ... .
> Stefan: Did you feel in any way an outsider ...?
> Jane: No – in a way. I used to say to them: 'You've got to be bloody born and bred and die here before they invite you in for a cup of tea.'

During the war Doris Daniels' family moved from Hull to Flemingate, just adjacent to Beckside, and remembered her mother falling out with a neighbour who called her 'Hull Bulldog' (Doris Daniels, interview, 16 December 2009). This kind of 'local xenophobia' (Snell 2006) will be discussed further in Chapter 7.

So where does all this leave 'traditional' working-class neighbourliness? Certainly we should not overemphasise the helpfulness and mutuality of neighbours in the period before affluence supposedly created 'privatised' families. We have seen evidence to support those authors who point out that in 'traditional' working-class settings, neighbourly relations could be characterised by polite cordiality and even enmity rather than warmth (Coates and Silburn 1970: 118–20; Bourke 1994: 136–70; McKibbin 1998: 203). However, whilst correctives to overly romanticist notions of the good old days of neighbourliness are welcome and necessary, it is possible to go too far in this direction. Evidence reported here corroborates research by Ellen Ross (1983), Elizabeth Roberts (1984: 87–92) and more recently Margaret Lane (2011: 146–176) showing how mutual assistance amongst neighbours could form an important plank of household survival strategies in the years before the post-war expansion of the welfare state and the elevation of living standards associated with the 'age of affluence'. To square these opposing points, it is important to remember firstly that mutual assistance might be a rational, calculative response to poverty and need not encompass sentiment (Roberts 1971: 26). Second, it seems that notions of a single type of 'traditional' working-class neighbourliness, like other supposed 'working-class' traits, are liable to be confounded by variety. Different streets might exhibit different patterns of mutuality and sociability, depending on variables such as population stability, lifecycle, socio-economic make-up and the vagaries of local economic life (Stacey *et al.* 1975: 83–103). Individual character and temperament could result in different responses to the common life of the street – we have heard Betty Carr describe her mother's social isolation in a Beverley street that other interviewees recalled was a paragon of traditional neighbourliness. This variability led at least one post-war social investigator to doubt that a standard type of working-class neighbourliness existed: 'The evidence is not very easily interpreted ... there is as much evidence that people do not get on with their neighbours as that they do' (Klein 1965:134). Finally, evidence of both enmity and warmth in neighbourly relations need not necessarily contradict. Both point to the fact that neighbours could be inescapable in highly localised lives.

Disruptions to neighbourliness, 1955–1980

It has often been supposed that the kind of neighbourliness we have seen above, which is associated with the 'traditional' working classes, declined amidst the purported individualism and 'privatism' of the post-war 'affluent society'. Neighbourly interdependence was eroded by the expansion of the welfare state, rises in real wages and new domestic technologies (Benson 1989: 117–131; Roberts 1984: 193–201). Workers had less contact with their neighbours as affluence eased the need for material mutual assistance, and private car ownership allowed sociability and leisure to spill the bounds of locality (Zweig 1961: 107, 208). Increased geographical mobility, post-war movement towards female employment outside of the home, larger and better equipped homes (meaning less time spent outside) all helped to erode the norms that had formerly oriented female neighbours towards each other (Roberts 1995:

201–219). Attention has often focussed on the effects of urban restructuring; social investigators noted that neighbours on new estates were unsure of each other and of what kind of neighbourly behaviour was appropriate, responding by limiting their contact (Klein 1965: 253–4) and by competing for status in materialistic display (Young and Willmott 1962/1957: 151–2). The Beverley evidence offered some support for the view that social and economic changes associated with the age of affluence could impact on neighbourly relationships; however, in many streets during this period, aspects of the so-called 'traditional' patterns remained undisturbed.

New neighbourhoods

A strong theme of what has been called 'architectural determinism' (Garrioch and Peel 2006: 667) runs through the literature on the mid-twentieth-century working classes. Although the state began to build homes and demolish slums after the First World War, the rate quickened in the 1950s and 1960s. Local authorities in Britain built 3,761,239 new dwellings between 1945 and 1970 (Hollow 2014: 2), and whereas in 1938, one tenth of the population lived in homes rented from their local council, by the 1970s this had risen to just under 30 per cent (Bernstein 2004: 310–11). Many of the old streets of terraced houses that had dominated the urban landscape since before the First World War were demolished, prompting anxiety about the fate of the communities they had once harboured (Moran 2012). In contrast to the dense and bustling old streets, threaded between industrial workplaces and dense with pubs, shops and wash houses, new estates offered low-density housing, were frequently many miles from workplaces and often lacked social amenities such as shops and pubs where people might meet each other casually (Todd 2014: 174–95; Klein 1965: 222–3, 229 Willmott 1963: 109). When shopping centres were later provided on the estates, many were designed with outmoded ideas about what tenants wanted and therefore were little used (Greenhalgh 2016). Michael Young was in no doubt about the impact of the new landscape on the neighbourliness of the working classes: 'Instead of the fierce loyalties of the turnings, there are the strung-out streets in which everyone is a stranger' (quoted in Moran 2012: 172). Recently, Ben Jones (2012: 202, 138–9) followed in the long tradition of social investigators and historians by declaring migration from inner-city neighbourhoods to suburban estates during the mid-century to be 'the most important socio-cultural change in working class life during the period'; in Jones' opinion, 'migration offered an opportunity for social reinvention in which inner-urban values and norms regarding respectability and neighbourliness were refocused through a new lens which allowed for a more restricted sociability ("keeping oneself to oneself")'. Of course, it was not simply the physical layout of the estates that led to a diminished sociability on the new estates. Whereas in the old streets, norms of easy public sociability arose because people were surrounded by long-standing neighbours, relatives and friends, on the new estates they lived (at first) amongst strangers, and experienced normative confusion regarding the correct levels and patterns of neighbourliness (Young and Willmott 1962/1957: 147–69; Klein 1965: 235–7). The Beverley evidence, however, suggests that the impacts of movement to new housing estates was not so disruptive in smaller towns.

Just as in the rest of Britain, Beverley's working classes experienced considerable change in their housing during in the post-war decades. Beverley's population increased only modestly in the 25 years from 1945 (from approximately 15,500 to 17,000), but 1,132 council houses were built in the town between 1945 and 1965, the majority of these on new council estates on green-field sites to the east of the town (HMSO 1964, 1973; *Beverley Guardian*, 20 August 1965; Brown 1989: 155–6). The effect was that much of Beverley's working-class population moved east into the large area of council housing estates (Brown 1989). New suburban private housing estates were also built in the 1960s and 1970s around the outskirts of the old borough, and some working-class interviewees bought houses on these estates (interviews: Les White 21 October 2010; Dennis Duke 14 July 2010).

Impacts of these shifts were felt in the old neighbourhoods. The demolition of older slum housing thinned out the long-standing populations of the older cohesive streets:

> Jack: [In the 1940s] If I looked at Beckside I could tell you everybody who lived from corner of Hull Road, where the fountain is, all the way down up to Potter Hill ... those families lived in them houses basically until the late sixties, early seventies, when basically them houses was seen as slum areas. They needed a lot of money spending on them to modernise them ... [a builder] bought all these properties up you see, as an investment, and he was doing them up as he was buying them you see ... late sixties, early seventies.
> Stefan: Would you say a lot of the old families moved out at that time?
> Jack: Yeah, yeah, yeah.
> Stefan: Where did they go?
> Jack: Council houses, moved into council houses on the estate most of them.
> (Jack Binnington, interview, 3 August 2010)

However, the normative disruption that the post-war researchers noted in new sub-urban council estates was not felt so strongly in post-war Beverley. In the 1960s, council estates had housed many of the unskilled workers whom I interviewed, because many of the more affluent skilled workers had been able to buy their own homes. Local women organised coach trips to take council estate children to the beach in the 1960s, as they had on Beckside in the earlier period (interviews: Peter Stephenson 27 May 2010; Pete Daniels 28 July 2010). Lending and borrowing of small items between different households continued amongst those living on council estates in the town at least into the 1960s (interviews: Keith Barrett 2 September 2010; William Vincent 25 May 2010). Keith Barrett's testimony (interview, 2 September 2010) regarding his

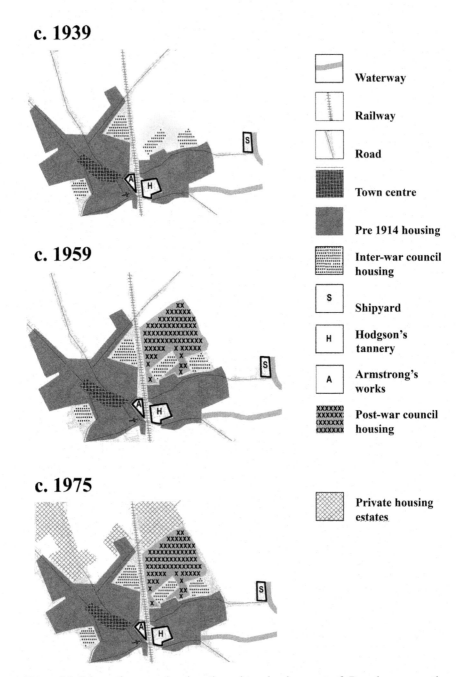

Figure 3.1 Schematic map showing the urban development of Beverley across the mid-twentieth century.

mother's sociability on Athelstone Road in the 1960s is worth reproducing at length since it captures the mixture of women's sociability and mutuality with neighbours and relatives, as well as the presumption towards the privacy of the home and against borrowing:

> They [mum's sisters] were only round the corner ... so they was always to and fro ... . My mum would get all the stories from King's Square off them ... . [My parents] both worked, we always had a coal house full of coal, and regularly in winter you used to get neighbours borrowing a bucket full of coal ... you used to get neighbours knocking all hours 'can you just lend us a couple of cigs while pay day' ... I've never seen them refuse anybody ... . People used to run what they called 'diddlums', which was like small savings things, and you'd maybe get someone up the street would save for people, maybe they'd put half a crown away a week ... . There was a woman across the street ... their mum lived with them as well and she was real old ... and my mum used to go out and help out with the old woman a lot ... and my mum as well, had like a bit of a name for, when people died, she used to go round and lay them out ... . One of my sisters lived down Athelstone Road as well ... and my mum would be, like, over at her house, or they'd be over at our house ... . It was usually relatives who used to be in your house for any length of time ... . Some neighbours, like Overtons next door, would knock and then open the door 'Hello Muriel' and then walk in, but others would just usually knock and wait ... . There was twenty houses down the street, and you knew everybody in every house ... but no, I've never known them borrow off neighbours ...my dad was dead against borrowing.

This kind of continuity does not appear to have been unique to Beverley. Rosalind Watkiss Singleton conducted oral history interviews in three small Black Country towns (Pensnett, Sedgley and Tipton) focusing on the period 1945–70, and found that:

> Pre-war behavioural patterns continued within these communities ... . Post-war affluence impacted minimally upon traditional mores of neighbourliness and community cohesion; kinship networks and matrilocality remained central tenets of life ... the Welfare State made scant impression upon the psyche of its potential recipients, or their customary habits.
>
> (Singleton 2010: 38–9)

One explanation for the continuity observed in Beverley's council estates, as well as in the Black Country towns studied by Singleton, may be size – the social disruption caused by slum clearance and the movement to new housing estates was probably not as great in smaller towns as in larger cities. Those who moved to new estates in Beverley were never more than a mile away from their old neighbourhoods and could therefore easily maintain existing social links; furthermore, most residents of Beverley's new estates were locals and were often known to each other. George Little (interview, 24 October 2008) claimed that '99 per cent' of those moved onto the new council estates in the 1950s were 'Beverley people'. Though the figure is rhetorical, the broad point was corroborated by other interviewees, including Janet Hill (interview, 3 March 2010) who recalled moving into a house on Swinemoor council estate in 1950s – the neighbours 'were all Beverley people', and she already knew some of them. This degree of population continuity probably helped to preserve aspects of working-class culture, including female patterns of neigh-bouring. Tebbutt (2012: 161) has made similar points in reference to continuity in 'traditional patterns of behaviour, neighbourliness and respectability' in 1960s Northampton, a town considerably larger than Beverley, but 'small enough for those who moved to outlying estates to maintain tight kinship and social links with the districts from which they had moved'.

Even in the larger cities, the rehousing of inner-city populations in suburban council estates may have only caused temporary disruption to patterns of neighbourliness. The analyses of Young and Willmott (1962/1957), John Macfarlane Mogey (1956) and Klein (1965) focussed on populations at the point of migration, when disruption might be expected to have been greatest. However, in the early 1960s Peter Willmott revised his own and Michael Young's earlier prognoses about the social effects of the move from inner-city London to suburban estates. Studying social practices on the large Dagenham council estate, Willmott (1963: 108–9) found, somewhat to his own surprise, that 40 years after its first tenants had moved in, residents had re-established many of the old features of working-class life, including cultures of neighbourly sociability and mutuality. Similarly, Mark Clapson's (2012) study of the Whitley suburban council estate in Reading between 1930 and 2010 also mounts a robust defence of the communality possible on English council estates across the later twentieth century.

Moreover, post-war housing estates were not bereft of social facilities. Though there was a lower density of shops and pubs on the new estates than in older Beverley streets – Beckside, for example, had four pubs and approximately twelve shops in the 1950s – the pubs in particular appear to have become social centres. The council built the Humber Keel pub on the Swinemoor estate in 1952 (conversation with landlord and customers, Humber Keel 29 April 2010). Peter Stephenson (interview, 27 May 2010) remembered that it was well used on Saturday nights by his parents and other neighbours from the estate during the 1950s. By the later 1960s the pub was attracting crowds from the estate and elsewhere, as a former barmaid recalled:

Lynne: It was a busy pub, yes it really was. There was cars up that street, all the car park used to be full … .
Stefan: Was that busy with people from the estate …?

Lynne: Yes. Actually a lot of people came from Hull ... they had a music room and the piano going, a sing along you see.

(Lynne Norton, interview, 9 November 2009)

Other venues for sociability were later added for use of council estate residents. The Methodists built a church on Queen's Road in the heart of the post-war estates in 1961 that lasted until 1982 (Brown 1989). The local authority opened an infant and a junior school on the estate in 1967 (Brown 1989). Residents, did, however, have to wait until the 1960s for a shopping precinct, and many used the mobile grocery vans that visited periodically (Joyce Sumner, interview, 13 August 2010). Once shops were built in the centre of the largest estate, Swinemoor, interviewees remembered a similar pattern of shopping to that in the older streets, with the local shops being used for some daily items, and trips into town for others (interviews: Jean Benson 14 January 2010; Joyce Sumner 13 August 2010). Singleton (2010: 330) suggests that housewives during the 1960s continued to prefer local shops because of the human contact and possibility for short-term credit.

Amongst those who moved to Beverley's new 1960s private housing estates there was more evidence of the kind of normative confusion suggested by post-war sociologists such as Klein (1965). These estates often contained a mix of those from different classes and social milieux. Les White (interview, 21 October 2010), a barge skipper, bought a home on the Model Farm estate in 1965 and recalled:

They wasn't my kind of people. They were bank managers or deputy bank managers, one was a customs man, one was a dock manager, you know, they were all above me, all above my stakes.

In addition to the class difference, the other denizens of Les's street 'were all outsiders, they'd all come in to live ... there was no Beverley kid down our street' (Les White, interview, 29 October 2010). Les recalled perplexity at his new neighbours' sociable priorities that were alien to his own background and expectations:

I didn't realise, when I used to say to them on a Friday night, maybe out doing something in the garden, 'coming for a pint tonight?' 'No', 'no', 'no'. [I] never thought, they were paid monthly, they had no money ... . [I thought] 'Why aren't they going for a pint, why aren't young men, as they've always done, going for a pint with your neighbours or your mates or whatever?'

Whereas Les expected, having bought his house, he would stay in it for many years, he found that his neighbours did not have such expectations:

We went onto Model Farm ... we get this new house and we were a happy family, and there was happy families around us, and after about five years, four years, people started to put their house up for sale, and I thought, 'hey up there, what they moving for?' And I got talking to one 'oh, we'll sell this house and we'll be able to buy a new car and then we'll go and get another 25 year mortgage' ... I didn't realise life worked like that.

Like Les, newly married Jim Fisher (interview, 16 December 2009) bought a house on a new Beverley housing estate in the 1970s and found the neighbours less friendly than those on Beckside where he grew up: 'It was one of those neighbourhoods where people are every Sunday out cleaning their cars.' In the later 1970s when they decided to have a family Jim and his wife moved back to the working-class east of the town where he felt more at home: 'We moved down here and the neighbours down here are just like they used to be in the olden days ... I mean you know everyone and they'll help each other.' However, a pub and shopping precinct was provided on the 1960s Model Farm private housing estate, an estate that housed a mixture of working-class and lower middle-class residents. Into the 1970s this pub provided a place for neighbours to meet and socialise: 'With it being an estate pub, you had all your mates ... I think he [dad] was in darts team ... I think in those days the pub was the hub of the community' (Michael Hudson, interview, 17 December 2010).

So, we see that the rehousing of large numbers of the working classes during the post-war age of affluence was not as cataclysmic for neighbourly relations as is often thought. Especially in smaller towns where the distances, geographical and social, between old and new addresses was not so great, there could be considerable continuity of neighbourly norms and practices (Singleton 2010; Tebbutt 2012). Even in council estates ringing larger cities, such as the Dagenham estate researched by Willmott (1963) and the Whitley estate studied by Clapson (2012), working-class people re-established practices not unlike 'traditional' patterns of neighbouring.

The decline of women's neighbourhood networks?

Married women moved into the workforce in significant numbers after the Second World War, and authors have posited a link between this phenomenon and a decline in older patterns of working-class life, including neighbourly interaction (Moran 2012: 182; Charles 2012). Nationally, the number of married women working outside the home rose from 22 per cent in 1951 to 51 per cent in 1971 (Wilson 2006), and the indications are that Beverley women participated in this trend. In 1951, 31 per cent of Beverley women aged over 15 were 'occupied'; by 1981, 58 per cent of married women aged 16–59 in Beverley were in employment (over half of whom were part-time) (HMSO 1956: 439; 1984). The new pattern established in the post-war decades was for women to work after marriage until having children, and then to work in part-time positions once children were older (Wilson 2006). A rough estimate on the basis of the Beverley interview evidence suggests that around one tenth of mothers in the 1930s worked while their children were younger than ten, whereas one third of interviewees or the wives of interviewees did so in the 1960s and 1970s. This left less time for interaction with neighbours. Jane Holland (interview, 11 November 2009) told how she had been too busy with her job in a local factory and bringing up children to have much involvement with neighbours in the 1960s and 1970s: 'By the time you've done your day's work and gone home and got your work done at home, we used to watch telly a bit and then it was time for bed.'

Post-war changes in women's domestic lives could also impact on their neighbourly sociability. Much of the inter-household mutuality conducted between neighbouring women in the early part of our period was not necessary in an era of rising living standards and the welfare state. Rising wages, the end of rationing in 1954, the increase in working-class ownership of fridges and freezers across the post-war decades all meant that many working-class housewives in the 1960s and 1970s had less need to borrow milk, sugar and other small items of food than had their mothers (Harrison 1961: 207; Roberts 1995: 22, 223; Kynaston 2015: 392). Approximately one third of interviewees recalled their mothers lending or borrowing foodstuffs and other small items in the 1940s or 1950s, but only about 10 per cent claimed that the households they themselves established in the 1960s practised such exchange with neighbours. Interviewees recalled that local women sometimes acted as midwives in the 1940s; this service became redundant with the National Health Service and the provision of a free professional mid-wifery service (interviews: Betty Carr 19 March 2010; Eva White 18 June 2010). Historians have connected women's mutual assistance with poverty (Ross 1983; Roberts 1995: 201); as wages and living standards increased, it seemed inevitable that the cultural preference for household independence noted throughout the Beverley interviews would lead to less reliance on exchange with neighbours.

Similarly, it seems likely that social worlds of many women expanded beyond the street during this period, both as a result of friendships struck up at work and through some softening of a gender divide in sociability. Conjugal joint sociability was often conducted with friends living at a greater remove than the immediate street or neighbourhood, as Vic and Sarah Baker (29 May 2010) described:

> Vic: You didn't socialise [with neighbours], but you had a good natter across garden fence … If you saw them you didn't ignore them …
> Sarah: But not like our parents, they used to go in each other's houses and have cups of teas, we didn't ever do owt like that …
> Vic: I think in our days people didn't socialise, not like our parents did …
> Sarah: You'd perhaps spend more time with your friends who lived a few streets away, and you didn't with your absolute direct neighbours.

This last quotation offers support to those who consider that post-war affluence allowed the working classes greater scope for keeping their distance from neighbours (Zweig 1961: 194; Roberts 1995: 199–231; Jones 2012: 201).

But 'traditional' mutuality or 'privatised' polite distance were not the only possibilities for neighbourly relations during the age of affluence.

New patterns of neighbourliness, 1955–1980

Focus on the decline of 'traditional' working-class neighbouring – the social practices of married women who were in the home full-time and whose limited social horizons and material poverty left them with little choice but to rely on neighbours for sociability and practical assistance – has led to a neglect of new ways neighbours might interact.

Although the necessity for borrowing consumables such as foodstuffs and coal from neighbours eased as the post-war affluent era progressed, other types of mutuality could come into focus. The rise in married women's work outside of the home meant that they needed more help with childcare. We saw in the previous chapter that relatives living locally often met this need. However, relatives were not always available, and neighbours were often called on for childminding of a short duration. Elaine Mateer (interview, 29 March 2010) remembered that as a child in the 1960s she would go round to a neighbours for half an hour on an evening after school before her mum finished work. Ellen Malster (interview, 21 May 2010), a working mother during the 1970s, said that the proximity of neighbours she knew well was a source of reassurance that allowed her to leave her 12-year-old child at home alone for five minutes every day between the end of the school day and her return from work (see also interviews: Jim Fisher 16 December 2009; Jean Benson 14 January 2010).

In the early part of the period, in the streets most resembling models of 'traditional' working-class community, most inter-household mutual assistance took place between women. But in the affluent era, the improved quality of working-class housing, and men's increasing concern with maintaining and improving their properties, underpinned new forms of mutual assistance between male neighbours. John Day (interview, 10 November 2009) and his neighbour in a street of post-war privately owned houses cooperated to build a double garage in the 1970s. John also helped his neighbour with wall papering. Skilled workers might use their skills to help neighbours – in the later 1950s and 1960s, George Hunter (interview, 14 January 2010), a painter and decorator, painted rooms for neighbours on the Cherry Tree council estate in exchange for a token payment of tobacco. The need to tend gardens on the council estate and in new private housing developments prompted exchange of tools, knowledge and labour (interviews: Sally Adams 21 June 2010; Lynne Norton, 9 November 2009). Vic Baker (interview, 19 May 2010) lived on the Cherry Tree estate with his young family in the 1960s:

> Where we lived in Cherry Tree, if you wanted a rabbit hutch, or a bit of fancy fencing, I was the lad. And I had two sheds full of stuff, and people used to come and say 'I'm looking for something like this'.

Dave Lee (interview, 9 November 2009) recalled how his father and other men on their council estate street would cooperate over gardening methods, lending each other seeds, tools and tips:

> There was a lot of guys then that was into gardening, and there was a guy at the end of the garden, Mr Horsley ... and there was another bloke, and all the gardens sort of merged, and before there was any digging, or any planting ... they had a meeting about see what was what, a chat about did you want some of this, and I've grown some of that.

Such examples were relatively commonplace in the testimony I collected about working-class life in the 1960s and 1970s in Beverley. In contrast, Singleton observed that stories of male neighbourly mutual assistance were rare in her oral history research in the Black Country (Singleton 2010: 99–100). Singleton focused on the post-war years up to 1970, whereas my research encompassed the 1970s. It may be that social and cultural changes associated with affluence and home ownership were translated more clearly into social practices by the latter decade. Certainly, the kinds of help that Beverley's male neighbours offered each other with tasks in their homes and gardens appears similar to that which Ian Procter (1990) documented taking place during the 1980s in the working-class Coventry suburb of Ivybridge. Procter denied that working-class households had become 'self-provisioning', as Ray Pahl (1984) had claimed; his social survey revealed that neighbours usually knew each other and proffered considerable mutual assistance including help with DIY and the loan of tools.

Procter's evidence also pointed to regular sociability between working-class neighbours. Similarly, in Beverley, neighbours were often incorporated into couples' shared sociability during the age of affluence. The improved quality of working-class homes, and their opening up as a venue of sociability, could contribute to this tendency. During the later 1950s, in contrast to the usual assertion that television contributed to privatised, home-centred lifestyles (Bedarida 1991: 209–13; Moran 2012: 176–7), ownership of a set could bring neighbouring couples together. Hilda Little (interview, 19 March 2010) recalled that the highlight of her and her husband's week during the later 1950s was popping next door on Monday night to watch *Wagon Train*. Dennis Duke (interview, 14 July 2010) remembered that his parents' sociability in the late 1950s involved entertaining neighbours and other friends at home, watching the television or sharing a meal. Ivy Shipton (interview, 17 May 2010) described how her and her husband's sociability with other neighbours included parties in their home in the 1960s:

> We had quite a social area in Norwood Far Grove, where we lived, and indeed we would gather at each other's houses and someone would cook and experiment with something, and we always had a Christmas party on Boxing night and it was like open house, the kids would sit up the stairs, they were suppose to be in bed but would end up sat at the top of the

stairs, and the kitchen was the bar and the living room was where the food was and the front room was for dancing.

Couples might also socialise with their neighbours by going out to a pub or club together (interviews: George Hunter 14 January 2010; Bob Garbutt 28 June 2010).

Many neighbours became friendly because they had children who played together. Dick Gibson (interview, 11 March 2010) remembered that in the council estate street where he lived in the 1960s, he and his wife became friendly with those neighbours whose children were the same age as their own (see also interviews: Margaret Day 23 November 2009; June and Dave Ireland 15 July 2010). Indeed, Dick and his wife became so friendly with one set of neighbours that he put a gate through the fence dividing their properties (Joan Gibson, interview, 17 March 2010). In the later 1950s and early 1960s William Vincent (interview, 25 May 2010) recalled family trips to the coast with a neighbouring family. Interviewees also recalled annual bonfire nights and occasional street parties:

> Helen: When we first got married in Grovehill [a relatively working-class street in the 1970s], once we had our children, I mean we got to know most of the people on the row, on the terrace, people with children growing up … .
> Eric: We organised a party at the twenty-fifth anniversary of the queen's thing [coronation], and we had all the people from all the row and we put bunting up and things like that … .
> Helen: We always had Guy Fawkes night we always had a bonfire, you always had a bonfire didn't you, and all the row again, they all came with their children and brought so many fireworks what you could afford, and I always, we used to do baked potatoes, mushy peas.
> (Eric and Helen Ross, interview, 16 February 2010)

Helen and Eric were from working-class backgrounds but attained social mobility through Eric's job in Hodgson's during this period. Theirs and others' memories of sociability with neighbours undermine Ferdynand Zweig's (1961: 116) proposal that 'the higher the level of prosperity, the higher the fences'.

It must be noted that joint conjugal sociability with neighbours was not new in the affluent era. During the 1940s, Jack Blakeston's mother and father exchanged home visits with a neighbouring couple, listening to *The Man in Black* on the radio together (Jack Blakeston, interview, 10 August 2010). The kinds of sociability with neighbours described here in the post-war decades may therefore represent the continuation of a longer twentieth- century trend, noted by Claire Langhamer (2000: 156), towards 'shared leisure within the marital relationship'. What I hope I have established here is that joint conjugal sociability did not preclude neighbourly sociability.

Conclusion

It is impossible to measure retrospectively, with any precision, levels of neighbourly interaction and mutuality over a particular historic period, and therefore either to securely prove or disprove a decline in neighbourliness amongst the British working classes during the age of affluence. But we can use oral history alongside other sources to take the temperature. The evidence discussed in this chapter provides grounds to doubt the declinist view.

First, portrayals of a 'traditional' type of working-class neighbourliness (Meacham 1977; Hobsbawm 1984; Roberts 1984: 183–201), thought to pertain during the first half of the century, and against which later decline is measured, are overdrawn. During the earlier decades recalled in this chapter (1935–1954), conflict, exclusion, social differentiation and indifference between neighbours were remembered alongside examples of kindness, mutuality and friendship. This wide variety in neighbourly relations in 'traditional' settings is also noted in some of the secondary literature, despite a prevailing impression that mutual assistance was the default for the 'traditional' working classes. Bourke (1994:162) presented evidence from inter-war social surveys to show that 'the isolated working-class family living in a predominantly working-class street was not as rare as the "community" theorists would have us believe'. Authors have also suggested regional differences in working-class cultures of neighbourly interaction, with working-class populations in wealthier areas in the English South and Midlands living more 'privatised' lives than those in northern industrial areas (Klein 1965: 135; Lawrence 2013; Massey 1995: 286). Though a simple north/south divide should not be assumed, local economic and historic circumstances must have impacted on neighbouring practices. Margaret Williamson (2009), for example, shows how women's sociability in a mid-century Cleveland coal-mining town deviated from the 'traditional' pattern documented by Norman Dennis, Fernando Henriques and Clifford Slaughter (1969) in a 1950s Yorkshire mining town, and explains this through reference to the greater availability of women's work in the Cleveland town. The impression given through the work of some post-war social investigators that the post-war era came at the end of a long and relatively unchanging 'traditional' period in working-class culture also seems unlikely. Adrian Franklin (1989) and Jon Lawrence (2013) point out that 'traditionalism' was little in evidence amongst working-class groups who were purchasing their own homes as early as the 1930s. Overall, it seems likely that there was considerable variability between individuals, socio-economic groups, regions, localities, as well as across time, in neighbourly behaviour. In the mid-century, no single type of working-class neighbourliness existed that might be acted upon and transformed by the onset of the age of affluence.

Second, the factors that authors have claimed reduced working-class neighbourliness during the age of affluence were uneven in strength and effect. The research reported in this book supports other recent voices (Singleton 2010; Tebbutt 2012) in suggesting that the move to new council estates was not everywhere as cataclysmic for social networks and local norms as it may have been in the larger cities. Similarly, gains in terms of 'affluence' were by no means universal during the period (for example: Coates and Silburn 1970; Garrioch and Peel 2006: 670). The Beverley evidence shows, like Singleton's (2010), that mutual exchange amongst neighbours continued to have an important role in day-to-day economic lives of many of the poorest amongst the working classes.

Finally, accounts that depict the decline of 'traditional' neighbourliness (for example, Roberts 1995: 199–231) frequently fail to discuss new ways in which neighbours interacted as affluence raised living standards. I do not wish to suggest that there were no changes in the ways working-class neighbours related to each other. The economic need for lending and borrowing did indeed become less pressing for many families as living standards rose, enabling the household independence that older norms had connected with respectability. More married women worked away from the home by the end of the period, thus broadening their opportunities for sociability. By the 1970s, fewer women were as dependent on neighbours for their sociability and mutual assistance as their mothers had sometimes been in the earlier part of the period. But the Beverley evidence suggests that change did not move in a single direction. Emphasis on the home and nuclear family as focus for working-class leisure could lead to new forms of social interaction and sharing between neighbours. In fact, where prosperity did lead to the building of fences between properties, neighbours often helped each other put up them up. Sometimes they even built in a gate.

References

Baines, Dudley and Paul Johnson (1999) 'In Search of the 'Traditional' Working Class: Social Mobility and Occupational Continuity in Interwar London', *Economic History Review*, LII:4, 692–713.

Bedarida, Francois (1991) *A Social History of England 1851–1990*, 2nd edition, London: Routledge.

Benson, John (1989) *The Working Class in Britain, 1850–1939*, Harlow: Longman.

Bernstein, George L. (2004) *The Myth of Decline. The Rise of Britain Since 1945*, London: Pimlico.

Birchall, Johnston (1988) *Building Communities: The Co-Operative Way*, London: Routledge & Kegan Paul.

Bourke, Joanna (1994) *Working Class Cultures in Britain 1890–1960: Gender, Class, and Ethnicity*, London: Routledge.

Brown, Lucy (1989) 'Modern Beverley: Beverley After 1945', in K.J. Allison (ed.), *A History of the County of York. East Riding: Volume 6: The Borough and Liberties of Beverley*, London: Oxford University Press, 154–160.

Charles, Nickie (2012) 'Families, Communities and Social Change: Then and Now', *The Sociological Review*, 60, 438–456.

Clapson, Mark (2012) *Working-Class Suburb: Social Change on an English Council Estate, 1930–2010*, Manchester: Manchester University Press.

Coates, Ken and Richard Silburn (1970) *Poverty. The Forgotten Englishman*, Harmondsworth: Penguin.

Colls, Robert (2004) 'When We Lived in Communities. Working-class Culture and its Critics', in Robert Colls and Richard Rodger (eds), *Cities of Ideas. Governance and Citizenship in Urban Britain 1800–2000*, Aldershot: Ashgate, 283–307.

Dennis, Norman, Fernando Henriques and Clifford Slaughter (1969) *Coal is Our Life: An Analysis of a Yorkshire Mining Community*, 2nd edition, London: Tavistock.

Franklin, Adrian (1989) 'Working-Class Privatism: An Historical Case Study of Bedminster, Bristol', *Environment and Planning D: Society and Space*, 7, 93–113.

Garrioch, David and Mark Peel (2006) 'Introduction: The Social History of Urban Neighborhoods', *Journal of Urban History*, 32, 663–672.

Greenhalgh, James (2016) 'Consuming Communities: The Neighbourhood Unit and the Role of Retail Spaces on British Housing Estates, 1944–1958', *Urban History*, 43:1, 158–174.

Hall, David (2012) *Working Lives. The Forgotten Voices of Britain's Post-war Working Class*, London: Transworld.

Harrison, Tom (1961) *Britain Revisited*, London: Victor Gollanz.

HMSO (1956) *Census 1951 England and Wales: Occupation Tables*, London: HMSO.

HMSO (1964) *Census 1961 England and Wales. County Report. Yorkshire, East Riding*, London: HMSO.

HMSO (1973) *Census 1971 England and Wales County Report. Yorkshire East Riding. Part 1*, London: HMSO.

HMSO (1984) *Census 1981: Key Statistics for Urban Areas: The North: Cities and Towns*, London: HMSO.

Hobsbawm, Eric (1984) 'The Formation of British Working-Class Culture', in Eric Hobsbawm, *Worlds of Labour*, London: Weidenfeld & Nicolson, 176–193.

Hoggart, Richard (1957) *The Uses of Literacy*, London: Chatto & Windus.

Hollow, Matthew (2014) 'The Age of Affluence Revisited: Council Estates and Consumer Society in Britain, 1950–1970', *Journal of Consumer Culture* (accessed 3 February 2016 from http://joc.sagepub.com/content/early/2014/02/05/1469540514521083.full.pdf).

Jones, Ben (2012) *The Working Class in Mid Twentieth-Century England: Community, Identity and Social Memory*, Manchester: Manchester University Press.

Klein, Josephine (1965) *Samples from English Cultures (Volume 1)*, London: Routledge & Kegan Paul.

Kynaston, David (2015) *Modernity Britain. 1957–1962*, London: Bloomsbury.

Lane, Margaret (2011) 'Women and Domestic Life in Hull, 1920s to the 1960s', unpublished PhD thesis, University of Hull.

Langhamer, Claire (2000) *Women's Leisure in England, 1920–1960*, Manchester: Manchester University Press.

Lawrence, Jon (2013) 'Class, "Affluence" and the Study of Everyday Life in Britain, c.1930–1964', *Cultural and Social History*, 10, 273–299.

Lummis, Trevor (1985) *Occupation and Society. The East Anglian Fishermen. 1880–1914*, Cambridge: Cambridge University Press.

Massey, Doreen (1995) *Spatial Divisions of Labour. Social Structures and the Geography of Production*, 2nd edition, Basingtoke: MacMillan.

McKibbin, Ross (1998) *Classes and Cultures: England, 1918–1951*, Oxford: Oxford University Press.

Meacham, Standish (1977) *A Life Apart. The English Working Class 1890–1914*, London: Thames and Hudson.

Mogey, John Macfarlane (1956) *Family and Neighbourhood. Two Studies in Oxford*, London: Oxford University Press.

Moran, Joe (2012) 'Imagining the Street in Post-war Britain', *Urban History*, 39:1, 166–186.

Pahl, Ray (1984) *Divisions of Labour*, London: Blackwell.

Procter, Ian (1990) 'The Privatisation of Working-Class Life: A Dissenting View', *The British Journal of Sociology*, 41:2, 157–180.

Roberts, Elizabeth (1984) *A Woman's Place: An Oral History of Working-Class Women 1890–1940*, Oxford: Basil Blackwell.

Roberts, Elizabeth (1995) *Women and Families: An Oral History, 1940–1970*, Oxford: Blackwell.

Roberts, Robert (1971) *The Classic Slum. Salford Life in the First Quarter of the Century*, Manchester: Manchester University Press.

Ross, Ellen (1983) 'Survival Networks: Women's Neighbourhood Sharing in London before World War One', *History Workshop*, 15, 4–27.

Schofield, Fred (1988) *Humber Keels and Keelmen*, Lavenham: Terence Dalton.

Seabrook, Jeremy (1973) *The Unprivileged. A Hundred Years of Family Life and Tradition in a Working-class Street*, Harmondsworth: Penguin.

Singleton, Rosalind Watkiss (2010) '"Old Habits Persist". Change and Continuity in Black Country Communities: Pensnett, Sedgley and Tipton, 1945–c.1970', unpublished PhD thesis, University of Wolverhampton.

Snell, Keith (2006) *Parish and Belonging, Community, Identity and Welfare in England and Wales, 1700–1950*, Cambridge: University Press.

Stacey, Margaret, Eric Batstone, Colin Bell and Anne Murcott (1975) *Power, Persistence and Change. A Second Study of Banbury*, London: Routledge & Kegan Paul.

Tebbutt, Melanie (1995) *Women's Talk? A Social History of 'Gossip' in Working-Class Neighbourhoods, 1880–1960*, Aldershot: Scolar Press.

Tebbutt, Melanie (2012) 'Imagined Families and Vanishing Communities', *History Workshop Journal*, 73, 144–169.

Todd, Selina (2014) *The People. The Rise and Fall of the Working Class 1910–2010*, London: John Murray.

Williamson, Margaret (2009) 'Gender, Leisure and Marriage in a Working-class Community, 1939–1960', *Labour History Review*, 74:2, 185–198.

Willmott, Peter (1963) *The Evolution of a Community: A Study of Dagenham After Forty Years*, London: Routledge & Kegan Paul.

Willmott, Peter and Michael Young (1967) *Family and Class in a London Suburb*, London: New English Library.

Wilson, Dolly Smith (2006) 'A New Look at the Affluent Worker: The Good Working Mother in Post-War Britain', *Twentieth Century British History*, 17, 206–229.

Young, Michael and Willmott, Peter (1962) *Family and Kinship in East London*, Harmondsworth: Pelican.

Zweig, Ferdynand (1961) *The Worker in an Affluent Society. Family Life and Industry*, London: Heinemann.

Primary sources

Bill Cooper, ERYMS interview.

Derek Mitchell, ERYMS interview.

Joan Binns, written reminiscences, ERYMS.

Mavis Martin, ERYMS interview.

Peter Cooper, ERYMS interview.

Beverley Guardian, 21, 28 April 1945; 20 August 1965.

Field notes from meeting with Beverley Day Club, 12 February 2010.

Field notes on conversation with landlord and customers of Humber Keel pub, Beverley, 29 April 2010.

4   Friends

He (Dad) had one good friend who he worked with, Bill Smith, he had a lot of other acquaintances ... he used to go up to British Legion, and he used to play snooker and have a couple of pints up there, and obviously he used to meet people. But he never, sort of, met up to go regularly out with anyone, that I can remember ... . There was a few people who used to come to the house occasionally, but not to be close friends ... just stay to have a chat, or bring something they'd found or pinched ... the odd rabbit and such as that ... . He had two brothers and a sister but they didn't really particularly [socialise] ... .

Mum's social life was mainly the family... she didn't like people encroaching on her little patch. She was friendly enough with the neighbours, but never sort of allowed them to come through the door.

In this way George Little (interview, 12 March 2010) described his parents' social lives in Beverley during the 1940s. His description evokes aspects of the 'traditional' working-class sociability. Husbands went out to see their mates in pubs or clubs, women chatted to neighbours; both chose companions largely from amongst those with whom they had a 'given' relationship – family, workmates, neighbours; sociability was conducted in specific contexts, with the home used rarely for entertaining those who were not related. George suggests that his parents had few relationships that we might think of as friendships – his father had one, his mother none. Like George, many post-war social investigators could not discern in the 'traditional' kind of sociability anything that looked like friendship as they understood it. 'Friendship is a category of behaviour which does not fit easily into traditional working-class life ... where people admit to friendship, the notion of a friend often has a sound unusual to the middle-class ear,' wrote Josephine Klein (1965: 137–8). Madeleine Kerr (1958: 104–5), in her psycho-social exploration of a deprived neighbourhood in 1950s Liverpool, also judged working-class friendship in relation to middle-class norms: 'The formal invitation to come for a meal between non-related people is almost missing from this group ... . Occasionally individuals have personal friends but this is not very common in adult life.' For these authors, friendship inhered in the making and maintaining of a long-term relationship; for the middle classes this often included entertaining in the home, something that the 'traditional' working classes were known to avoid. Peter Willmott and Michael Young argued that making friends was a skill more relevant to the more mobile lifestyles of the middle classes; the 'traditional' working classes did not need to develop this skill, since they mostly lived in neighbourhoods where they had grown up and were well known (Willmott and Young 1967: 108–15).

George described how he and his wife shared friendships in a way that his parents had not. George and Hilda greatly valued their friendship with a close-knit group including two other couples who had all socialised together since the 1960s; this sociability included entertaining at home and going on holidays together (interviews: George Little 12 March 2010; Hilda Little 19 March 2010). Certainly, it has appeared to some observers that the working classes began to place a greater emphasis on sociability with 'chosen' friends during the age of affluence. A shift in emphasis from casual sociability within 'given' relationships – extended family, neighbours and acquaintances – to friendships carefully chosen, nurtured and maintained, has been seen as part of the dissolution of 'traditional working-class community'. For example, Klein (1965: 265) suggested that affluent workers who moved to new post-war council estates often exercised greater freedom of choice in selecting friends than was usual in traditional working-class neighbourhoods. Because they travelled beyond the bounds of particular estates to socialise with friends, they were less likely to engage in the informal sociability with neighbours that created the solidarity of 'traditional' communities. Klein's interpretation was largely speculative, but it has since gained some empirical support. Adrian Franklin's historical case-study of affluent tobacco workers in mid-century Bristol showed that these workers were often able to purchase homes away from their 'natal communities', and that they used their homes for sociability in ways that were not reported for 'traditional' neighbourhoods (Franklin 1989). Friendships were shared between husband and wife, maintained over a long period of time and a wide geographical area, and friends were entertained in the home. Franklin considered that these patterns of sociability were 'historically significant', contrasting as they did with the 'poorly developed' sociability of the 'traditional' working classes.

Franklin's study has received little attention from historians but has influenced sociological thinking. Allan (1996: 86–90) cited Franklin's work as evidence of a shift in prevailing patterns of working-class friendship in the latter half of the twentieth century, away from what he described as 'mateship'. Allan drew a distinction between 'mates' and 'friends', and considered that the traditional working classes had more of the former and relatively few of the latter in comparison with the middle classes. Mates were social ties largely restricted to a particular context, such as workplace, pub, sports teams, and neighbourhood. Because they did not want to enter into potentially expensive obligations of reciprocal entertainment, many working-class people rarely invited neighbours into their homes, and did not socialise with workmates outside of work.

Such 'mateships', tied to specific contexts, tended to be transitory – moving job or neighbourhood usually resulted in loss of contact with mates from that context. The more affluent, especially the middle classes, did not have the same anxieties about reciprocity and therefore were able to invite workmates out for a drink or into the home to socialise. Those who socialised in multiple contexts in this way were more likely to use the term 'friend' to describe their relationships, and these relationships were more likely to be durable. Graham Allan (1996: 129) referenced Franklin's study as evidence that rising levels of affluence allowed working-class people to develop friend-like social ties. But he argued that a corollary of a shift towards chosen friendships was a decrease in network density – an individual's friends were less likely to also know and to be friends with each other. Thus close-knit communities centred on particular neighbourhoods would be weakened by the tendency to socialise with chosen friends made in a variety of contexts.

A purported increase in 'friend-like', chosen relationships amongst the working classes during the age of affluence sits within *longue durée* socio-logical interpretations of change. Anthony Giddens (1990: 112–24) argued at the end of the twentieth century that affective relationships had replaced older institutional and communal allegiances as the central link articulating indivi-dual and society. Giddens suggested that there had been a change in the meaning of friendship, part of a wider 'transformation of intimacy': whereas 'friend' was formerly a loose term denoting those encountered daily in the contexts of family, locality and workplace, by the late twentieth century friendship had become a project, requiring constant reflexive attention. Ray Pahl (2000: 172) argued that the informal, freely chosen ties of friendship became the defining social bond of late modernity: 'we are increasingly socially and culturally determined by our friends … this was not the case 100 years ago'. Such sociological interpretations are reflected in the judgements of Mark Peel (2009: 317), one of the few historians to consider the contemporary history of friendship, who commented that 'the second half of the twentieth century saw the triumph of … [a] particular form of intimate and reciprocal friendship' characterised by 'a greater emphasis on emotional and private rather than practical and public obligations'. For Peel, increased affluence and state provision of social and health care in most western societies since 1945 meant that it became less incumbent on many people to enter into relation-ships of mutual assistance with family and neighbours, and that they were therefore free to prioritise and nurture chosen friendships.

So, a number of authors have argued that post-war affluence helped to encourage new forms of sociability amongst freely chosen, geographically dispersed friendship groups, hastening the decline of 'traditional' community-of-place. However, the empirical bases for such interpretations are relatively scant, and feature populations that had recently uprooted and moved to new settings (Klein 1965; Franklin 1989). By contrast, Beverley provides a case-study of relative stability during this period, an alternative perspective from which to consider the impact of rising levels of affluence on patterns of sociability with friends, and the implications of any such changes on the ways local community was practised.

Before considering what the Beverley evidence might reveal about changing modes of friendship and their impact on working-class community, it is necessary to note some of the conceptual problems that beset the study of informal relationships. Allan noted that 'friend', unlike 'sister', 'spouse' or 'neighbour', is not easily defined. Friendship does not exist as a structural relationship and depends on subjective conceptions. Notions of friendship not only differ between groups (as we have seen, social class and gender differences have often been posited), but individuals are also inconsistent in their use of terms such as 'friend' and 'acquaintance', and may use both terms at different times to describe the same person (Allan 1996: 84–5). Pahl (2000: 61) pointed out that the meaning of friendship is also historically variable, and friendship patterns cannot be discussed 'without recognizing the distinctiveness of the social, political and economic circumstances of the time'. Furthermore, empirical research by Liz Spencer and Ray Pahl (2006: 167–71, 181–9) showed no simple correlation between the different patterns of 'personal communities' they discovered and social class or gender, belying sometimes simplistic notions of working-class and middle-class patterns of friendship. Indeed, Pahl (2000: 167) has suggested that there is an elusive quality to the topic of friendship, which has often evaded 'the heavy-handed intrusions of social science'.

For the sake of the present chapter, a common-sense approach will be adopted, led by interviewees' own uses of the terms – 'friends' and 'acquaintances' are seen as stronger and weaker variations of social ties with people who were not family, although it is recognised that the borderline between friends and acquaintances is fluid. Despite the provisos detailed above, some themes can be observed in the data relating to patterns of sociability with friends and acquaintances in Beverley across the period of the study. As in the previous chapters, it will be seen that change was more evolutional than was implied in some portrayals of novel patterns in working-class life in the affluent era. In particular, the idea that 'given' relationships began to be replaced by 'chosen' relationships for many in the working classes is complicated by the evidence discussed here. In the early, pre-affluent part of the period there was evidence of chosen, friend-like relationships even amongst the groups who might most be expected to conform to the 'traditional' model; the affluent period did bring more opportunities to choose and develop friendships, but friendships were still structured by lifecycle and by place.

The chapter is organised as follows: section one explores some of the ways in which lifecycle influenced sociability with friends, showing that in adolescence and young adulthood sociable leisure with friends was particularly important; section two explores the ways marriage could limit the social worlds of women in the early, pre-affluent part of the period; section three outlines some of the emerging possibilities for sociability with friends in the affluent era; section four argues that whilst networks of social ties were usually spread over a wider area than the street or immediate neighbourhood in this later period, these networks were still largely contained within the town itself.

Sociability with friends in the early life-stages, 1935–1954

In this and the following section I will concentrate on female patterns of sociability during the pre-affluent decades. This is partly because male sociability in workplaces, clubs, pubs, sports teams and hobby associations will be dealt with further in Chapters 5 and 6. But it is also because it is often thought that working-class women in traditional neighbourhoods had few friends. Klein (1965: 139) wrote that in working-class communities 'men have traditionally had their own male groups outside the home, leaving the main responsibility for kin and neighbourly relations to their womenfolk' and quoted one of Young and Willmott's interviewees: '"Men have friends, women have relatives".' For the Beverley context during the early part of our period, this formulation correctly points to limitations on the sociable worlds of working-class married women, but it passes over the importance of friends to women in young adulthood, and also underestimates the ability of married women, even in more 'traditional' settings, to choose and sustain friendships. Some degree of choice was always exercised in whom, and how, one engaged in friendly relationships.

As described in the preceding chapter, children drew their friendship groups almost exclusively from the streets in which they lived. Younger Beverley children attended different neighbourhood schools, but the opening of Longcroft Secondary School in 1949 meant that a large proportion attended the same school from the age of 11 to 15 (Brown 1989). This opened up access to a wider pool from which to select friends. Fred and May Peters (born 1937 and 1938) recalled:

> May: I went to St Nicholas School ... then to Minster Girls, and then Longcroft, that's how I got to know you then. I didn't know you [Fred] before then, no, 'cause you lived in a different part of Beverley to me ... .
> Stefan: When you went to Longcroft, did you get to know people from other parts of Beverley?
> (Both): Oh, yes.
> Fred: And from out in the country, yes.
> (Fred and May Peters, interview, 24 June 2010)

Other testimony corroborated this point (interviews: Keith Barrett 2 September 2010; James and Peggy Alexander 18 February 2010; William Vincent 25 May 2010).

Sociability in adolescence and young adulthood was conducted amongst a wide group of acquaintances known from school, workplace and the town more broadly. Interaction often took place in communal settings containing large numbers of others, such as dance halls, youth clubs, or in the open-air spaces, and so enabled wide-ranging social contact and the possibility of meeting members of the opposite sex. In the 1940s, groups of teenaged friends congregated to walk in certain parts of the town. George Hunter (interview, 14 January 2010) recalled this activity in the mid-1940s, which he called 'galling':

'Galling'[was] looking for lasses on Westwood [an area of common land] ... . Westwood was popular then ... you used to walk around ... with your mates, like, and try and pick a lass up ...and they used to all walk over there, gangs of them ... it was so popular, especially in summer.

This practice continued into the 1950s, and was known by some of the older respondents as 'the monkey walk' – the same name was given to this custom in other northern towns in the early twentieth century (Reid 2000: 762). From the 1950s, mixed-gender youth clubs were held in church halls, schools and in purpose-built accommodation (interviews: Ivy Shipton 17 May 2010; Margaret Day 9 November 2009; Pete Daniels 28 July 2010). Other clubs existed for young men and women, including religious and political groups, sports clubs, Church Lads' Brigade and youth clubs attached to workplaces (see Chapter 6). From the age of 16 or 17, the majority of interviewees began to attend dance halls on Fridays and Saturdays with friends of their own age (interviews: Evelyn Frith 10 February 2010; Ellen and Harry Malster 21 May 2010; Ellen Watton 8 March 2010; Les White 29 October 2010). Younger teenagers learned to dance at Hodgson's dancehall, but then progressed to the Regal. Ellen Watton (interview, 8 March 2010) met her husband there in the early 1950s and remembered:

Ellen: Regal dance on a Saturday night, that's where most people were ... .
Stefan: Would you know most people there?
Ellen: Yeah, yeah, usually the same crowd.

Not only locals, but servicemen stationed near the town attended these dances, as Betty Carr (interview, 19 March 2010) remembered in the early 1950s:

I knew a lot of local boys ... but then, when you got a bit older and started going to Regal, to dance, you met up with the lads from the RAF Leconfield, or the army. And then the local lads didn't like it you see ... it was exciting meeting someone from a different part of the country, who had lots of different things to talk about.

Adolescents thus participated in leisure that brought them into contact with a number of others at the same life-stage, but this wider 'communal' sociability was experienced and mediated through smaller peer-groups, as Gwen Harris (interview, 30 July 2010) intimated:

> The Regal or Hodgson's … we'd just meet other girls inside, or talk to different ones. But we never went out in big gangs, groups.

Although she did not consider herself to be particularly sociable, the following quotes from Gwen's testimony illustrate the range of social activities enjoyed with a few close friends, typical of other interviewees who recalled this life-stage in the early 1950s:

> One of my friends, Sylvia, who's died now, her and me we got on really well, we used to go on our bikes, and I had a cousin who lived near Thirsk, sometimes we'd go on our bikes and cycle there for the weekend. We'd go on a Saturday afternoon after the shift finished, come back on a Monday morning before next week's shift started at two o'clock … . She was the main friend at that time, and we just used to go bike riding out together, or just go to the pictures, or just wander about, go up to the Westwood for walks, or, just like kids do … .
>
> Sylvia and me mainly were together, and occasionally Margaret, and then later on Mary, she came from Sunderland with her family, and I made friends with her, and so they were the main ones, and then there was a girl called Pauline … oh, and there was Betty, she used to come dancing with us sometimes … .
>
> Mary, she came from Sunderland … she kept in touch with one of her friends, and there was one year her friend Audrey came down and there was myself, and this other girl Dorothy and we all went to Llandudno on holiday, and that was sort of something special, it was really a first holiday away with friends … I must have been about eighteen … that holiday was a really good one … .
>
> We went to the cinema a lot … nearly every week, sometimes every week, depending on the pictures, you see. Mostly on a Saturday nights, sometimes during the week … Sylvia by that time was married, or she was going out with Les, so mostly that time it was Mary and me, and sometimes Dorothy.

I have concentrated above on the early, pre-affluent part of the period to make the point that at a time when 'traditional' working-class restricted sociability might be thought to pertain, young people did not conform to this model. Later generations recalled a similar period of sociability in early adulthood. Although the content of youth culture – fashions, music styles – were to change radically across the affluent era, structural changes were perhaps less significant. The Regal, despite name changes, remained the central venue for youth sociability, popular with successive generations. Les White (interview, 29 October 2010) recalled of the 1960s:

Your community, your dance night, that was Beverley Regal, that was your centre ... . That was your youth club, that's where you all went.

The hall became the 'Beverley Hills' discotheque in 1979 and continued to attract the town's youth until its closure in 1986 (*Beverley Guardian*, 3 January 1980; interviews: Les White 29 October 2010; Peter Stephenson 27 May 2010).

Mothers' sociability, 1935–1954

As Gwen's testimony quoted above indicates, peer-group sociability with friends was reduced once steady courtship began (see also interviews: Matthew Walton 22 July 2010; Vic Baker 29 May 2010). Marriage could complete this process of separation from friends (see Kerr 1958: 101). Gwen recalled that after her old friend Sylvia got married, 'of course, we lost touch'. She suggested that her principal social period of 'concert going and pictures' had been early adulthood: 'from me being 16 to 22, getting married, it was sort of condensed in those few years'. Gwen was married at the age of 22 in 1958, after the period of affluence commenced, but her experience mirrored that of those married in the austerity years and seemed to confirm cultural expectations that courtship and marriage reduced women's contact with friends. Like others, Gwen felt it was only natural that marriage had significantly reduced or brought to an end her sociability with her female friends. It was perhaps significant that the one friend from her single days who Gwen continued to see was unmarried.

The practice of women giving up work after marriage, commonplace in the early part of the period (1935–54), could reinforce the separation of women from networks of friends and acquaintances. Joyce Sumner (interview, 13 August 2010) married in 1948 and gave up work. During young adulthood Joyce had a friend who worked in greenhouses with her, whom she regularly visited at her home in Hull and went out to the pictures, but after her wedding they lost touch:

> Stefan: Did you have a social life with your husband, did you have friends who you saw together?
> Joyce: No, no, didn't seem to have a social life like that, no. I don't know, it didn't seem to be a done thing in them days, not like it is today ... [I used to] just stay in, read or knit... my mam used to come or my sisters would come along ... I hadn't any close friends, what you could call close-knit friends at all.
> Stefan: Not these friends you met through work, you didn't continue with them?
> Joyce: No, no, well no, 'cause they was in Hull and we was in Beverley, they was sort of, a different class type of thing, we didn't keep a close relationship or anything like that ... if you saw anyone from school you'd say hello but wasn't close to anybody.

Women's opportunities for sociable leisure were further restricted by parent-hood; but their domestic role was not necessarily viewed negatively by women themselves, as Eva White (interview, 18 June 2010), who had her first baby in 1946, recalled:

> I never went out, no. I never left them ... it was very rare. When they got older [I sometimes did]. I would never leave them when they were babies, ooh no ... . You were content. I mean, [you had] lived through the war, and you get a house and children, and you were content with your life ... women didn't go out.

For more testimony about women bringing up families during this period, it is helpful to turn to interviewees' memories of their own mothers. Interviewees often remembered that their mothers in the 1930s through to the 1950s did not have extensive social lives. Peggy Alexander (interview, 18 February 2010) remembered that although her father regularly went to the pub, 'I don't recall her [my mother] having a babysitter ... I don't recall mum going out socially.' Dick Gibson (interview, 11 March 2010) recalled of his mother and other women of her generation in the 1940s:

> They didn't have a social side, not as married women do now. They were bloody slaves really ... she did belong Coop [Society] ... but that was later in life as we were growing up. All I remember at home was her working – ironing, washing, getting food ready, baking.

In this respect, the interview findings confirmed Claire Langhamer's portrayal of women's leisure in the period 1920–1960: After a period of sociability in early adulthood, married women's notions of leisure were limited by ideologies of femininity and motherhood, and structured around the demands of domestic work and childcare (Langhamer 2000: 25–6).

In a study utilising oral history testimony and court-case evidence in a Cleveland town between 1930 and 1960, Margaret Williamson (2009) suggested that some married women regularly went dancing with friends, leaving their husbands at home. Although there was little evidence of Beverley women with children in these years 'going out' in terms of visiting social venues such as pubs, cinemas, dance hall and clubs, this did not mean they could not still find some time and space for socialising with chosen friends. Friendly companions were often sought from amongst 'given' social contacts – neighbours and family. These were the women who were closest at hand or with whom kinship made a casual, 'dropping in' form of sociability more conducive. But such relation-ships were not devoid of choice and friendship. Klein (1965: 137), developing her model of traditional working-class 'communal' sociability, suggested that in traditional working-class districts, distinctions between neighbours in terms of 'friends' and 'not friends' were irrelevant since all were engaged at a similar level, with companionship and help required at some times but a degree of social distance always maintained:

The fact that neighbours are 'familiar figures in the landscape' does not mean that they are 'friends' in the sense in which that word is used by middle-class people. Nor indeed, should it be assumed that neighbours are 'not-friends'. Friendship is a category of social behaviour which does not fit easily into traditional working-class life.

However, Beverley interviewees describing their own or their mothers' relations with neighbours in the pre-affluent years indicated that relationships with particular neighbours were closer and more friend-like than with others. Matthew Walton (interview, 22 July 2010) recalled that in the 1940s his mother was:

> very friendly with Mrs Lawson on one side, [whereas] Mrs Ford on the other side, they were on sort of, conversational terms occasionally, but they were not in and out of each other's houses. But Mrs Lawson on the other side, in fact I can remember my father putting a gate in the fence so they could get through to each other.

Similarly, Jack Binnington (interview, 22 June 2010) recalled that a particular neighbouring couple provided his mother with emotional support in the early 1950s. As we saw in Chapter 2, supposedly 'given' relationships with relatives were also 'chosen' to some extent, since favoured relatives were visited regularly and others not at all.

Some busy mothers maintained a small number of friendships with others who were neither kin nor neighbours. Janet Hill (interview, 3 March 2010) recalled that from the 1930s through to the 1950s her mother had a friend who lived a few streets away with whom she was particularly close: 'Aunty Molly, I called her, and she used to come down every night … for years. She used to knit all my jumpers for school.' Judy Whittles' mother had a friend who visited once a week for a coffee in the 1940s; others recalled their mothers popping round to a friend's home (Judy and John Whittles, interview, 10 May 2010). This pattern of women's sociability – female friends engaged independently of their husbands, visited usually in homes whilst husbands were out at work or in the pub – resembled the 'callin' that Norman Dennis, Fernando Henriques and Clifford Slaughter (1969: 170) described as women's principal form of social interaction in 'Ashton'.

As noted in Chapter 2, 'Families', many working-class women socialised at least occasionally with their husbands in the 1930s and 1940s in venues apart from the home, for example spending Saturday nights in their husband's favoured pub or club. In the 1940s, Anna Mason's mother and father had friends whom they regularly met in the pub to play dominoes (Anna Mason, interview, 12 July 2010). There was also occasional testimony of couples with shared friends whom they visited or entertained at home in ways that anticipated the forms of conjugal sociability that will be described below for the later part of our period. Hannah Witham (interview, 16 April 2010) recalled that in the 1930s and 1940s her parents often played whist in the homes of shared friends who lived nearby:

> Most days someone had a whist drive in their house ... and they just used to go from house to house. It was a pleasant evening and they enjoyed it ... they'd stop and have a cup of tea and sometimes fish and chips.

Ellen Ingleton (interview, 20 April 2010) remembered that her parents called on friends casually and were called on in turn: 'We often had people in the house who just called.'

Although Allan (1996: 17) considered that there was 'little evidence of organised female sociability' in traditional working-class districts, some interviewees remembered women's informal clubs, whist nights and trips away (see Chapters 3 and 6 of the present book), which certainly seemed to constitute communal organised sociability. For example, Doris Daniels (interview, 16 December 2009) remembered a women's club held in a room of the Foresters' pub on Beckside, organised by the landlady, which she attended with her mother in the 1940s and 1950s. Activities included organised trips away, and rehearsing and performing for charity concerts in the pub.

The evidence discussed above, from the early part of our period, paints a mixed picture. We noted the importance of their friends to young unmarried women, something that is often ignored in the wider literature of the 'traditional' working classes. However, as the 'traditional' model suggests, friendships developed during early adulthood could be set aside as women married and started a family. But any idea that working-class sociable relationships were simply 'given' in this period seems inherently unrealistic. Even in the years in which they were busy bringing up children, married women exercised choice in selecting companions from amongst neighbours and relatives. Some married women maintained one or two long-standing friendships. Furthermore, there was evidence of the conjugal joint sociability, often associated with the later age of affluence. It is also worth noting that in later life-stages, many women said that they again picked up older friendships. Gwen Harris (interview, 30 July 2010) recalled that in later life she again struck up a friendship with her friend from young adulthood, Sylvia:

> When she got married of course, we lost touch ... we always sent a card at Christmas but we didn't often see each other in those years, but later on, I suppose after her family had grown up and my family had grown up, we just wrote a bit sometimes to each other, telephoned each other ... I think by the time we really got involved her husband had retired.

New forms of sociability, 1955–1980

As living standards rose from the 1950s, and increasing numbers of married women went out to work, there was more scope for working-class women to conduct sociable leisure with friends. This was partly in the context of shared conjugal sociability with friends drawn from beyond the neighbourhood and family, as authors such as Klein (1965: 263–4) and Franklin (1989: 110) have suggested.

A pattern of couples socialising with other couples might begin in court-ship. Jack Binnington (interview, 13 July 2010) remembered that in the 1960s:

> Your mates came first until you got seriously courting ... you didn't see your mates so often and you saw the girl a little bit more ... if your best mate, he was courting, then you meet up in the pub and talk ... obviously there was times when I'd probably not like my mate's girl-friend, and so you didn't meet up because there'd be an atmosphere, but by and large you all generally got on together and talked and socialised together.

Elaine Mateer (interview, 29 March 2010) began seeing a member of a local rock group in the late 1960s:

> Stefan: Did you stop seeing your girlfriends as much?
> Elaine: Yes, yes, totally. It was exciting to go off with groups where they were playing and all like that for a while, and then meet the other lads' girlfriends and so you'd hang around all together.

Many interviewees spoke of 'our' friends from their early married life in the 1960s and 1970s, some of whom they still saw:

> We had lots of friends that I made and that Jen had and we are still friends now, from then, some friends who were Jen's best friends ... and friends of mine.
>
> (Gerald Ibbotson, interview, 7 July 2010)

> When we had the children, we did more family things didn't we? ... With friends who had families as well ... . And you used to play golf with Tom didn't you? And I met Brenda [Tom's wife] – I didn't know Tom and Brenda before I had the children, and we both had [our first children] Tom and Jonathan within three weeks of each other, and then we've sort of been pals.
>
> (June and David Ireland, interview, 15 July 2010)

> Dennis: Yes, [my wife and I] we always socialised together, we was very close. Obviously we used to go out occasionally on our own, you know what women are, their shopping and that, you know, but we used to go out a fair bit, for meals and what have you.
> Stefan: Did you have a group of friends who you saw?
> Dennis: Yes, yes, various couples we knew.
>
> (Dennis Duke, interview, 14 July 2010)

Janet Thompson (23 November 2009) remembered that after she and Pete were married in the early 1970s they shared a social life based around the pub and a group of shared friends:

> It didn't seem to make a lot of difference, just carried on the same ... we still went out on the Friday and Saturday night ... we both went out together ... . When I met Pete there was a load of them in the George and Dragon, and he'd got quite friendly with a particular two or three of these gentlemen, who we are still very good friends with nowadays.

Although for financial reasons the couple were not able to go out together as much while the children were young, Pete was keen to ensure that Janet was able to socialise whilst the children were small during the 1970s. The couple had a rule that they each spent at least one night out a week with their friends, and throughout their adult life the couple socialised either together or as a pair with the same peer group. Other couples had a similar shared social life in pubs (interviews: Peter Lawson 4 May 2010; Sally Adams 23 June 2010; Ellen and Harry Malster 21 May 2010). For example, Jim Fisher (interview, 16 December 2009) recalled that his parents in the late 1950s and 1960s went out to pubs and Hodgson's social club together most nights, and that he was himself practically brought up by his grandparents.

Whereas in the 1940s and early 1950s conjugal shared sociability might be limited to particular contexts, such as a regular pub or club night, couples in the affluent era often socialised with shared friends in several contexts. In addition to their pub sociability, Janet and Pete Thompson (interview, 23 November 2009) also went on holidays with their friends in the 1970s: 'We used to rent a cottage there in Kettlewell, Wharfedale, slept ten, and we used to go, us four, Pat and Bruce and their two girls and two of the chaps that I've just been talking about.' In the later 1970s, Dennis Duke (interview, 14 July 2010) began working as a driver at a local haulage firm and he and a fellow driver became friendly, socialising together with their wives in a number of settings:

> Sandra got on very well with his wife, and we just used to go out socialising, you know. Out for meals ... restaurants, pubs, wherever we fancied ... further afield sometimes, we'd go for a day, you know.

Couples' sociable leisure practices increasingly involved the use of cars. Nationally, the number of domestic households with use of a car doubled between 1955 and 1965 (Gunn 2011: 524). Interviewees recalled driving with friends to country pubs during the 1960s and 1970s (interviews: Ivy Shipton 17 May 2010; James and Peggy Alexander 18 February 2010; Ron Matthews 2 December 2010). The rise in sociable eating out was perhaps connected with this increased mobility, with couples travelling to go for 'basket meals' with friends in the 1970s (interviews: James and Peggy Alexander 18 February 2010; Ron Matthews 2 December 2010). Gerald Ibbotson (interview, 7 July 2010) and his wife in the 1970s would sometimes leave their children with babysitters whilst they went out with friends to pubs or restaurants in villages or in Hull. A 1973 'advertorial' piece in the *Beverley Guardian* (26 January 1973) claimed that 'more and more' people were eating out and that more establishments – clubs, hotels and inns – were serving food.

Some interviewees saw differences between their own more wide-ranging sociability and that of their parents. Sarah and Vic Baker (29 May 2010) recalled that neighbours were less important for their own generation:

> Sarah: We got on with them all [neighbours] ... but we never used to go socialising with them ... I think in our days, people didn't socialise [with neighbours], not like our parents did ... .
> Stefan: Did you have friends round to the house?
> Sarah: Yes, we'd have Christmas parties and things like that.
> Vic: You'd probably spend more time with your friends who lived a few streets away, and you didn't with your direct neighbours.

Asked whether she had been involved in the Townswomen's Guild like her mother, Margaret Day (interview, 8 December 2009) compared her own generation's expanded range of sociable leisure opportunities with their parents' more limited pallet:

> I didn't [want to get involved with the Townswomen's Guild]. I used to like socialising, and I played golf for a little while ... . In those days [when mother was young] there wasn't other things to do, you know what I mean, it was a real good night out for them wasn't it?

These interviewees clearly felt that there was some degree of novelty in aspects of their own generation's sociability.

One clear difference between earlier and later generations was the use of homes for sociability. Increased use of the home for entertaining friends appeared to be connected to the post-war rise in home ownership. Although few interviewees who grew up before the Second World War lived in homes that their parents owned, at least 60 per cent of the interviewees born after 1940 had eventually bought their own homes. If their parents had used their homes for sociability with friends at all, this was typically casual, of short duration, and usually took place during the day (interviews: Keith Barrett 2 September 2010; Ellen Ingleton 20 April 2010). Interviewees who married in the 1950s onwards often entertained shared friends in a more structured way, with this entertaining taking place on an evening. John and Margaret Day (interview, 23 November 2009) regularly entertained friends in their semi-detached home in the east of Beverley in the 1960s and early 1970s:

Margaret: We used to come back after here after we'd been out for a drink or something ... we've always had people round, haven't we? And we used to go to other people's houses ... .

Stefan: Did you cook meals for people?

Margaret: You didn't do that sort of thing then, did you? We did more things like buffets, you know, sandwiches and sausage rolls, chicken legs, pineapple and cheese on sticks, and that sort of thing, we did lots of little buffets and things. But we now, more, if anybody comes you have a meal, you know.

Stefan: Buffets, what were they for birthdays, or – ?

Margaret: Yes, or if you had anyone over on a Saturday night, 'come round to us on a Saturday night', and there might be six, seven or eight of you, and I used to set the table up and make a bit of a buffet.

By the 1970s, some interviewees were cooking meals in their homes for friends. Gerald Ibbotson (interview, 7 July 2010) recalled:

I can't remember them [parents] having hardly anybody round for a meal, they might have been round for a scone and a cup of tea, but that was about it. But I think from the ... early seventies, we had a circle of friends from the [music] group and people that used to knock around with us from the group, but we've all got married, or just before we've got married or whatever, we've been to their houses for a meal, and they've been to our house for a meal, and it just built up.

Allan (1996: 87) saw home-based sociability as particularly significant in differentiating 'friends' from 'mates' – inviting people into the home signified an extension of the relationship beyond the original context in which it was established (pub, club or workplace, for example). In Beverley the working classes used their homes in this way in the 1960s and 1970s – somewhat later than amongst the affluent working-class population in Bristol whose use of their homes for entertaining friends in the inter-war period Franklin (1989: 108) described as 'historically significant'. For the Beverley residents, home-based conjugal sociability with shared friends may have been part of the post-war cultural emphasis on the home noted by some historians (Langhamer 2005; Tebbutt 1995: 150–3). The time and money invested in purchasing and improving homes meant that they might be shown off rather than kept private (Tebbutt 1995: 81).

Friends shared between husband and wife were usually chosen from a wider range of contacts than just the neighbourhood or family (although people from these contexts might well be accommodated in friendship networks). Many of Margaret and John's friends were from the golf club (Margaret Day, interview, 23 November 2009); Gerald's and his wife's friends were from their pre-married social networks (Gerald Ibbotson, interview, 7 July 2010); Vic and Sarah Baker (interview, 29 May 2010) regularly socialised with a group of friends in the 1960s and 1970s who were an assortment of current and former workmates and people Vic 'had grown up with'.

Other developments helped to bring about new patterns of sociable interaction with friends. The rise in married women's work outside of the home in the post-war decades brought opportunities for women to forge friendly relationships away from the neighbourhood and family. Doris Daniels married immediately after the Second World War and had a large family. Much of her sociability in the 1950s and 1960s resembled that often attributed to working-class women: informal outdoor chatting with neighbouring women and closer relationships with her mother and sister. However, she returned to work in the 1970s in Skelton's bakery in the town, a move that brought new friends and social opportunities:

> Now we all did good years at Skeltons, and Madge ... she said, 'oh Doris, do you fancy going to Blackpool?' I said 'I can't go to Blackpool and leave all them!' [husband and children] "Course you can!' And I said 'oh I don't know, I'll have to see', like. I had to look into it, and Jim said 'I don't see why not' ... and, course, I had a bit of pocket money and things like that, and you're thinking, 'oh, I can do' – anyway I decided to go ... and I thoroughly enjoyed it ... and the next year, 'eh, shall we go again?' well of course, it ended up twelve years ... I thoroughly enjoyed it, I really, really did. Of course, they were devils you know, and we used to go out all hours dancing, you really filled the weekend in ... Elaine, Jackie, Linda, Me, Elaine ... Jackie would only take eight.
>
> (Doris Daniels, interview, 13 November 2009)

In the early part of the period, married women socialising together often had to arrange whist nights or informal clubs in the back rooms of pubs, as it was taboo for respectable younger women to go to the pub without their husbands (Tom Potter, 24 October 2008). However, during the affluent period married women gained some limited access to pubs on their own terms, through women's darts teams (interviews: Janet Hill 3 March 2010; Jean Benson 14 January 2010; ERYMS interview with Mary Elizabeth Miles). Janet Hill (interview, 3 March 2010) recalled that this was a way to socialise with friends she made while working at Armstrong's part-time when her daughter was young in the 1960s:

> Stefan: Did you see these ladies outside of work ...?
> Janet: Yes, you used to play darts. I didn't play a lot, I did the adding up and marking up ... .
> Stefan: What team were they in?
> Janet: It was a pub, a pub team ... Mariners Pub. Real good it was ... once a week, darts night.

Janet Thompson (interview, 23 November 2009) first became involved in ladies' darts in the early 1980s, but her testimony chimed with that of other women who played in earlier decades in emphasising the social aspect of the game:

> I mean, we don't profess to be able to play, we never have done. And I think everybody's about the same, they just go to have a night out and have a natter and a laugh ... . It's nice to catch up, because they're normally somebody who you maybe don't see all the time, apart from Helen [workmate], the rest of them I wouldn't see from one week to the next, and yet they're lovely girls, they're lovely ladies, so it's nice to have a get together and all have a good natter together.

Friends were clearly important to the generations who reached adulthood in the 1950s onwards; many friendships that interviewees discussed had been nurtured and maintained over decades. Janet and Pete Thompson (interview, 23 November 2009) shared a long-term friendship group since the 1960s:

> Pete: We're more friends-oriented than relatives to be truthful ... .
> Janet: They're long term friends as well, aren't they?
> Pete: One of 'ems just died, been a friend for over forty-two year, he was older than us but he was still a good friend, he just died ... it hit me about as much as it hit me when my mum and dad died ... I used to really go out with him more times than with my mum and dad ... .
> Janet: Our really close-knit ones [friends], which we call our family, you know, they're always there and they always will be.

That such a high valuation was placed on friends corroborated sociologists' suggestions of an increasing emphasis on friendship in the latter half of the twentieth century. Spencer and Pahl (2006: 117–20), for example, commented that amongst those they interviewed in the early twenty-first century, many had the kinds of close bonds of support and mutual obligation with friends that are often associated with families. The authors described these as 'chosen-as-given' relationships – what began as 'chosen' friendships became invested with the characteristics of 'given', family relationships. Similarly, Giddens (1990: 117–20) posited a 'transformation of intimacy' during late modernity – individuals increasingly channelled energy into their friendships as older, more solid and less self-conscious sources of 'ontological security' (family, local community) were eroded.

In previous chapters it was seen that affluence loosened the necessity for some types of mutual material assistance amongst neighbours and family, but that new forms of support could develop. It is suggested here that a further corollary of changes associated with the affluent era – improved housing, more time and money for leisure, emphasis on the conjugal bond – was the extension of what Franklin (1989) termed 'external' sociability for married couples. Although the evidence from the Beverley study does not allow secure conclusions about long-term developments in friendship patterns, it was certainly the case that some couples marrying in the 1950s, 1960s and 1970s appeared to have placed more emphasis on sociability with friends than had their parents. If, as Allan (1996: 90) suggested, poverty led people to limit the contexts in which they engaged with friends for fear of entering into obligations of reciprocity, then rising levels of affluence appeared to lead to a more relaxed attitude towards, for example, sociability in the home.

Friendship and acquaintanceship in a geographical context

The discussion above may therefore appear to lend some support to those authors who saw an increase in 'non-local social networks' amongst the affluent working classes, and thus a weakening of working-class community-of-place centred on particular streets or groups of streets (Klein 1965: 264–5; Zweig 1961: 104–7; Franklin 1989). However, the extent to which the new social networks were geographically scattered is not often stipulated. The Beverley evidence suggests that, though immediate neighbours in particular streets may have become less important for some interviewees during the affluent era, the town itself continued to contain a large part of the social networks of most of the interviewees.

Surprisingly often, interviewees stated that they had not had any friends from outside of the town during the period of the study (interviews: Amy Easterling 15 February 2010; Ivy Shipton 17 May 2010; Jean Benson 14 January 2010). This was true across the age range of interviewees. Even those relatively affluent workers who owned homes and reported a wide range of friends nevertheless usually said that the majority of these friends lived in the town. Ellen and Harry Malster (interview, 21 May 2010) were married in 1953. Harry was a skilled electrician and the couple built their own house. They reported a varied social life, from the 1950s through to the 1970s, with a range of friends:

> Stefan: Did you have friends who lived away from Beverley who you went to visit or was all your social life in Beverley?
> Ellen: I should think it would be wouldn't it? Yes, I'm sure it was.

Similarly, in the 1960s and 1970s Margaret and John Day (interview, 23 November 2009) had a full and active social life, with shared friends from work and associational life, but the great majority of these friends also lived in Beverley. Margaret valued the proximity of friends: 'I can't imagine all these people who want to move away, and retire ... you're leaving all your friends and your surroundings'. Although Margaret was here speaking in the present tense, Les White (interview, 29 October 2010) indicated that his own attachment to local friendships was the reason for a brief relocation to London in the 1970s coming to an end:

> Why would you want to move and leave all your mates? I wouldn't dream of moving to London and living in Hackney ... I went there, they were all strangers in flats from all over the place.

The simple material fact of proximity and ease of interaction helps explains the concentration of friends within the town. Even movements over a small distance could be significant: 'A few of my friends married farmers [in the 1960s], so they went out, I've got a friend lives in [the nearby village of] Holme on Spalding Moor ... [and friends in] Thwing ... Scorborough, they went away, so it's sort of sending cards for so long and then you just break away, don't you?' (Margaret and John Day, interview, 8 December 2009). Elaine and Patrick Mateer (interview, 13 January 2010), who also had an active social life, nevertheless recalled that upon moving to a village about ten miles away in the 1970s they lost contact with most friends in Beverley, and that when they moved back to the town more recently they stopped seeing friends they had made in the village. Similarly, many of those who left Beverley in their youth and later returned said they did not maintain ties with friends made whilst they were away. Mick Underwood (interview, 16 June 2010) did national service in the early 1950s:

> Stefan: Did you make any friends in the army?
> Mick: Yes, tremendous, unbelievable ... that's why it annoys me that, I've got pictures of them all ... .
> Stefan: Was it difficult to keep in touch with them afterwards?
> Mick: I lost touch with them immediately I got back to Beverley.

In the 1960s and 1970s, Iris Brown (interview, 21 May 2010) spent many years away from the town, serving in the armed forces herself and bringing up a family as the wife of a serviceman, but when she returned to the town did not maintain friendships with the people she met during these years, and instead took up again with friends from her youth in the town.

However, rising standards of living, larger homes, the possession of cars and money for travel facilitated the maintenance of some long-distance relationships. Particularly close and valued friendships could withstand geographical separation. Hilda Little (interview, 19 March 2010) moved to Beverley with her family as a young girl in the 1940s, and soon after went to grammar school in Bridlington, 20 miles from Beverley. She did not make many friends in Beverley, but shared experience of grammar school appeared to underpin her close friendship with a small group:

> From going to Brid, that's when I became friends with who was, and who has always been, my best friend. And her sister went to Beverley High, and another girl who lived near them, so there were the four of us ... sadly Anne has died, and her sister Gwen is still, is now, my closest friend. I don't have a lot of friends as such, I've a lot of acquaintances, but they are really the only people who I would go to see unannounced ... it wouldn't matter, or if I needed anything.

When her friends married servicemen and left the town in the 1950s, Hilda married George, a maintenance engineer who worked at Hodgson's, and she stayed in Beverley. However, she always stayed in touch with her friends who had moved away. The friendship group incorporated their husbands and then children into their sociability, with the families making visits to each other's homes.

But long-distance friendships were reported rarely, and were usually maintained not instead of, but alongside, local friendships and acquaintances. Thus in the 1960s and 1970s, most interviewees' networks of sociable friendships, if not so closely centred on particular streets, were still largely contained within the town. Furthermore, there was still a role for the informal 'effortless' sociability that Klein (1965: 265) suggested was central to traditional working-class communities. Informal interaction with casual acquaintances in the public spaces of the town remained important, helping make the town feel like a knowable community.

Because they had been to school, socialised and worked in the town where members of their extended family also lived, many interviewees had lots of casual acquaintances in Beverley. I showed Lynne Norton (interview, 9 November 2009), born in 1942, a random selection of photos of local sporting teams, workplaces and public events from the decades from the 1950 to the 1980 (copied from the local museum's collection), and asked her to identify people she knew and to talk about how she knew them. She cited a range of reasons for her recognition of many of the faces. Family connections were important: one woman had been known to her mother; one man's nephew married Lynne's niece; another man was an acquaintance of her father; a younger person was a friend of her nephew. Some were familiar because of Lynne's knowledge of former neighbours and their families: one of those pictured had lived in the same neighbourhood Lynne had grown up in; a man was related to a former next-door neighbour; a girl had married a man who lived around the corner. Others were familiar because of a public role: a woman had worked as doctor's receptionist; several were 'well-known' local personalities (councillors for example); some had been owners of local shops. Lynne knew many of the faces in the photos simply as a result of a lifetime lived socially within the town: one person was a friend of a friend of a friend; some women were members of her ladies' group; several had been to the same school as Lynne; one man went into the same pub she had used; some she had met and spoken to 'round town'. Summing up, Lynne said:

> I've lived in Beverley all my life. 'Cause he [son] used to say to me, 'Do you know everybody?' I said 'no', but I know an awful lot of people. People you've been to school with, people you've worked with.

It was likely that residents of Beverley who had grown up in the town, and had family and work locally, stood a good chance of bumping into acquaintances whilst shopping in town or drinking in pubs in and around the market square. Across the period, from the 1950s to the 1970s, there was a sense that the faces in the crowd were familiar:

Yes, you could walk down the shopping street and you knew everybody, everybody. So it was like a big family really.

(Ellen Watton, interview, 8 March 2010)

You could go into town when I was younger and you would know more or less, not everybody, but, you know, you recognised most people.

(Sally Adams, interview, 21 June 2010)

At one time Beverley, it was a small town, hell of a lot smaller than what it is now. And, to be quite honest with you, most people knew each other by sight.

(Peter Lawson, interview,4 May 2010)

A shopping trip into town could involve multiple minor social interactions, as William Vincent (interview, 25 May 2010), recalled of the late 1950s: 'We'd go shopping with Mum into town to the market or whatever, and every few yards along the road: "oh hello" "hello" "hello so and so" – everybody knew everybody.' Although interviewees did not give much detail about the content of these interactions, occasional accounts of more recent meetings suggest something of the flavour of these casual encounters: 'I went for my paper, about three or four days ago, and he [a councillor known since youth] was in there, and I said "ah, I want a word with you."'; 'I met Betty [old school friend], she's nearly the same age as me, I met her in Morrison's … I see more people from working at Skelton's for twenty year, you see I get girls who were sixteen coming up and saying "you don't remember me do you Doris?"'; 'I was telling a bloke this morning, in Netto's [supermarket], an old shipyarder' (interviews: Vic Baker 19 May 2010; Doris Daniels 13 November 2009; Bob Garbutt 28 June 2010).

Interviewees had often valued this sense of familiarity. Ivy Shipton (interview, 17 May 2010) moved away from Beverley in the 1960s (and again in the 2000s), and realised that she missed familiar faces:

Ivy: I went to live in Liverpool. I didn't settle … it was like an alien environment really … you don't realise, do you, until you do start talking about it, how intertwined with a community you actually, actually were really.

Stefan: So what did you miss about Beverley, can you remember?

Ivy: (pause) You couldn't put your finger on it, I think it came home more to me when we moved from Beverley to here [Driffield], two years ago, the fact that I was used to walking down the street and I was used to seeing faces that I knew, either people I went to school with, or somebody, a relative.

Mick Underwood (interview, 16 June 2010) gained a sense of worth from his position as well-known local personality (partly achieved through his involvement in local cricket and football teams): 'There must be some people if they were listening, honestly Stefan, would think "who does he think he is?", but that is fact, you know, I mean, everybody knows me.' The sense of belonging gained from being part of a knowable community was just as strong for those whose leisure time was focused around spouse and family:

> If we went up town [my wife and I in the 1960s] we'd go on our own, and if we bumped into them [friends] so be it. So, my circle of friends was very small. Very, very small. And is now. Although I know a lot of people, and talk to a lot of people ... I've never been unhappy with Beckside or people who live around. I've never been unhappy with people who live on the [council] estate. In my opinion they're my people and I'm part of it ... it's a belonging thing for me ... I know the people around this area [east Beverley].
>
> (Jack Binnington, interview, 13 July 2010)

That people whose lifestyles might appear 'privatised' could nevertheless derive a sense of belonging from local social networks is something not often captured in the historiography and sociology of the 'age of affluence'. Those who valued their close friends during this period could also derive satisfaction from being situated in a knowable community. Since the 1960s George and Hilda Little (interview, 24 October 2008) had maintained close friendships with Hilda's childhood friends, visiting each other in their homes; but the couple also expressed regret that since the town's expansion in the 1990s (the population grew by just under a third between 1991 and 2001) they now knew few of the other people they saw when they went out shopping.

Friendship networks continued to be largely located within the town during this period. Many in Beverley, as in the British working classes more generally, continued to live in localities in which they were born and where they were able to remain due to the abundance of working-class employment in traditional industries (Pahl 1984: 313; Franklin 1989: 94; Offer 2008). The post-war building boom expanded the range of housing stock available for rental and purchase in Beverley as elsewhere, but many people did not move far in their search for improved housing. Their networks of friends and acquaintants were thus concentrated in the town, even if many did not live in the street or neighbourhood in which they were born. These were still social worlds contained within a relatively small local area, and in which network density (the chance that any two people within a person's social network would also know each other) was high. This fact provides a corrective to narratives in which 'community' is conceptualised purely in terms of the social networks of the residential street and immediate neighbourhood (for example, Benson 1989: 131–2; Roberts 1995: 199–231; Jones 2012: 120). Beverley was and remains a small town and therefore, of course, it was more likely that any two people would know each other than in a large city. Nevertheless, even in larger towns and cities it is likely that the continuing localness of social networks has often been missed because of the tendency to associate community only with the residential street and immediate neighbourhood. Robert Putnam (2000: 93) argued that even small and superficial daily interactions such as nodding to a fellow jogger have social and psychological benefits, adding to the stock of 'social capital' that makes people feel comfortable in places, engage positively with society and invest trust in social institutions. Casual interactions with acquaintances living in the same town may not have been of the same intensity as the daily gossiping amongst neighbours reported in 'traditional' communities, but nonetheless helped create a sense of the town as a knowable community. This contact was valued by interviewees.

Conclusion

The purported shift towards chosen, friend-like relationships in the age of affluence (Allan 1996, 1998; Peel 2009) dovetails with the narrative of the demise of 'traditional working-class community': chosen friendships replaced given relationships with kin, neighbours and workmates. Although empirical research into working-class friendship is sparse, there is some support for the suggestion that sociability with chosen friends may have been more important at the beginning of the twenty-first century than it had been in the first half of the twentieth (Spencer and Pahl 2006; Phillipson *et al.* 2001: 251–65). The evidence from Beverley suggests additional support for, but also some modification of, the thesis that friendship practices changed in the second half of the twentieth century.

Generalisations about working-class friendship need to be qualified by consideration of lifecycle variation. Both before and after the onset of the age of affluence, young adulthood was a period of intensive sociable leisure. Young adult peer groups socialised against a backdrop of broader communal sociability in the town's public spaces and dance halls (see also Davies 1992: 82–3; Langhamer 2000: 49–113). For women in particular, marriage and child-rearing limited this sociability, and often brought at least temporary disengagement from friends. This was perhaps more marked amongst women in the early part of the period (c.1935–54). Women in these years who did not work outside of the home and whose husbands pursued extensive sociability away from the household often had limited opportunities to engage with friends.

There is little doubt that new forms of sociability came into focus during the age of affluence. Those who married in the 1950s onwards were more likely to engage in novel types of joint-conjugal sociability with friends from beyond the immediate neighbourhood. From the 1960s, it appears that homes were sometimes used for evening sociability. Interviewees recalled that during the 1970s they had friends over for dinner – a hallmark of middle-class, 'friend-like' relationships according to some post-war social investigators (Goldthorpe *et al.* 1969: 92; Kerr 1958: 104–5). Furthermore, the steady post-war rise of married women's employment outside of the home brought increased opportunity for women to meet and socialise away from their streets and independently of their husbands.

However, the evidence described in this chapter complicated any conceptual divide between limited, given social relationships (associated with the pre-affluent 'traditional' working-class communities) and freely chosen relationships with friends (arising as a result of affluence). Chosen friendships amongst the working classes were not new to the affluent later 1950s and 1960s. Married women in the older streets in the early years of the period developed closer relationships with some neighbours rather than others; they also chose which relatives they would socialise with, and many had at least one friendship with a woman who was neither neighbour nor relative. Similarly, the suggestion that working-class preference for 'chosen' relationships during the age of affluence was necessarily antithetical to community-of-place (Klein 1965: 261–4; Franklin 1989: 111; Allan 1996: 87–8) underestimates the ways that geographical considerations continued to limit friendship ties. Friends in the town during the 1960s and 1970s might not be neighbours, but they *were* usually Beverley residents. The continuing localness of working-class sociability meant that 'chosen' friendships were embedded in, and continued alongside, 'given' networks of acquaintanceship spread across the town. Furthermore, the frequency with which acquaintances were met in the course of day-to-day life represented some continuity of the 'effortless sociability' which authors attributed to 'traditional' working-class communities (Klein 1965: 142; Roberts 1995: 202).

References

Allan, Graham (1996) *Kinship and Friendship in Modern Britain*, Oxford: Oxford University Press.

Allan, Graham (1998) 'Friendship and the Private Sphere', in Rebecca G. Adams and Graham Allan (eds), *Placing Friendship in Context*, Cambridge: Cambridge University Press, 71–91.

Benson, John (1989) *The Working Class in Britain, 1850–1939*, London: Longman.

Brown, Lucy (1989) 'Modern Beverley: Beverley After 1945', in K.J. Allison (ed.), *A History of the County of York. East Riding: Volume 6: The Borough and Liberties of Beverley*, London: Oxford University Press, 154–160.

Davies, Andrew (1992) *Leisure, Gender and Poverty. Working-class Culture in Salford and Manchester, 1900–1939*, Buckingham: Open University Press.

Dennis, Norman, Fernando Henriques and Clifford Slaughter (1969) *Coal is Our Life. An Analysis of a Yorkshire Mining Community*, 2nd edition, London: Tavistock.

Franklin, Adrian (1989) 'Working-Class Privatism: An Historical Case Study of Bedminster, Bristol', *Environment and Planning D: Society and Space*, 7, 93–113.

Giddens, Anthony (1990) *The Consequences of Modernity*, Cambridge: Polity.

Goldthorpe, John Harry, David Lockwood, Frank Bechhofer and Jennifer Platt (1969) *The Affluent Worker in the Class Structure*, London: Cambridge University Press.

Gunn, Simon (2011) 'The Buchanan Report, Environment and the Problem of Traffic in 1960s Britain', *Twentieth Century British History*, 22:4, 521–542.

Jones, Ben (2012) *The Working Class in Mid Twentieth-Century England: Community, Identity and Social Memory*, Manchester: Manchester University Press.

Kerr, Madeline (1958) *The People of Ship Street*, London: Routledge & Kegan Paul.

Klein, Josephine (1965) *Samples from English Cultures (Volume 1)*, London: Routledge & Kegan Paul.

Langhamer, Claire (2000) *Women's Leisure in England, 1920–1960*, Manchester: Manchester University Press.

Langhamer, Claire (2005) 'The Meanings of Home in Postwar Britain', *Journal of Contemporary History*, 40:2, 341–362.

Offer, Avner (2008) 'British Manual Workers: From Producers to Consumers, c. 1950–2000', *Contemporary British History*, 22:4, 538–571.

Pahl, Ray (1984) *Divisions of Labour*, London: Blackwell.

Pahl, Ray (2000) *On Friendship*, Cambridge: Polity.

Peel, Mark, with Liz Reed and James Walter (2009) 'The Importance of Friends: The Most Recent Past', in Barbara Caine (ed.), *Friendship. A History*, London: Equinox, 317–356.

Phillipson, Chris, Miriam Bernard, Judith Phillips and Jim Ogg (2001) *The Family and Community Life of Older People. Social Networks and Social Support in Three Urban Areas*, London: Routledge.

Putnam, Robert D. (2000) *Bowling Alone: The Collapse and Revival of American Community*, New York: Simon & Schuster.

Reid, Douglas A. (2000) 'Playing and Praying', in Martin Daunton (ed.), *The Cambridge Urban History of Britain. Volume III. 1840–1950*, Cambridge: Cambridge University Press, 745–807.

Roberts, Elizabeth (1995) *Women and Families: An Oral History, 1940–1970*, Oxford: Blackwell.

Spencer, Liz and Ray Pahl (2006) *Rethinking Friendship. Hidden Solidarities Today*, Princeton, NJ: Princeton University Press.

Tebbutt, Melanie (1995) *Women's Talk? A Social History of 'Gossip' in Working-Class Neighbourhoods, 1880–1960*, Aldershot: Scolar Press.

Williamson, Margaret (2009) 'Gender, Leisure and Marriage in a Working-class Community, 1939–1960', *Labour History Review*, 74:2, 185–198.

Willmott, Peter and Michael Young (1967) *Family and Class in a London Suburb*, London: New English Library.

Zweig, Ferdynand (1961) *The Worker in an Affluent Society. Family Life and Industry*, London: Heinemann.

Primary sources

Beverley Guardian, 26 January 1973; 3 January 1980.

ERYMS interview with Mary Elizabeth Miles, November 2005.

5 Workplaces

For authors concerned with the 'traditional' working-class culture thought to have prevailed in the first half of the twentieth century, the link between industrial workplace and local community seemed axiomatic. John Clarke (1979: 240), wrote that in the nineteenth and twentieth centuries, working-class communities developed in those places where there was a 'close, dove-tailed relationship between work and non-work'; similarly, the traditional close-knit working-class communities described by Eric Hobsbawm (1984: 180) were those that cohered around the more-or-less settled locations of industrial manufacturing from the late nineteenth century onwards. But to many observers of working-class life in the decades that followed the Second World War, the link between working-class community life and the industrial workplace has seemed less clear. Contemporary observers like Ferdynand Zweig (1961: 117–9), Michael Young and Peter Willmott (1973: 28–9) and John Goldthorpe et al. (196: 108) noted a separation between workers' social lives at work and away from it, and suggested that 'traditional' working-class culture, oriented around industrial production and a highly gender-divided, localised sociability, was in decline. For these authors, the home rather than the workplace had become the key locus of working-class culture since post-war 'affluence' enabled a turn towards more family-oriented, 'privatised', consumerist lifestyles. This is a narrative to which social and cultural historians of the post-war period have added nuance (Langhamer 2005; Jones 2012) but generally do not challenge. This narrative is reflected in the fact that recent historiographical discussions of post-war working-class community utilise case-studies of places where community was a matter of 'belonging to and identification with particular neighbourhoods' (Jones 2012: 120) rather than working in particular industries (Clapson 2012; Rogaly and Taylor 2009; Todd 2014: 174–95).

The relatively low prominence of industrial workplaces in sociological and historiographical discussions of working-class community can be contrasted with the weight given to industry in many personal recollections. The people I interviewed in Beverley often considered that industry had been crucial to the sense of community that had once pertained in the town:

When I worked at the shipyard, everyone knew each other, a lot of people were related to one another, but they grew up, their father was a plater there, and they took over when their father retired, or worked alongside his father ... . The tanneries, that employed hundreds of people ... [workplaces are] the heart and soul of a town.

(Peter Lawson, interview, 4 May 2010)

Of course, in them days there'd be a lot of work people from Shipyard would be in the pub ... . Get to be a community don't they.

(Dick Gibson, interview, 11 March 2010)

I think it goes back to the fact there was a lot of industry in Beverley, and people who lived in Beverley worked in Beverley. You worked with your neighbours ... the community was you lived and you worked and you played together.

(Hilda Little, interview, 24 October 2008)

Having a community seemed to somehow come to an end in the seventies ... Beverley lost a lot of its industry then, and that seemed to strip a lot of it out, that sort of thing.

(Dave Lee, interview, 9 November 2009)

Similarly, a study of six low-income neighbourhoods across Britain found that working-class people connected a perceived decline in the quality of community life with 'historical decline in specific sectors of industry and the particular dependence of some neighbourhoods on a small number of predominant firms' (Batty, Cole and Green 2011: 32).

Historians should pay more attention to these claims about the social and cultural role of industrial workplaces in post-war community life. The immediate post-war decades saw an upsurge in employment in Britain's manufacturing sector, and the numbers (if not the proportion of the population) employed in manufacturing continued to rise until 1966 (Howlett 1994: 337). Historically low levels of unemployment up until 1973 – usually below 3 per cent (Howlett 1994: 320–1; Bedarida 1991: 254) – gave some communities an almost unprecedented degree of stability, allowing young working-class people to remain living in the areas where they had grown up amongst social networks of family, friends and acquaintances. In these communities, industrial workplaces continued to be key contexts for sociability and were an important constituent of local identity.

To some extent, the under-reporting of the role of workplaces by sociologists and historians of post-war working-class community is a matter of geography. Post-war sociologists who had little to say on the integration of workplaces in community life were often those who wrote about working-class life in London (Young and Willmott 1962/1957), or in the new suburban council estates many miles from old workplaces (Willmott 1963; Klein 1965). Bridge

(1990) drew on network analysis of middle- and working-class Londoners to argue that, though work continued to be an important context for creation of social ties for both classes, these ties were now largely divorced from local community settings. Recent historians have also focussed on case-studies other than supposedly stereo-typical northern industrial working-class contexts. Ben Jones (2012: 34–50) utilises a case-study of Brighton as the basis of his history of the mid-twentieth century working classes, a town that was not heavily industrialised in the mid-century; works by Mark Clapson (2012) and Ben Rogaly and Becky Taylor (2009) describe life on council estates on the edge of Reading and Norwich. On the other hand, my case-study town of Beverley was an industrialised northern town, the type of context where Avner Offer (2008: 538) argues that 'the proletarian mode of production continued to dominate' during the 1950s and 1960s. Some important post-war sociological works did explore such contexts (Dennis, Henriques and Slaughter 1969/1956; Jackson 1968). But, as Mike Savage (2010: 137–64) has pointed out, most post-war sociologists were more interested in change than in continuity in working-class life. Of particular concern were the effects of 'affluence' and suburbanisation on the working classes, and the places where these contours of new working-class changes could best be seen were often in the south or in the midlands (Young and Willmott 1962/1957; Willmott 1963; Klein 1965; Gold-thorpe *et al.* 1969). Historians of the mid-century working classes have also been more interested in places where dramatic change was apparent – particularly towns where large numbers moved from inner-city neighbourhoods to suburban council estates – than in 'traditional' (often northern) industrial towns that appeared redolent of an earlier phase of working-class history (Jones 2012: 34–50; Clapson 2012; Rogaly and Taylor 2009; Todd 2014: 174–95).

The omission of work from historiographical discussions of post-war working-class community is also related to scale at which 'community' is conceptualised. Whereas 'community' for many of my interviewees could include networks of acquaintanceship and sense of belonging at a town-wide scale, historians of mid-twentieth century working-class life (as noted above) often treat community solely as the interaction between immediate residential neighbours. Neighbours get to know each other and interact regardless of where they work, and hence workplaces have been passed over by authors who prioritise neighbourhood as the framework for their discussion of com-munity. But as Mark Granovetter (1973) suggested, workplaces become important if we want to examine why some wider urban entities, such as towns or districts, come to think of themselves and to act as 'communities'.

In this chapter I will use the Beverley case-study evidence to show how industrial workplaces in the post-war decades could play an important role in underpinning local social networks and sense of belonging at a town level. These workplaces represented a thread of social and cultural continuity for many working-class communities in a period that as we have seen, is often characterised as one of fundamental change. I will begin with a description of the industrial dimensions of Beverley in the age of affluence, before examining the role of workplaces in the social worlds of employees and the contribution local factories made to the collective life and identity of the town in the three post-war decades. I finish with a consideration of ways in which the relationship between work and community developed across this period.

Industry and social ties

During the age of affluence, much working-class employment in Beverley was in traditional industries present in the town since the nineteenth and early twentieth centuries. A Local Government Commission (1960) report gives a snapshot of employment in these industries. R. Hodgson and Sons tannery employed 729, Cook, Welton and Gemmell Beverley Shipyard employed 570, and Armstrong Patents, a modern factory manufacturing car components, employed 1,987. In addition, Beverley in 1960 contained many smaller manufacturers, including: Deans and Son, making parts for musical instruments and fittings for buses, trains and Rolls Royce engines (436 employees); Overton Brothers' ropery (119 employees); Barkers and Lee Smith animal feed manufacturers (118 employees); and Melrose tannery (employing 70). Women as well as men worked on the shop floor in all of these factories apart from the shipyard in the post-war decades; indeed, 45 per cent of Armstrong's workers were women in 1960. The oral history evidence shows that women from working-class backgrounds were also employed in clerical positions in many factories. Through the 1950s the town's factories had boomed – in 1951, 47 per cent of Beverley's workforce worked in manufacturing industries (HMSO 1956: 246). This reflected the national picture – in 1955, British industrial employment, driven by the post-war export drive, stood at the historic record level of 48 per cent of total civilian employment (Howlett 1994: 337). Although the shipyard closed and reopened with a smaller workforce in 1963, Beverley's industrial sector as a whole continued to thrive into the 1970s, and unemployment remained low (Brown 1989). Change came suddenly when the larger factories (the shipyard, Hodgson's and Armstrong's) all closed between 1978 and 1984 (Brown 1989: 154–60).

The vitality of manufacturing industry in Beverley across the post-war decades corroborates Offer's observation about the continuity of 'a proletarian mode of production' away from the south during this period. Beverley certainly appeared to have more in common with other northern communities where the persistence of traditional industries underpinned continuity in local culture (Brown and Brannen 1970; Dennis, Henriques and Slaughter 1969/1956; Jackson 1968) than with those towns and cities of southern England and the midlands where economy and society were often subject to change at a faster pace (Lawrence 2013; Marwick 1990: 22–32). Of course, industry was not the only source of employment in the town. Beverley is the county town for the East Riding of Yorkshire, and in 1951 35 per cent of the town's workers were employed in the service sector (HMSO 1956: 246). Local government offices provided clerical work for young working-class women and administrative employment for grammar school boys (Marianne Woolly, interview, 22 February 2010). A hospital provided work and nurse training for girls, and a mental hospital employed mainly male nurses (interviews: Anna Mason 12 July 2010; June and Dave Ireland 15 July 2010). Smaller employers included building firms, shops, solicitors' offices, utility companies and the railway. Granovetter's influential concept of 'weak' and 'strong' social ties helps to explain how the town's large factories could contribute to feelings of community. Granovetter (1973) theorised a range of social ties – from the 'strong ties' between family and close friends who form 'peer groups', to the 'weak ties' between acquaintances. He argued that weak ties are particularly important to community since they form 'bridges' linking separate peer groups. Places with an abundance of the bridging weak ties are more likely to feel like a community: residents know a large number of people other than those in their own peer groups or immediate neighbourhood, and invest trust in local leaders to whom they are linked through social networks. Conversely, where there are fewer weak ties, sociability is 'clustered' – restricted to the peer group of family and friends – and a district is less likely to feel or act like a community. Granovetter suggested that the presence of large workplaces within a town or neighbourhood could aid the creation of weak ties amongst residents.

But it is important to note that one of most important contributions made by Beverley's local industries to the social ties that make up community was simply the provision of employment: The ready supply of jobs in the town in the post-war decades allowed young people to remain living in the town in which they had been brought up, amongst networks of family, friends and acquaintances. The general consensus among interviewees was that 'if you left a job on a Friday you could guarantee to start on a Monday' in the three post-war decades (Peter Stephenson, interview, 27 May 2010). Of interviewees who started families of their own in the 1960s and 1970s, 80 per cent had at least one parent who was also born and bred in Beverley, suggesting the extent of inter-generational continuity that this abundance of employment enabled. This degree of family continuity was in itself important for the creation and maintenance of networks weak ties, as Willmott and Young discovered in Bethnal Green in the 1960s:

> When a person has relatives in the borough, as most people do, each of these relatives is a go-between with other people in the district. His brother's friends are his acquaintances, if not his friends; his grandmother's neighbours are so well known as almost to be his own. The kindred are ... a bridge between the individual and the community.
>
> (Young and Willmott 1962/1957: 104)

But industrial employment contributed more to community life than simply providing the economic means for young adults to remain living and working where they had grown up. The oral evidence from Beverley shows that workplaces were important in their own right as contexts for sociability and the formation of 'weak ties' of acquaintanceship. Industrial workplaces were social worlds, as John Whittles (interview, 27 April 2010) recalled of Hodgson's tannery in the 1950s:

> There was so many different departments and all the people got on pretty well together ... they had interdepartmental football, interdepartmental cricket, and then they had, Whit Monday was the factory sports, and all that. And to play football there or cricket or any sport you had to be an employee, there was no outsiders, unless you worked there you couldn't play, so it was all sort of interwoven. And that's another thing about the interaction of the employees, probably why they got on so well, they had contact, probably the whole factory covered a square mile ... you've got to sort of be there really, to understand how people got on.

Many interviewees clearly prized the sense of camaraderie and large social network of workmates that industrial workplaces provided. John Day (interview, 10 November 2009) left his first job in an office because the man he worked with rarely spoke, and began an apprenticeship at the shipyard where he enjoyed the male company and atmosphere of comradeship and joking:

> Always plenty of fun and banter. It was always a good laugh going to work, there weren't many miserable days ... you knew everybody, you knew them all. I mean, if someone said to me 'can you name a hundred fellas who worked at shipyard' I bet I could.

Sally Adams (interview, 21 June 2010) worked at Melrose tannery three decades later in the early 1980s but recalled that a family atmosphere prevailed:

> I knew everybody. There was about, probably a hundred or so workers, and about six women out of all that and the rest were men really ... yes, real good, got on with everybody, I can remember loads of different people there. I can't remember anyone I didn't like, it was always a big friendly place, you know, there wasn't any bitchiness ... at Christmas a big raffle in the canteen ... big long benches laid out and absolutely full of raffle prizes, and everybody down the pub for drinks after and stuff like that, real close.

Works' provision of social and sporting facilities burgeoned across Britain after the First World War (Fitzgerald 1988: 16), and most of Beverley's larger industrial workplaces provided such amenities in the post-war decades. Industrial employers in Beverley entered sporting teams into local leagues for football, rugby, cricket and darts. Works provided rooms in which workers could run their own clubs. There was a boxing club and a horticultural club run by employees at the shipyard in the 1950s; because many shipyard employees kept birds, rabbits and mice, or had gardens and allotments, 'fur and feather' shows and vegetable shows were held on works premises (*Beverley Guardian*, 2 and 9 February 1946; John Day, interview, 10 November 2009). The *Beverley Guardian* in 1950 reported that there were 800 entries in a rabbit show held at the shipyard (*Beverley Guardian*, 28 October 1950). The shipyard, Armstrong's, Deans and Hodgson's tannery had social clubs with snooker tables and a bar. The larger factories had inter-departmental sporting matches (Hodgson's held theirs on Whit Monday) (John and Judy Whittles, interview, 10 May 2010). Hodgson's tannery was the most generous of the Beverley works providing sports and social facilities. The firm opened the grounds of their nineteenth-century owner Richard Hodgson as a sports field for employees' use in 1948 (*Green's Household Almanack*, 1949). Hodgson's sports and social club hosted a wide variety of the firm's sporting teams and clubs, including football, hockey, rugby, golf, tennis, cricket, darts, snooker, bowls, netball, table tennis, angling and shooting (*Beverley Guardian*, 14 February 1948, 28 February 1948; John and Judy Whittles, interview, 10 May 2010). Former Hodgson's workers considered that the social element of sporting clubs helped employees from all over the large factory get to know one another. Eric Ross (interview, 16 February 2010) worked in the laboratories in Hodgson's in the 1960s and discussed how the works sports and social club could bring people together:

> It was a good way of people mixing, you went in the club and you knew everybody ... . The nice thing about it was we used to have football competitions between the departments, we had ... cricket between the departments, we had darts ... . So as long as someone was willing to organise them, the firm would actually stump up money for it and things and let it go on because they wanted it to happen.

In addition to the sporting and social clubs, firms provided a range of social events including annual trips and Christmas parties for employees and their families, retired workers' outings. When Keith Barrett (interview, 2 September 2010) was a child in the 1960s his father worked at Hodgson's:

> Hodgson's, where my dad worked, they used to do a daytrip every year, and there was like seven coaches every year used to go, and it was a real big event ... [we went on that] every year without fail ... everyone [went], and even nephews and cousins and all sorts. Yeah, they were real big family do's.

An employees' 'monthly bonus' dance was held at Armstrong's social club, and the *Beverley Guardian* reported that more than 1,000 attended an Armstrong's works' dance in 1955 (*Beverley Guardian*, 16 February 1955). The range of social and sporting facilities provided by Beverley's industrial employers in the post-war decades was not unique; similar activity was described in oral history interviews conducted by Rosalind Watkiss Singleton (2010: 138–9) and David Hall (2012: 98–9) in the Black Country.

Workers had their own workplace social cultures apart from those activities arranged or encouraged by employers. Beverley's traditional industrial workplaces were the setting for rich cultures of sociability and mutuality that resembled the 'occupational communities' described by Richard Brown and Peter Brannen (1970) in shipyards in 1960s Tyneside. Male shipyard and tannery workers were involved in illicit but well-organised shop-floor betting networks (Bob Garbutt, interview, 16 June 2010), and women in workplaces often ran savings clubs, known as 'diddlums' (Sally Adams, interview, 21 June 2010). Workplace culture for skilled workers in particular was tinged with the trade union ethos of collectivity. As Brown and Brannen (1970) also noted, shipyard workers sometimes held 'whip rounds' for those who were off work. John Day (interview, 10 November 2010) recalled that in the shipyard in the 1950s and early 1960s, when a worker died the trade union would call a meeting:

> The union man, there'd be two of them on the gate and they'd say we're meeting, on the boards, and you had to go straight to the boards ... that was an area of the shipyard where they marked off frames, and then they'd just say 'I'm sorry worthy brothers, I have to tell you about the death of so and so, and the funeral's next Tuesday, and we'd like four volunteers for bearers' ... and they'd get four volunteers and there'd be a levy of two shillings, and everybody used to give two bob for the funeral, and then the blokes who'd taken say half a day off work'd get their pay and the rest'd go to the widow or whatever.

As we have seen in the preceding chapters, many accounts of 'traditional' working-class life in the first half of the twentieth century suggest that the workplace was the central community experience of men whereas women were defined socially by family and neighbourhood ties (Dennis, Henriques and Slaughter 1969/1956; Tebbutt 1995). This 'traditional' pattern was particularly notable where the 'family wage' meant men went out to work while women stayed at home. We will see below that an increasing number of married women went out to work in Beverley across the three post-war decades; but many still did not, and there was undoubtedly some of the gender division of community experience associated with the 'traditional' model. Even those married women who worked in factories during this period remained reliant on family and neighbourhood networks for childcare (see also Glucksmann 2000: 63). Men continued to spend more time than women away from the home and neighbourhood – at work, in the pub, engaging in hobbies or works sports and social clubs. However, in a small town like Beverley, the social worlds of workplace and neighbourhood were not as separate as they appear in some sociological and historiographical accounts. Many workmates socialised outside of the workplace, away from the more formal social and sporting activities organised by works bosses and employees. Keith Barrett (interview, 2 September 2010) recalled how his father cooperated with friends from work on home DIY projects: 'Dad was friends with some people at work – they used to help each other put sheds up and greenhouses and things, and he would go and help them. I don't know if it was expected, but he did.' Neighbours were often also co-workers and this could enhance the moral obligation to help in times of need. Bob Garbutt (interview, 25 June 2010) followed his father into the shipyard in the 1940s and remembered how the foreman, who lived nearby and whose wife was friendly with his mother, gave him overtime immediately after his father's death to help the family finances. Albert Newby (interview, 12 January 2010) recalled how he felt obliged to help a neighbour who was the widow of a former work colleague. In a small town, those who knew each other from the workplace would also meet casually in shops, pubs and street, contributing towards the sense of familiarity many expressed, the feeling that 'everyone in Beverley knew everyone else' (Eva White, interview, 18 June 2010).

The Beverley evidence supported Granovetter's suggestion that weak ties made in contexts such as workplaces could encourage community cohesion by providing personal links to those in leadership roles in the town. From the 1940s until the 1970s two prominent working men in Hodgson's, James Smedley and Harold Godbold, who were also involved in the organisation of the works social club and well-known to many employees, were local councillors and could be approached with issues (interviews: Hannah Withham 26 April 2010; Bernard Hunt 12 January 2010). Hodgson's director, George Odey was an MP for several years in the 1950s and also a county councillor in the 1960s, and many men and women who worked at Hodgson's felt they had at least some personal connection to him – an impression he liked to cultivate by learning workers' names (Bill Johnson, interview, 8 July 2010). Through such examples we see how the social worlds of industrial workplaces were entwined with the broader community life of the town.

Industry in public life

Industrial workplaces were not only important for the social lives of those who worked in them. Beverley had few publicly owned rooms or sports facilities, and factories sometimes put their facilities at the service of local residents. In 1945, many local firms, including Hodgson's, Armstrong's and Hall's Ropery, allowed their buildings to be used for VE day celebrations (*Beverley Guardian*, 26 May 1945). Beverley had no sports field of its own, and Hodgson's tannery made their social club and sports ground available for a number of other groups to use – the East Riding police rugby team, Barkers and Lee Smith's factory football team and the Beverley Whippet Club used Hodgson's sports field in the 1960s (interviews: Bernard Hunt 12 January 2010; Vic Baker 29 May 2010). The Sea Angling club were offered use of a room in Hodgson's social club for their meetings in 1967 (Beverley and District Sea Angling Club minutes). In 1978 the *Beverley Guardian* (27 July 1978) described Hodgson's as the foremost sports and social club in the town; thirty organisations were then using the firm's facilities, 95 per cent of which did not pay room hire. Hodgson's also had a dance hall that was used for public functions, and many interviewees fondly remembered attending the weekly dances there in the 1950s and 1960s. Bernard Hunt (interview, 12 January 2010) remembered that the secretary of the Hodgson's sports and social club Harold Godbold donated a minibus to the Church Lads' Brigade in the 1970s.

Harold Birch (1959: 183–4) observed that in the northern town of Glossop in the 1950s, industrial leadership had passed from local families to 'national combines'; many local people missed 'the sense of belonging that came from living in a community in which they could look up to a small group of clearly recognized leaders who took the initiative in nearly all spheres of activity'. By contrast, in post-war Beverley there was still local leadership spanning industrial and civic spheres. The larger industrial firms – Hodgson's tannery, Cook, Welton and Gemmell Beverley Shipyard, Armstrong Patents Co Ltd, Deans and Lightalloys – had long roots in the town and to a surprising extent, their owners and managing directors continued to live locally, patronise local associations and hold public office in the town. George Odey, Chairman of Hodgson's parent company Barrow, Hepburn and Gale from 1933 until 1974 (Barrow, Hepburn and Gale Ltd 1948), was a particular visible presence in the public life of the town over the three post-war decades and was mentioned by many of the interviewees. Odey lived in Beverley and dedicated himself to the town's fortunes through involvement in local politics and associational life. He was at various times MP for Beverley, County Councillor, and president of various bodies including the Beverley Chamber of Trade, Beverley and Hornsea District Scout Council, and Beverley Operatic Society. He sat on the boards of Beverley Consolidated Charities, Beverley Minster Old Fund and the Minster Restoration appeal and was involved with conservation movements in the town – during the 1960s Odey used his own money to purchase a house in order to thwart council demolition of a historic street (*Beverley Guardian*, 20 January 1977; Joan Walsh, interview, 21 November 2014). Though not quite so dominant, other industrial bosses were also involved in local political and civic life. Harold Sheardown, chairman of the Beverley Shipyard from 1926–1953 (Thompson *et al.* 1999: 7–8), was president of the Hull Works Sports Association (to which many local works sports teams were affiliated) from 1935 to 1950 and also served as a member of the East Riding County Council (Cook, Welton and Gemmell, 1953). Ken Ingleton (interview, 20 April 2010) described how local industry bosses patronised the Scout group he led in the 1950s: George Odey, as chairman of the Scout District Association, made sure that local troops got 'a lot of bits and pieces'; Gordon Armstrong, of the large local car components manufacturer Armstrong's, 'backed us quite a lot'; Bobby Dean of Deans and Lightalloys, a manufacturer of musical equipment among other things, provided instruments for a drum and fife band.

Industrial leaders fulfilled the role of local dignitaries. In 1945, Harold Sheardown, his new shipyard managing director Ambrose Hunter and their wives attended the prize ceremony for the Turner domestic service charity (*Beverley Guardian*, 20 January 1945). Odey and his wife were prominent guests at the annual St John's Day ceremonies organised by Beverley Borough Council in 1958 (Beverley Borough Council, ERALS, BOBE 2/15/1/191). Those industrial leaders with a long and demonstrable concern with Beverley contributed to a sense that local people had some control over the town's destiny:

> (Odey) had Beverley at heart really. 'Cause I mean he, when he was in charge of the tannery there, as other tanneries came up for sale he bought them up, and sort of closed them up and that got rid of a bit more competition didn't it, and kept Beverley going a long while.
>
> (Ken Ingleton, interview, 20 April 2010)

Industry and town identity

Beverley's prominent industries registered at a physical and emotional level in residents' sense of place and local patriotism. A consciousness of the industrial character of the town was unavoidable for those who lived in the eastern, industrialised part of the town, where the sounds, smells and sights of manufacturing were an integral part of daily life. Large numbers of workers on bicycles occupied the roads in the east of the town in the morning and evening – 'When shipyard buzzer blew on a night, you was best out of road, there was five abreast on bikes coming home, just a mass of bikes, if you were going t'other way, well you had to get off and go back' (John Day, interview, 10 November 2009) – and buses and trains disgorged workers from Hull each morning. Residents of the Beckside neighbourhood lived surrounded by the manufacturing process. Not only were there a number of small industries alongside the Beck, but a fleet of barges unloaded coal and other products for Hodgson's tannery into warehouses on the quayside, which were then transported through the neighbourhood to the nearby tannery (Jack Binnington, interview, 3 August 2010). Hodgson's was upwind and upstream of Beckside, and in addition to giving out a strong smell the tannery released effluent that polluted the Beck (*Beverley Guardian*, 18 June 1965). Even residents living some distance away from factory sites could hear the sounds made by factory buzzers; the noise of shipyard riveting was audible a mile away (George and Hilda Little, interview, 24 October 2008).

Beverley's traditional industries were implicated in the rituals and symbolic vocabulary through which community identity was constructed (see, for example, Cohen 1985). Shipyard launches, of which there was at least one a month during busy years in the 1950s, functioned as communal ritual. The sideways slide of a new ship into the River Hull was attended by the shipyard workforce, town dignitaries (the mayor and industrial bosses), and assorted onlookers including employees from other industries and school groups:

On launch days everybody stopped and even where I worked at Deans we all went out on launch day to see them being launched. They always let us out to see the launch.

(May Peters, interview, 24 June 2010)

At a launch in 1948, local dignitaries made speeches lauding Beverley's ship-building tradition and the connection shipbuilding provided to the wider world (*Beverley Guardian*, 3 January 1948). Products of Beverley's manu-facturing industries were included in harvest festival displays in the town's Minster church in 1948, emphasising the importance of factories to the identity of the town (*Beverley Guardian*, 2 October 1948). The *Beverley Guardian* ran a series in 1948 highlighting the achievements of the town's industries and the part they played in the national economy (*Beverley Guardian*, 17 January 1948). Closure of Beverley Shipyard and its reopening with a smaller work-force in 1963 prompted much comment in the local paper asserting the importance of the firm to Beverley's distinctive character, including a speech by the mayor: "'The shipyard is part of the Beverley tradition … the threa-tened closure of the yard seemed like someone was taking a knife and cutting the town right in two'" (*Beverley Guardian*, 11 January, 28 June, 23 August 1963). Such claims resonated with residents such as Tom Chambers for whom employment at the shipyard was a family tradition: 'I was sixteen when I started … . My dad had been there all his life, and his father was there before him' (ERYMS recorded interview, Tom Chambers).

Changing social role of industries

Although industrial workplaces continued to contribute socially and culturally to a sense of community in the town in the post-war years, the relationship between workplace and wider community was a developing one. Rising living standards and the increasing availability of private transport meant that many became less dependent on the kinds of leisure that industrial workplaces had provided (sports and social clubs, annual works outings). Robert Fitzgerald (1988) noted that works leisure facilities were highly valued in the 1920s when there were often few alternatives. By the 1950s and 1960s, relative affluence and expanded leisure opportunities meant that many workers had other interests that reduced their reliance on works' social and sporting provision. As early as 1950, the shipyard's sports and social club secretary bemoaned workers' 'couldn't care less' attitude towards the club and urged them to 'redouble their efforts' (Cook, Welton and Gemmell 1950). Instead of joining works clubs, many employees were gaining access to sports clubs that had in the interwar years been seen as middle-class, including the town's golf and cricket clubs (John Day, interview, 10 November 2009). Ray Stocks (interview, 20 May 2010) worked as an engineer at both Hodgson's and Armstrong's in the 1950s through to the 1970s and made little use of their works sports and social club because his principal interest was sub-aqua diving, which he pursued in amateur clubs unconnected to any workplace. Ken Ingleton (interview, 23 March 2010), employed as a maintenance engineer in the 1970s, recalled that 'Armstrong's had a very good social club but I never really got too involved' – Ken already had a busy social life as a scout leader and member of a local vintage motor club.

In the three post-war decades, younger workers were developing interests in new kinds of pastimes – to the above examples we could add playing in rock bands – and the appeal of a game of dominoes in a works social clubs was waning. Furthermore, the number of domestic households with use of a car doubled between 1955 and 1965 (Gunn 2011: 524), and those with cars or motorbikes could easily travel beyond the town for leisure. Personal transport enabled some workers to put distance between home and workplace, reducing the likelihood of socialising with workmates outside of the factory gates:

> I mean, Hodgson's [sports club] gradually dropped away as people spread out, started to travel in from the villages probably … it was starting to break down, the sports side was starting to break down … . I think the rugby league team was first to feel this, they couldn't raise enough from the factory, but they had a sister factory in Hull, Thomas Holmes, another tannery, and they had a combined rugby league team, and then the football team started to take outsiders in as well, whereas they'd all been employees … . It was a result probably of mobility, people becoming more and more, "oh we'll go and live out in Cherry Burton, I can get to work on my motorbike," and that what started to happen.
>
> (George Little, 24 October 2008)

But whilst for some workers at least, links between work and wider sociability may have been declining, a new group was using industrial workplaces to enhance their local social networks. Married women were entering the work-force in greater numbers in the post-war decades (Thane 1994: 393). Many were employed in the growing service sector, but changes in manufacturing industry, including the rise of newer 'light' engineering (Newell 2007: 40) created job opportunities for married women. Though working-class women had always worked, by the 1980s they were more likely to be employed in factories than at any time in the past (Pahl 1984: 64). Armstrong's, a Beverley manufacturer of vehicle components, grew its workforce from 400 in 1938 (Dodd 1978: 41) to almost 2000 in 1960, at which point over 45 per cent of the firm's employees were women (Local Government Commission 1960). In 1965, the *Beverley Guardian* (21 May) reported that 'the biggest and most urgent demand [for labour] is for full time female factory and laundry workers'. Women made use of the sociable and networking opportunities afforded by factory employment. For example, Ferdinand Zweig (1961: 172–3) noted that most of the married female operatives he interviewed in the Millard radio assembly plant in London in the late 1950s gave companionship as an important benefit of their employment, and that many had contact with workmates outside of the workplace. Similarly, an oral history research project carried out in Sterling, Scotland, during the 1980s found that women remembered work as 'a site for socializing, song and gossip, of friendships and contact which was much missed in later life' (McIvor 2013). The social importance of work for women was corroborated in the Beverley interviews. Linda Roberts (interview, 19 April 2010) worked in Armstrong's for a year as a young woman in the mid-1960s and remembered the sociability of the line and canteen, including raucous group sing-alongs with the other women on her line, as well as pub lunches and nights out. Janet Hill (interview, 3 March 2010) recalled that sociability with workmates on her evening shift at Armstrong's in the 1960s included pub trips, and Jean Benson (interview, 14 July 2010) recruited female co-workers onto her pub darts team when working at Armstrong's in the 1970s. Like male employees, female workers' social integration with the wider community could be strengthened through the 'weak ties' they acquired through their employment. Eva White (interview, 18 June 2010) recalled of her work in Armstrong's in the 1940s: 'When you work in a factory you get to know people, don't you?' and Lynne Norton (interview, 9 November 2009) gave the fact that she had worked locally throughout her life as one of the reasons she knew lots of people in the town: 'he [son] used to say to me, "Do you know everybody?" I said, "No" but I know an awful lot of people. People you've been to school with, people you've worked with.'

Women's increased profile in union activism by the 1970s may also hint at a growing identification with the role of factory worker. Linda Roberts (interview, 29 April 2010) worked in Armstrong's in the mid-1960s and recalled that at this point there was a relatively weak sense of commitment to factory life on the part of her fellow female workers. Most were not union members, and saw factory work as very much a temporary interlude between school and marriage:

> We understood in the '60s that you never, that a woman didn't have to work all their lives, and your job was to get married and to bring the children up … . I can remember having a conversation with someone about women who go to work when they've got children at home, and thinking: oh, it's not right is it? You know, you shouldn't have to work when you're married, should you?

However, female union membership was to grow rapidly from the mid-1960s – nationally, women made up 70 per cent of new union members between 1964 and 1970 (McCarthy 2010: 111). Janet Howarth (2011) and Arthur McIvor (2013: 270–80) point out that though industrial workplaces were often segregated according to the different jobs undertaken by men and women, both could react in a similar way when they felt their rights or conditions threatened. Linda Roberts (interview, 29 April 2010), though not unionised, led an informal walk-out of women workers in protest at the inappropriate behaviour of a male charge-hand. Linda thought that she may have been inspired by the T.V.

sitcom *The Rag Trade*, set in a clothing factory and featuring a female shop-steward who blew a whistle and shouted 'everybody out!'. Beverley interviewees recalled that by the 1970s a group of women working in Armstrong's were very much at the forefront of union activism, led by a strong female union convenor: 'She got all these people out, all these women followed her and followed her like mad' (Ken Ingleton, interview, 20 April 2010).

Conclusion

Though some significant post-war sociological studies (Dennis, Henriques and Slaughter 1969/1956; Jackson 1968; Brown and Brannen 1970) did explore the connections between workplace and community, much British sociology of the 1950s and 1960s was more concerned with the sociability of neighbourhoods. This emphasis helped to magnify the impression of a funda-mental shift towards individualistic lifestyles centred on the consumption prac-tices of the family unit (Young and Willmott 1962/1957, 1973; Goldthorpe *et al.* 1969). Historiographical discussion of post-war working-class communities has tended to follow suit, focussing on change in the timbre of neighbourhood life with little consideration of industrial workplaces (Roberts 1995: 199–231; Jones 2012:120–54; Todd 2014: 174–95). From the perspective of contemporary 'post-industrial' Britain, communities still cohering around manufacturing workplaces in the 1950s and 1960s appear to have been left over from an earlier age, and historians of the post-war working classes search elsewhere for the harbingers of today's social and cultural arrangements.

But the degree to which British manufacturing industry was to collapse in the 1970s and 1980s would not have been predicted by most people living in the 1950s and 1960s, and we are wrong to ignore the experiences of those inhabiting industrial working-class communities, often in the north, which now seem to us to have been living on borrowed time. Industrial workplaces represented a considerable strand of continuity in the social worlds of many across the age of affluence. It may be true that those workers who moved to the suburbs did see some separation between the spheres of work and home/ leisure; however, in other localities the decades following the Second World War represented a period of economic stability during which the connection between industrial workplace and community life was maintained and arguably even strengthened. Post-war Beverley was no more 'typical' of wider Britain than any other case-study town or area, but neither was it particularly excep-tional in terms of its industrial base or population. There were no doubt many places like Beverley where a mixed manufacturing sector employed a high proportion of the local population and where factories remained important for building social networks, sense of place and communal identity.

The broader social and cultural changes of the age of affluence – new forms of sociability, the rise of car ownership, married women working outside of the home in growing numbers – were of course felt in Beverley. But we have seen that such changes did not only serve to erode the importance of industrial workplaces in community life. This book seeks to challenge the prevailing narrative that a monolithic 'traditional' proletarian culture crumbled amidst the unprecedented conditions of post-war 'affluence'; the present chapter contributes to this endeavour by pointing out a key continuity in working-class life from earlier decades – the importance of industrial workplaces for many communities. Given the social and cultural role of factories at the heart of such communities, industrial decline – which played out at different speeds in different localities across the later decades of the twentieth century – probably represented a greater dislocation in their collective life than any post-war rise in affluent individualism.

References

Barrow, Hepburn and Gale Ltd (1948) *Everything in Leather*, Bermondsey: Grange Mills.
Batty, Elaine, Ian Cole and Stephen Green (2011) *Low-Income Neighbourhoods in Britain: The Gap Between Policy Ideas and Residents' Realities*, York: Joseph Rowntree Foundation.
Bedarida, Francois (1991) *A Social History of England 1851–1990*, 2nd edition, London: Routledge.
Birch, A.H. (1959) *Small Town Politics. A Study of Political Life in Glossop*, Oxford: Oxford University Press.
Bridge, G. (1990) 'Gentrification, Class and Community: A Study of Sands End, London', unpublished DPhil thesis, University of Oxford.
Brown, Lucy (1989) 'Modern Beverley: Beverley After 1945', in K.J. Allison (ed.), *A History of the County of York. East Riding: Volume 6: The Borough and Liberties of Beverley*, London: Oxford University Press, 154–160.
Brown, Richard and Peter Brannen (1970) 'Social Relations and Social Perspectives Amongst Shipbuilding Workers – A Preliminary Statement', *Sociology*, 4, 71–84.
Clapson, Mark (2012) *Working-Class Suburb: Social Change on an English Council Estate, 1930–2010*, Manchester: Manchester University Press.
Clarke, John (1979) 'Capital and Culture: The Post-war Working Class Revisited', in J. Clarke, C. Critcher and R. Johnson (eds), *Working-Class Culture. Studies in History and Theory*, London: Hutchinson, 238–253.
Cohen, Anthony P. (1985) *The Symbolic Construction of Community*, London: Routledge.
Dennis, Norman, Fernando Henriques and Clifford Slaughter (1969/1956) *Coal is Our Life: An Analysis of a Yorkshire Mining Community*, 2nd edition, London: Tavistock.
Dodd, R.M.J. (1978) 'The Changing Structure of Industry in Beverley, North Humberside 1801–1978', unpublished BA thesis, University of Durham.
Fitzgerald, Robert (1988) *British Labour Management and Industrial Welfare 1846–1939*, Beckenham: Croom Helm.
Glucksmann, M. (2000) *Cottons and Casuals. The Gendered Organisation of Labour in Time and Space*, Durham: Sociologypress.
Goldthorpe, John Harry, David Lockwood, Frank Bechhofer and Jennifer Platt (1969) *The Affluent Worker in the Class Structure*, London: Cambridge University Press.

Granovetter, Mark S. (1973) 'The Strength of Weak Ties', *The American Journal of Sociology*, 78:6, 1360–1380.

Gunn, Simon (2011) 'The Buchanan Report, Environment and the Problem of Traffic in 1960s Britain', *Twentieth Century British History*, 22:4, 521–542.

Hall, David (2012) *Working Lives. The Forgotten Voices of Britain's Post-war Working Class*, London: Transworld.

HMSO (1956) *Census 1951. England and Wales. Industry Tables*, London: HMSO.

Hobsbawm, Eric (1984) 'The Formation of British Working-Class Culture', in Eric Hobsbawm, *Worlds of Labour*, London: Weidenfeld & Nicolson, 176–193.

Howarth, Janet (2011) 'Classes and Cultures in England After 1951: The Case of Working-Class Women', in Clare Griffiths, V.J. James, J. Nott and William Whyte (eds), *Classes Cultures and Politics: Essays on British History for Ross McKibbin*, Oxford: Oxford University Press, 85–101.

Howlett, Peter (1994) 'The "Golden Age", 1955–1973', in Paul Johnson (ed.), *Twentieth-Century Britain: Economic Social and Cultural Change*, London: Longman, 320–340.

Jackson, Brian (1968) *Working Class Community. Some General Notions Raised by a Series of Studies in Northern England*, London: Routledge & Kegan Paul.

Jones, Ben (2012) *The Working Class in Mid Twentieth-Century England: Community, Identity and Social Memory*, Manchester: Manchester University Press.

Klein, Josephine (1965) *Samples from English Cultures (Volume 1)*, London: Routledge & Kegan Paul.

Langhamer, Claire (2005) 'The Meanings of Home in Postwar Britain', *Journal of Contemporary History*, 40:2, 341–362.

Lawrence, Jon (2013) 'Class, "Affluence" and the Study of Everyday Life in Britain, c.1930–1964', *Cultural and Social History*, 10, 273–299.

Marwick, Arthur (1990) *British Society Since 1945*, 2nd edition, London: Penguin.

McCarthy, Helen (2010) 'Gender Equality', in Pat Thane (ed.), *Unequal Britain. Equalities in Britain Since 1945*, London: Continuum, 105–123.

McIvor, Arthur (2013) *Working Lives. Work in Britain Since 1945*, Basingstoke: Palgrave Macmillan.

Newell, Andrew (2007) 'Structural Change', in Nicholas Crafts, Ian Gazeley and Andrew Newell (eds), *Work and Pay in Twentieth Century Britain*, Oxford: Oxford University Press, 35–54.

Offer, Avner (2008) 'British Manual Workers: From Producers to Consumers, c. 1950–2000', *Contemporary British History*, 22:4, 537–571.

Pahl, Ray (1984) *Divisions of Labour*, London: Blackwell.

Roberts, Elizabeth (1995) *Women and Families: An Oral History, 1940–1970*, Oxford: Blackwell.

Rogaly, Ben and Becky Taylor (2009) *Moving Histories of Class and Community. Identity, Place and Belonging in Contemporary England*, Basingstoke: Palgrave Macmillan.

Savage, Mike (2010) *Identities and Social Change in Britain Since 1940: The Politics of Method*, Oxford: Oxford University Press.

Singleton, Rosalind Watkiss (2010) '"Old Habits Persist". Change and Continuity in Black Country Communities: Pensnett, Sedgley and Tipton, 1945–c.1970', unpublished PhD thesis, University of Wolverhampton.

Tebbutt, Melanie (1995) *Women's Talk? A Social History of 'Gossip' in Working-Class Neighbourhoods, 1880–1960*, Aldershot: Scolar Press.

Todd, Selina (2014) *The People: The Rise and Fall of the Working Class 1910–2010*, London: John Murray.

Thane, Pat (1994) 'Women Since 1945', Paul Johnson (ed.), *Twentieth Century Britain: Economic, Social and Cultural Change*, London: Longman, 392–411.

Thompson, Michael, Dave Newton, Richard Robinson and Tony Lofthouse (1999) *Cook, Welton and Gemmell. Shipbuilders of Hull and Beverley, 1863–1963*, Beverley: Hutton Press.

Willmott, Peter (1963) *The Evolution of a Community: A Study of Dagenham After Forty Years*, London: Routledge & Kegan Paul.

Young, Michael and Peter Willmott (1962/1957) *Family and Kinship in East London*, 2nd edition, Harmondsworth: Pelican.

Young, Michael and Peter Willmott (1973) *The Symmetrical Family. A Study of Work and Leisure in the London Region*, London: Routledge & Kegan Paul.

Zweig, Ferdynand (1961) *The Worker in an Affluent Society. Family Life and Industry*, London: Heinemann.

Primary sources

Beverley and District Sea Angling Club minutes, ERALS, DDX 1150/2.

Beverley Borough Council. File on St John of Beverley Day, 4 May 1958. ERALS, BOBE 2/15/1/191.

Beverley Guardian, 20 January, 26 May 1945; 2 February, 9 February 1946; 3 January, 17 January, 14 February, 28 February, 2 October 1948; 28 October 1950; 16 February 1955; 11 January, 28 June, 23 August 1963; 21 May, 18 June 1965; 20 January 1977; 27 July 1978.

Chambers, Tom. East Riding of Yorkshire Council Museums Service recorded interview.

Cook, Welton and Gemmell Annual Review, 1953. East Riding of Yorkshire Council Museums Service collections. ERYMS: (Guildhall) 2007.13.6.

Cook, Welton and Gemmell Ltd. Shipyard Journal, vol 1. No.7, 1950. ERYMS: (Guildhall) 2007.13.5.

Green's Household Almanack, 1949, ERALS: Y/914–274/Bev.

Local Government Commission 1960 'Summary of number of employees in major industrial undertakings in Beverley May 1960', ERALS: CCER/9/2/1.

6 Civil society and associational life

In his final speech after a year as mayor of Beverley in 1960, Albert Meadley said he had been surprised by 'the many charitable institutions, youth organisations and associations doing work to the benefit of the community existing in the town' (Councillor Meadley correspondence, ERALS). Albert Meadley was himself an example of the extent to which Beverley's working classes could become enmeshed within the civil society of the town. He grew up in the working-class Beckside neighbourhood, the son of a lorry driver (*Beverley Guardian*, 7 May 1965). Albert began his political career as a Labour councillor before switching to become an Independent. His correspondence reveals him to have been an active mayor, campaigning on issues of industrial pollution, visiting hospital and industrial workplaces, founding the Beverley Lions, and generally personifying the notion of service to the local community (Councillor Meadley correspondence, ERALS).

Not only did the town have many associations undertaking charitable work, but a search through editions of the *Beverley Guardian* from the period reveals a wealth of sporting, cultural, religious, political and sociable associations. The extent to which the working classes were involved in associational life of their neighbourhoods, towns and cities is sometimes passed over in a literature, which has tended to assume that working-class sociality could be understood through the more homely lens of family and neighbourhood. Michael Young and Peter Willmott (1962/1957: 115–6) did not investigate membership of clubs and societies in their influential account of working-class life in East London, describing instead the informal sociability between kin in the home and acquaintances in the public spaces of established neighbourhoods. John Macfarlane Mogey (1956: 155) argued that in an old working-class area of Oxford in the 1950s:

> Everybody participates in the very minimum of group activities. Only the family, the kindred, workmates and the well-accepted neighbourhood set of cronies are commonly accepted groups.

Josephine Klein (1965: 206–9) suggested that the preferred form of associational life was 'non-committal' – the working classes shied away from the commitment necessary for membership of formal associations. Herbert Gans (1962: 41, 246), reviewing this literature, considered that the working-class populations of the industrialised west were inclined by virtue of their class experience to conduct sociality primarily in small 'peer-groups' – made up of, for example, of family, neighbours, workmates – with little time or inclination for clubs, societies and the civic organs of the wider community. Historians of the working classes have often been similarly dismissive of associational life. Joanna Bourke's (1994: 136–69, 164) chapter on working-class community during the period 1890–1960 limits consideration of working-class associations to church and youth groups, claiming that 'in many districts, clubs and gangs for the young were the only locally based groups'; Ben Jones (2012: 120–54) claimed that only a minority of residents of mid-century council estates in Brighton joined clubs and associations, and that associational life divided as much united the residents.

These authors draw attention to the fact that many among the working classes did indeed have little time or energy to commit to the life of clubs and associations. But emphasising solely family and informal relationships in discussions of working-class community surely underplays the extent to which working-class people formed angling and cycling clubs, played in football teams, volunteered for service in St John Ambulance, attended political party meetings and helped raise funds for the parish church – before, during and after the age of affluence. Rather than envisaging working-class society fragmented into isolated peer-groups, some historians have depicted instead a rich associational culture. Ross McKibbin (1984) argued that one of the reasons British workers did not show much enthusiasm for Marxism was that since the nineteenth century much of their spare time was absorbed by involvement in hobby and sports clubs. Robert Colls (1995) argued that the working classes in the North East of England in the first half of the twentieth century engaged in associational life that not only joined individuals to each other but also communities to each other, constituting a regional, cross-class civil society.

Indeed, ethnographic detail from post-war social investigations shows how both visions – the working classes as peer-group society, and as engaged members of civil society – contain elements of truth. The working classes have of course always been various in their interests, energy and propensity to engage with issues beyond those of immediate existential concern. Norman Dennis, Fernando Henriques and Clifford Slaughter (1969: 144–45) depicted the different conversational zones in a working men's club in the Yorkshire mining town of 'Ashton' (Featherstone) during the 1950s. Whilst some groups were content to talk about what happened at work that day, or about sports, others were debating national and international politics. From this latter group came the men who were also engaged with public life as local councillors. In a similar vein, Brian Jackson and Dennis Marsden (1966: 78–80) noted that the parents of grammar school students were often 'the articulate and the energetic'. Frequently with skilled manual jobs or from the foreman 'aristocracy', these were parents who held multiple positions in the associational life of their communities. One example was Mr Bleasdale: 'in him a host of local group-ings join together. He is a Labour councillor, president of his union branch, director of the local Co-op, secretary of the allotment association and a member of the district youth committee. His father was an active Socialist and his mother a suffragette.' It is likely, or course, that for many people participation in one area of associational life would have been enough (McKibbin 1984: 306); the point is that alongside the 'non-committal', there was also a sizeable minority of working-class people ready to breathe life into a variety of clubs and societies.

Since many post-war social investigators gave little space to working-class associational life, it is not always possible to discern whether they believed this to be in decline along with aspects of 'traditional working-class community' such as neighbourliness and close propinquity of kin. Later, retrospective, laments for the decline of the working-class collectivist values that had founded trade unions, Labour politics and cooperative societies, assume the decline of associational life (Seabrook 1984; Colls 2004). However, there is quantitative and qualitative evidence to suggest that, though the types of associational life that the working classes engaged in may have changed over the latter half of the twentieth century, there was no net decline (Bernstein 2004: 454–5; Andersen, Curtis and Grabb 2006; Clapson 2012: 182–214).

The present chapter will use the Beverley evidence to explore continuity and change in working-class involvement in associational life and civil society during the age of affluence. This evidence is central to my refutation of the notion that working-class people withdrew into privatised individualism during this period. Instead of simply pursuing private ends alone or in the company of immediate family and friends, the working classes remained actively engaged in public life through membership of a plethora of clubs and societies; many also sought to serve the wider community through their involvement in civil society.

In the first section, I outline the range and extent of working-class associa-tional life in Beverley during the three post-war decades in order to demonstrate that working-class community-of-place should not be conceptualised only as neighbourliness, family propinquity and informal sociability. In the second section, I focus on civil society, showing how some from the working classes joined groups in order to further a public service ethos. Since the organs of civil society were shaped and often led by the middle classes, conservative hegemonic values emphasising acceptance of local and national societal hier-archies were foremost in many such groups. The final section concentrates on changes in the content of associational life across the period, revealing some shifts in the contours of local class relations. Throughout the chapter, 'asso-ciational life' is understood broadly, as formal or semi-formal groupings established to further social, sporting, cultural, charitable or political ends. 'Civil society' is conceived here as the strata of local associational life con-sisting of groups seeking to enhance the public good and/or provide service to the wider community. Although the state is not conventionally included in discussions of civil society, I have included some consideration of the town council here, since borough councillors were active players in the public life of the town and their activity often dovetailed with other local associations.

In the club

Some authors consider working-class associational life primarily in terms of involvement in specifically *working-class* associations (Williams 1982: 5–7; Hobsbawm 1984). The working classes across the nineteenth and twentieth centuries did indeed create many institutions for self-help in political and social spheres, including friendly societies, trade unions, cooperative societies, working men's clubs (Hobsbawm 1984; Cherrington 2009). But there were also many associations with a much less explicit class component. People joined sporting and hobby clubs not because they had a working-class membership but because they facilitated interesting and enjoyable leisure activity. Martin Johnes (2007), for example, showed that pigeon-racing clubs in twentieth-century England and Wales, contrary to stereotype, often contained middle-class as well as working-class members. Here, I survey the array of associational life in which Beverley's working classes participated during the three post-war decades. We will also glimpse the range of motivations for engagement with such groups.

Traditional working-class associations

Traditional working-class institutions of mutual assistance and political solidarity (friendly societies, trade unions, the Cooperative Society and Labour Party) still existed in the post-war decades in Beverley, but did not appear to play a large part in the lives of most interviewees. Whilst friendly societies continued in a reduced form as charitable and social institutions, they had lost their former importance as a source of help in sickness and infirmity due to increasing state welfare provision. Interviewees who worked as tradesmen were usually members of unions but few were involved in an organisational capacity; only two interviewees had any history of trade-union activism (interviews: Jack Binnington 26 October 2010; Mick Underwood 16 June 2010). Many interviewees displayed apathy, and occasionally even hostility, towards unions (for example, interviews: Sally Adams 21 June 2010; Dennis Duke 14 July 2010). Whilst the Labour Party gained seats in the borough council for the first time in 1951, and always enjoyed a majority of Minster ward votes in local elections subsequently, attendance at local Party meetings fluctuated between 12 and 20 in the 1950s and 1960s (Beverley Labour Party Minutes, 1947–1960, 1964–1970).

This relatively muted involvement in the traditional institutions of working-class self-help and defence in the latter half of the twentieth century was in part a result of rising living standards and welfare state provision; certainly, friendly societies lost much of their vitality along with their function as primary working-class institutions of insurance against sickness and old age (Neave 1990). Contemporary commentators (Abrams, Rose and Hinden 1960: 105) considered that post-war affluence was leading the British working classes to disengage from class-based politics:

> They now have opportunities for leisure, for the enjoyment of most of the good things in life ... the day is gone when workers must regard their station in life as fixed ... . Is it any wonder that in these circumstances we should be reaching the limit of the old class appeal?

But it may also have been the case that in Beverley, class-based 'images of society' (Lockwood 1994) were in any case relatively undeveloped. Lockwood (1994 – first published in 1966) suggested that workers took their views of the way in which society was structured from the evidence available in their immediate social context. Small towns were likely to produce a 'traditional deferential' view, in which an evident local hierarchy was seen as justified and natural. We will see below that a hierarchical and consensual image of local community did indeed pervade Beverley's civil society; there is some evidence that many of Beverley's working classes did not demur. In 1945 an incomer compared his previous home, 'the progressive industrial town of Manchester', with Beverley, where many councillors were 'conservative and parochial in out-look' (*Beverley Guardian*, 9 June 1945). Jerry Young (interview, 18 May 2010), a member of the Beverley Labour Party since the 1960s, recalled a streak of working-class conservatism in the town in the 1960s and 1970s, especially evident amongst Hodgson's tannery workers who were impressed by the paternalism of their director, George Odey. Furthermore, he suggested that during the 1950s and 1960s, such labourist sentiment as there was (amongst workers in the ship-yard) was partly a result of workers migrating from Tyneside and Wearside and bringing their political traditions with them. These observations gained some support from interviews with former workers (interviews: Hannah Witham 26 April 2010; John and Margaret Day 8 December 2009; John Cooper, ERYMS interview 2; Les White 21 October 2010; Peter Cooper, ERYMS interview 2a).

Leisure-based associational life

Whilst there was limited engagement with traditional working-class institutions and politics in post-war Beverley, there was enthusiasm for all kinds of leisure-based associational life. John Day's recollection of a shipyard strike in the 1950s is indicative of this:

> When I was on strike, I painted golf club ... they wanted volunteers to paint it, there was me and someone else from shipyard who played golf ... I used to do a bit of painting and then get washed and changed and have a shower and have a game of golf in the afternoon.
>
> (John Day, interview, 10 November 2009)

A letter-writer to the *Beverley Guardian* (30 October 1948) suggested that the town was partaking in renewed national enthusiasm for culture: 'There is evidence of this in the local clubs and societies and guilds which are supposed to serve such a purpose'. It is difficult to quantify these clubs and societies. Surveying editions of the *Beverley Guardian* from 1948 suggests that there were least fifty clubs, associations and sports teams. This figure does not include the twelve churches in Beverley in the late 1940s, most of which had a range of auxiliary groups catering separately for women, children and men. Nor does it count works sports and social clubs. The figure also probably misses many darts, snooker and football teams, as well as informal groups described in the oral interviews. Beverley may have been comparable with the slightly larger town of Glossop, (18,000 people in 1953), surveyed by Birch in 1953–4, where there were nearly 100 voluntary associations (Birch 1959: 195). In Beverley, oral evidence suggests associational life in the town remained healthy across the period; in 1977 the Humberside County Council listed seventy-seven groups in the town (*Beverley Guardian*, 10 March, 17 March 1977).

Strata of associational life

Much that we might term associational life – i.e. organised groupings with a specific purpose and regular meetings – took place at only one step up from informal, non-committal, peer group sociability, and therefore would not be enumerated in official lists or reported in newspapers. Across the period, working-class people formed groups to organise neighbourhood coach trips, plan bonfires and coronation parties, as well as to undertake charitable activities and collections (see Chapter 3 'Neighbours', also interviews: Bill and Alice Andrews 20 January 2010; Iris Brown 21 May 2010; Derek Mitchell, ERYMS interview). Women sometimes established neighbourhood social clubs. The club that Lynne Norton (interview, 9 November 2009) remembered in the 1950s appeared a simple gathering of friends but also had a formal element in that activities were organised and fees collected:

> Lynne: We used to go to this lady's house, and a few of us would play cards, rummy, you know ... dominoes, and we had a cup of tea ... it was a good gathering.
> Stefan: Who was the lady?
> Lynne: Mrs Johnson, who, her and her husband used to keep Foresters Arms at one time ... . We just used to put something in, I suppose to help with the trips and that.

Jack Blakeston (interview, 10 August 2010) remembered that his mother organised a regular whist night for women living in the Beckside area in the upstairs room of a local pub in the 1940s. In neighbourhoods and workplaces women ran 'diddlums' or savings clubs; small amounts were deposited weekly, to be withdrawn when needed, perhaps at Christmas (interviews: Sally Adams

21 June 2010; Keith Barrett 2 December 2010). One interviewee was still paying regularly into a 'diddlum' at the time of the interview (Sally Adams, interview, 21 June 2010). Across the period, many pubs arguably acted as clubs: regulars joined darts and dominoes teams, went on pub outings, and took a proprietorial attitude towards their own chairs on busy Saturday nights (interviews: Lynne Norton 9 November 2009; Jim Fisher 16 December 2009; Vic Baker 29 May 2010). One interviewee described how the group cohesion of regulars in one pub during the 1970s was so strong that in recent years they had organised reunions (Les White, interview, 29 October 2010).

Involvement with churches and church youth groups was a form of working-class associational life at one stage further removed from the informality of peer group, but still with a connection to the community of the neighbourhood. During the 1950s and 1960s, the majority of a church's congregation usually lived within the parish (there were three parish churches in the town) (Janet Thompson, interview, 27 November 2009). In 1952, five of the six voluntary officers at St Nicholas Church lived in the same working-class district in the east of Beverley; the sixth lived just to the west of the railway lines (St Nicholas Church Magazine, January 1952). Churches had a range of associated groups – for example, in 1955 the Latimer Congregationalist Church had a Sunday School, a Girls' Bible Class, and young Men's Bible Class, Life Boys, Women's Own, a meeting for boys aged 6 to 8, teacher training classes, a Prayer Meeting, Brownies, Guides and a choir (*Green's Almanack* 1955). Many youth organisations were connected to particular churches, including the Church Lads' Brigade, the Life Boys, and Girls' Friendly Society.

Associations organised on a town rather than neighbourhood level were often in the leisure sphere. In the 1940s, 1950s and 1960s these included a caged bird society, two pigeon clubs, a whippet-racing club, a rabbit club, a sea-angling club, motor clubs, a model aeroplane club, an allotment society, as well as clubs and teams dedicated to the sports of rugby union, cricket, tennis, football, snooker, darts, cycling and boxing. Though Beverley only had one working men's club – the Grosvenor – many working-class men attended the British Legion, the Catholic Club and the Conservative Club, as well as the various works clubs (Neil Cooper, interview, 14 April 2010). Across the period, working-class men were more likely than women to participate in this kind of associational life, although wives were often involved in a supportive capacity, attending and catering for functions as well as washing kit or volunteering in the club tea house (interviews: Hilda Little 19 March 2010; Marianne Woolly 22 February 2010).

Clubs and sociability

The variety of associational life was reflected in the complexity of motivations for engaging in particular voluntary activities. Most groups had a social element. For example, although political belief motivated those involved with the Trade Union and Labour movement, activities were also laid on that were purely social. The Beverley Labour Party held regular social events (annual dinners, garden parties, fundraising dances), and monthly meetings (often in pubs) were a social activity (Beverley Labour Party Minutes, 1947–1960, 1964–1970). Similarly, membership of sporting teams was not only about the sport. Football teams went to the pub after matches, darts and snooker matches were held in licensed premises, the golf club had a bar and the rugby and cricket club held regular social events (interviews: Bob Garbutt 28 June 2010; John Day 10 November 2009; Hilda Little 19 March 2010). Women's involvement in darts teams from the 1960s often had little to do with competition and everything to do with getting out of the house for the evening and socialising with other women (interviews: Sally Adams 21 June 2010; Janet Thompson 27 November 2009). The competitive aspect of many hobby clubs – pigeon clubs, the Allotment Society and the Caged Bird Club – should be seen as evidence of their social role (interviews: James and Peggy Alexander 18 February 2010; Marianne Woolly 22 February 2010).

The Beverley and District Sea Angling Club minutes offer an insight into the motivations of working-class men setting up a sporting club. At a public meeting in the King's Head pub to launch the idea of the club in 1967, a Mr Stephens appealed both to the instrumental and social instincts of his audience:

> They had to get together these days when everything seemed to be more expensive and pocket money remained stable. By cooperating, he said, they could get cheaper sport … . He thought the club could provide a service to every one of its members who would be able to travel to the coast with new friends and meet new friends from other parts of the Riding.

The minutes of subsequent meetings record this mix of instrumentalism and sociability. In 1968 the meeting discussed members who never attended club meetings but nevertheless obtained places on the club's boat fishing excursions. The club failed to gather sufficient support to hold an annual dinner in its first year, but in the 1970s held a social evening attended by 'more than 200 anglers from many parts of the East Riding'. Letters to and from other sea angling clubs in the area referred to an 'interclub social and prize presentation', an 'inter-town angling meeting' a 'fisherman's evening' and a 'casting competition'. A former club member testified to the range of social activities (Dick Gibson, interview, 11 March 2010).

The working-class members of the Sea Angling Club followed the conventions of associational life, appointing officers and a president (the mayor of Beverley), holding regular, minuted meetings and printing a rule book. Meetings were conducted in a formal way, with motions proposed, seconded and amended. The working classes had long experience of formal associations gained through union and labour movements, local politics and friendly societies. This fact has sometimes been missed by authors who concentrate on community solely in terms of neighbourhood and kinship (Roberts 1995; Bourke 1994). David Neave (1990: 54–6, 95–6) described how the friendly society movement in nineteenth-century East Riding adopted some of the formal language and processes of association from middle-class culture. By the middle of the twentieth century, formal practices of associational life appear to have been well-known, and working-class people reached for them naturally when setting up groups.

Associational life and 'weak ties'

As outlined in the Chapter 5, 'Workplaces', Mark Granovetter (1973) argued that workplaces and associations could contribute to 'weak' social ties. Sociability in clubs helped build networks of acquaintanceship across the town. Contacts from clubs could connect people to resources (such as information about jobs) and to individuals with some local power, such as borough councillors (interviews: Andrew Tyler 1 July 2010; Lynne Norton 9 November 2009). Dorothy Jackson (interview, 10 February 2010) recalled that she got to know lots of people in the town from visits to the British Legion with her husband on weekends in the 1960s and 1970s. Mick Underwood (interview, 16 June 2010) stated that he was well known in the town from a lifetime playing cricket in the local club. Sports teams competed in leagues and therefore met members of other teams, and angling clubs cooperated to organise matches (Beverley and District Sea Angling Club records). Groups sometimes worked together for charitable and philanthropic purposes, or loaned each other facilities and equipment (which will be discussed further in the section below). Associational life was therefore one of the contexts, along with work, school, neighbourhood and family, through which individuals got to know others, and contributed to the sense, often mentioned by interviewees, that in the 1940s through to the 1970s 'everybody in Beverley knew everybody else' (interview, George Little, 12 March 2010).

Lifecycle variation in associational involvement

Involvement in clubs and societies varied across the lifecycle. Childhood and adolescence was a period in which youth groups provided diversion for most. In the 1940s and 1950s for example, there was a range of clubs for children and adolescents. Many of these were connected to a greater or lesser extent with various churches, including the Church Lads' Brigade, the Life Boys, Girls' Friendly Society, several Scouts, Cubs troops and Guides companies, as well as church youth clubs. In addition, the St John Ambulance brigade had strong youth divisions, and there were army cadet groups and a short-lived Labour League of Youth (Beverley Labour Party minutes August 1948; interviews: Andrew Tyler 1 July 2010; John Whittles 26 April 2010; Anna Mason 12 July 2010). The local authority became involved with youth provision in the post-war era, and from the later 1950s interviewees remembered youth clubs run by the local authorities (*Beverley Guardian*, 21 January 1945; interviews: Elaine Mateer 29 March 2010; Dennis Duke 14 July 2010). In the 1940s, 1950s and 1960s, the parents of interviewees had usually insisted on Sunday school attendance, even though their own religious commitment might be ambiguous at best. In later adolescence there was often a reduction in the attraction of clubs and more emphasis on peer group sociability. Across the period, child-rearing years were usually the low point of associational involvement, particularly for women. However, children's involvement in youth groups could often bring their parents some voluntary duties – for example, sitting on parent committees or helping run sports teams (interviews: Bernard Hunt 12 January 2010; Louise Christopher 25 November 2010). Once their children had grown up, there was again time for parents to become involved in voluntary activity. Studies that have downplayed the extent of associational life amongst the working classes have often based their assessment on the activities that research participants were engaged in at the time of the study (Mogey 1956; Gans 1962); but it is possible to suggest that the benefits of club and society membership in terms of local social ties continued after the period of member-ship ended. People continued to encounter others in their locality whom they had first met through clubs and societies.

None of the interviewees failed to mention contact with voluntary associa-tions at some point in their lives, whether it be work's club, darts team or Sunday school; nevertheless, it is important to note that many people had only fleeting contact with associational life. Some described themselves as not suited to this kind of sociability (interviews: William Vincent 25 May 2010; Peter Lawson 4 May 2010). Typical of these interviewees was Ellen Ingleton (interview, 20 April 2010) who, although she liked 'being with people', claimed: 'I've not really been a person ... just to go in and join a club'. This corre-sponds with the distinction made by Robert Putnam (2000: 93–9) between those who engaged in an organised and structured sociability through clubs and societies and those who preferred personal sociability in less structured ways. Putnam suggested age and class continuums in connection with these tendencies, with the young and working classes tending towards informal sociability, and older people and middle classes more likely to join clubs and societies. My research suggests the abundance of both kinds of sociability amongst the working classes in this period, although as noted above, membership of formal clubs and societies was more prevalent amongst males than female.

Civil society

Robert Colls (1995) argued that civil society in many industrial areas of Britain across the first two thirds of the twentieth century incorporated asso-ciational life that was specifically working class – trade unions, brass bands, coops – as well as the sphere of the 'bourgeois civic'. This latter included areas of public life dominated by the middle classes, but also associations through which the working and middle classes joined forces to carry out service to the wider public. Colls gives the Wesleyan Methodists as an example of associational life in the 'bourgeois civic' sphere, which involved face-to-face interaction and cooperation between classes. I have argued above that associational organs of 'traditional' working-class self-help and politics played a relatively minor part in the day-to-day lives of many of Beverley's working-class residents during the three post-war decades. However, the 'bourgeois civic' sphere was apparently alive and well in Beverley, and many working-class people played a part.

Many working-class Beverley residents committed considerable time and energy to civil society associations that might be considered 'bourgeois civic'. Ken Ingleton (interview, 23 March 2010) volunteered for almost sixty years leading local Cub Scout packs; John Whittles (interview, 27 April 2010) gave forty years' service to the St John Ambulance Brigade. Like Jackson and Marsden's Mr Bleasedale, those who acted in a voluntary capacity often did so in a number of contexts. The *Beverley Guardian* (15 November 1947) reported the many public roles of the new mayor, James Smedley, a labourer at the tanyard. Many of these roles, though not all, fell within the sphere of the 'bourgeois civic'. Smedley had been a long-term councillor, a member of the Working Men's and Women's Committee of the Beverley Cottage Hospital, was currently serving as secretary of the local branch of the Manchester Unity of the Independent Order of Oddfellows, had 'held every office a layman could enjoy' in the Baptist church, and was a founder member of the Hodgson's Recreation Club, playing 'a great part in the creation of that well-known and helpful organisation'. The paper praised Smedley's contribution to 'the good of the town'. Harold Godbold, also a Hodgson's worker, was a councillor from 1940s until the 1970s, a committee member at Hodgson's Recreation Club and held other voluntary posts such as secretary of the snooker league (*Beverley Guardian*, 7 May 1955).

Working-class women also played roles in civil society organisations, though often in a less formal capacity. Women from all classes volunteered to help run children's groups, including the Brownies, Guides, Cubs, Girls' Friendly Society and Sunday school groups (interviews: Bernard Hunt 12 January 2010; Louise Christopher 25 November 2010; Eliza Wood 18 November 2009; June and Dave Ireland 15 July 2010). Mothers sometimes became involved in these groups as a result of their children's membership. Wives of youth group leaders often helped in an informal way, providing support at camps and outings (interviews: John Whittles 27 April 2010; Ken Ingleton 23 March 2010). Women were also members of the voluntary fire service and the Red Cross (interviews: Hannah Witham 26 April 2010; Bernard Hunt 12 January 2010). Mothers with young children across the period perhaps had less time and inclination to engage in voluntary activity, especially as many worked part-time in addition to looking after children and running the home (interviews: Sally Adams 21 June 2010; Vic Baker 29 May 2010).

The borough council

As noted above, some men (and increasingly across the period, women) sought to serve the wider community by becoming borough councillors. Definitions of civil society usually exclude the state, but borough councillors are included in the discussion here because they acted in a voluntary capacity and were often involved in, and supported, wider civil society. Borough councillors were integrated into civil society through the performance of public roles beyond the representation of their constituents in the council chamber. Mayors were kept busy ensuring that the borough council was represented in public life; they attended fund-raising events, sports league prize evenings, cultural performances and visiting almshouses and hospitals at Christmas time. Milestone wedding anniversary celebrants could even find themselves beneficiaries of a mayoral visitation (*Beverley Guardian*, 3 January 1948). At busy times, other councillors assisted. Councillors attended the many street parties held to celebrate VE day, distributing small cash gifts to children (*Beverley Guardian*, 26 May 1945). Councillors judged an annual garden competition for council housing tenants in the 1940s and 1950s (Eva White, interview, 18 June 2010; *Beverley Guardian*, 16 October 1948).

The borough council supported wider civil society in the town morally and materially. The council gave cash grants to community organisations and loaned out meeting rooms in their Guildhall to clubs and societies (interviews: Bernard Hunt 12 January 2010; Ed Byrne 24 May 2010). Borough councillors worked in partnership with the many local people and organisations undertaking charitable work. For example, in the 1950s the mayor helped run the 'Boots for Bairns' charity in conjunction with the local police superintendent (Beverley Borough Council file on 'Boots for Bairns' 1928–1959). In 1955, the Beverley Station Christmas Tree Appeal distributed gifts to local children's homes with the assistance of the mayor (*Beverley Guardian*, 15 January 1955). In turn, councillors initiated their own charitable activities that attracted support from other associations. In 1945, the Rotary Club, the residents of Anne Routh's almshouse and a darts league all donated money to the borough council's 'comforts fund' for sending gifts to Beverley men serving abroad (*Beverley Guardian*, 6 January 1945). Most local firms and many shops donated prizes to the mayor's charity ball in 1957 (*Beverley Guardian*, 6 April 1957). Mayor Albert Meadley noted that he had been supported by the Rotary, Lions (of which he was a founder member) and Round Table during his year in office in 1960 (correspondence to and from Councillor Meadley 1954–1973). The borough council's partnership with the assorted associations of local civil society often worked informally through interpersonal networks. For example, both Ken Ingleton and John Whittles considered that the considerable personal social capital of the leader of the Church Lads' Brigade (CLB), Neville Hobson, helped ensure that his organisation was favoured over the Scouts and St John Ambulance when it came to handing out council grants. Bernard Hunt recalled that in the years after Hobson's retirement it became necessary for the new CLB leadership to lobby councillors to secure grants (interviews: Ken Ingleton 23 March 2010; John Whittles 27 April 2010; Bernard Hunt 12 January 2010).

Councillors were frequently active as members and leaders in other associations; membership of a club could therefore bring you access to the town's decision makers. John Day (interview, 10 November 2009) recalled that as a young man in the 1950s he knew many of the local councillors, often through their involvement in clubs he attended:

> Stefan: Did you know any of the councillors?
> John: Yes, Harold Godbold, Smedley, Roberts, Burgess.
> Stefan: How did you get to know them?
> John: Well, Beverley Swimming Club, I was a big member of Beverley Swimming Club, I was junior captain there and was on committee, and there was a councillor there used to go, and I was a member of Conservative club, Snooker Club, and Dennis Dunn he used to be a member, he was a vet, and he used to be member of the Golf Club, he only used to go for a drink on a Sunday dinner time.

The fact that working-class people were borough councillors in the post-war era also had benefits for those who were not personally involved in associational life. Many interviewees had known local working-class men who were borough councillors in the period of the study, and could approach them with issues. In the early 1970s, Lynne Norton's husband obtained the help of a councillor in order to get the family a council home:

> It was a councillor who helped us get this house. Now, you could walk down Beverley and you would maybe run into one. You could sort of ask him ... I think it was ... George Nelson ... went to see him when we wanted that house ... . You could walk down the street and you'd probably see them, just going about their business, and you could have a word with them.
>
> (Lynne Norton, interview, 9 November 2009)

Such connections, and the feeling that one had personal links to local decision makers, were important for creating a sense of community across the town as a whole, transcending the isolation of fragmentary peer groups.

Inter-associational giving

Susan Eckstein (2001) argued that community coherence was revealed in the ways that local organisations exchanged gifts and services. She drew on anthropologist Bronisław Malinowski's notion that the exchange of gifts could help cement social bonds. She reported that community organisations in a working-class area of Boston across the last three decades of the twentieth century had a strong culture of inter-associational giving, frequently exchanging or loaning labour and money. Eckstein saw this as evidence that American working classes were not always the individualised 'peer group' societies that Herbert Gans had claimed, and that a collectivist ethos could animate local life in some areas, given factors including class homogeneity, stable residence and insularity. Beverley was not class-homogenous, but it did have relatively stable residence and some degree of insularity (see Chapter 7) during this period. We have seen that the town council collaborated with civil society associations, and it was also the case that these associations collaborated with each other, including through exchanging gifts. Clubs and societies loaned each other facilities – for example, Hodgson's social club (run by the tannery workers) allowed other groups to use its meeting rooms (*Beverley Guardian*, 21 September 1978). Others exchanged gifts of money or help. In 1948, the Beverley and District Oddfellows friendly society gave money to the Beverley Town Nursing Fund and the Unity Orphan Fund and in 1977 raised funds for the Church Lads' Brigade to make a trip to London (*Beverley Guardian*, 21 April 1977). Groups whose purpose was not primarily philanthropic nevertheless gave charitably to other groups within the town. For example, in 1945 the Beverley and District Rabbit Club gave funds to the cottage hospital, and in 1955 the Beverley Racing Pigeon Club raised funds for the hospital through their annual Cottage Hospital Cup competition (*Beverley Guardian*, 17 March 1945; *Beverley Guardian*, 14 May 1955). Beverley pub darts teams raised money to help support the East Riding Branch of the Forces Help Society in 1955 (*Beverley Guardian*, 19 March 1955). Left-wing associations had their own mutual networks of support; the Beverley Labour Party minutes recorded cash donations from local trade union branches and the Cooperative Society toward expenses incurred fighting local elections, as well as loans of equipment such as loudspeakers (Beverley Labour Party Minutes 1947–1960, 2 July 1959).

The values of civil society

Though a large proportion of Beverley's population was working class during the three post-war decades, the town also had a sizeable middle class. In 1961, 13.4 per cent of the town's residents were employed in middle-class occupations (socio-economic groups 1–4), exactly the same percentage as in England and Wales as a whole (HMSO 1966). Beverley was a popular residential town due to its county-town atmosphere, medieval churches and scenic ancient common pastures. A long history as county town has bequeathed attractive Georgian buildings, including some substantial town houses in the west and south of the town. As well as incoming middle classes, including those moving to the town for work or simply to live in an attractive setting, Beverley had its native 'burgess' class of shopkeepers and businessmen. Both incoming and native middle classes participated in local associations, and where those associations included working-class membership, it was the middle classes who often held the leadership roles. The prevailing ethos of civil society therefore tended to be conservative, supportive of existing institutions (including church and state) and of the notion of stable, harmonious community. In this respect, Beverley's civil society played its role into the hegemonic work of legitimising society's dominant institutions (Castells 2004: 8–9). Many members of the working classes did not appear to challenge the hegemonic ethos, though we might question extent to which they actively supported it.

As an example of the prevailing conservative ethos of civil society, we can consider youth organisations, most of which had both regimental and religious overtones and often aimed moral instruction at the young working classes. The Scouts celebrated King (or Queen), country and church; Scout troops and Guide companies were attached to a particular church and during the 1950s were required to attend services regularly (interviews: Ken Ingleton 23 March 2010; June and Dave Ireland 15 July 2010). Discipline emanated from the senior officers of the Scouting and Guiding organisations. Ken Ingleton's father believed he had been forced out of his role as scout leader in the interwar years by Admiral Walker because he had left-wing political sympathies and because he had admitted 'rough kids' into the troop (Ken Ingleton, interviews, 23 March 2010, 20 April 2010). Ken Ingleton was himself a Cub Scout leader from the 1950s until the 2000s, and remembered that during the 1960s and 1970s there was pressure from further up in the organisation to maintain dress standards in his troop. He himself was told to fix a tooth he had broken in an accident before he was allowed to become a King Scout. Local authority figures made a show of support for the values of the Scouts – the mayor wrote to the *Beverley Guardian* (12 April 1963) to commend the Scouts' 'bob a job' week for inculcating in youth the necessity of earning their keep. In the same year, the headmaster of the Beverley Grammar school praised the Scouts' 'ideal of helping other people at all times' (*Beverley Guardian*, 17 May 1963). Similarly, the Church Lads' Brigade promoted respectable values and behaviour amongst its charges and was thus deemed worthy of broader support from the other civil society associations. The Beverley CLB troop leader from 1908 until the 1960s, Neville Hobson, a solicitor and an established member of the town's burgess class, was keen on discipline. When he entered the brigade's headquarters the boys were expected to stand to attention; those who did not submit to the organisation's military standards of discipline or who resisted the pressure to 'look smart' were asked to leave (George Little, interview, 12 March 2010). Ken Ingleton (interview, 23 March 2010) said that Neville Hobson's discipline on occasion extended to giving children a dressing down that could reduce them to tears, and remembered that his father called CLB 'Hitler Youth' and Neville Hobson 'Charlie Chaplin – the great dictator'. While George Little enjoyed the CLB's discipline and marching practice, Keith Barrett remembered that his spell in the brigade was brief because he felt that he didn't fit in (Keith Barrett, interview, 2 December 2010). Ben Curry (interview, 19 April 2010) justified the Lions' long-standing support for the Church Lads' Brigade: 'I'm particularly involved with CLB, funnelling money from Lions through the CLB because they do a good job, they're looking after 140 kids, the majority of whom live on the other side of the railway lines, and they're really strict with them.'

These conservative values were dramatised in civic parades, when civil society came together to symbolise an ideal, unified town community supportive of national and local institutions. Ed Byrne remembered four civic parades a year in the 1950s, 1960s and 1970s. These were Mayor's Sunday, St John of Beverley Day, Battle of Britain Day and Remembrance Sunday. Parades included the uniformed children's church groups (Cubs, Scouts, Guides, Church Lads' Brigade), St John Ambulance brigade, town councillors, and for the remembrance parades, units of the armed forces. Oral evidence and surviving film from the period attests that parades were attended by large crowds (Ernest Symmons, 'Picture Playhouse News 1942'; interviews: George Little 12 March 2010; Andrew Tyler 1 July 2010). Parades often featured the mayor taking the salute from the marching column at the Market Cross, the ceremonial centre of the town, and procession to one of the town's churches (usually the Minster) for a religious service (John Whittles, interview, 27 April 2010). Parades encompassed all classes in a display of community harmony – working-class and middle-class children were present in the uniformed youth groups, borough councillors came from the working and middle classes, higher status members of the community such as George Odey were invited as guests and seated close to the front for the church ceremony (Beverley Borough Council file on St John of Beverley Day, 4 May 1958).

Alternative values

In the Beverley evidence, we also witness examples of the consensual community values of the 'bourgeois civic' sphere coming into conflict with the class-based visions of society prevalent in working-class institutions. Beverley's Labour Party, gained their first borough council position in the town in 1952 (Beverley Labour Party Minutes 1947–1960: 14 May 1952). Labour councillor Ed Byrne found himself caught between the political imperative of Labour Party organisation and his own sense of the tradition and the dignity of local institutions in an argument over his candidacy for the mayoralty in 1957. He was thrown out of the Beverley Labour Party because he was not willing to withdraw from this candidacy, which had not been sanctioned by the party. He clearly had an affinity with Labour's politics, and remained the Haltemprice Constituency Labour Party's chairman during his year as Mayor in 1958 (*Green's Almanack* 1958). But Ed was a proud Beverlonian, born and bred in a working-class part of the town, and 'regarded the position of the Mayor of the Borough – as an honour: He stressed that he regarded the Mayor as the Mayor of Beverley, not as Mayor of the L.P.' (Beverley Labour Party Minutes 1947–1960: 18 February 1957). Ed was at ease in local civil society; as mayor he enthusiastically supported the St John of Beverley day celebrations (Ed Byrne, interview, 24 May 2010). Significantly the borough council's Labour group opposed expenditure on this celebration in 1959 (Beverley Labour Party Minutes 1947–1960: 5 March 1959). When interviewed in 2010, Ed said that he disliked the interjection of national party politics into the local council (Ed Byrne, interview, 24 May 2010).

Whilst not all interviewees recalled sustained involvement with the formal associations that constituted Beverley's civil society, many did. It is therefore a mistake to discuss working-class community purely in terms of informal sociability amongst family, peer groups and neighbours and to overlook working-class contribution to the public life of the places in which they lived. Working-class people were part of associations who interacted with each other and through collaboration and gift exchange constituted a town-level civil society. Much of this level of associational life, which we have termed 'bourgeois civic', was inflected with conservative hegemonic values.

Change and continuity in associational life

We turn now to consideration of changes in associational life during the age of affluence. Historians have noted that rising living standards during the mid-twentieth century presented the working classes with increasing freedom of choice in the sphere of leisure (Reid 2000; Bernstein 2004: 316–17); others have linked the age of affluence, and especially the 1960s, to a rising culture of choice and individualism that undermined respect for hierarchies (Morgan 1990: 207–9; Bedarida 1991: 249–52; Marwick 1990: 141–53). Such changes helped to move the invisible boundaries that delimited class interaction in associational life; nevertheless, we will see that class remained important.

Stacey (1960: 171) found in her first study of Banbury, beginning in the late 1940s, that class structured many aspects of community life, including associational membership. Although she found distinctions between 'traditionals' who had been born and brought up in the town and 'non-traditionals' who moved in and brought new ideas, class trumped these divisions. However, by the time Margaret Stacey *et al.* (1975: 130–33) restudied the town in the later 1960s, she found that class distinctions were no longer so clear. There was evidence of a greater mixture of classes in associational life. A similar development appears to have taken place in Beverley. Although many clubs and associations had distinct class memberships, with rising affluence there was some blurring of lines. Working-class men and women gained access to clubs that had previously been middle-class.

Some authors in the 1950s and 1960s considered that working-class adoption of types of leisure formerly beyond their reach was part of a wider move away from working-class culture and an embracing of middle-class culture and identity – this became known as the '*embourgeoisement*' thesis (Abrams, Rose and Hinden 1960: 23, 100; Klein, 1965: 422–429; Goldthorpe *et al.*, 1969: 21–23). The evidence here, however, suggests that in a small town like Beverley there was some overlap between working-class and middle-class cultures in terms of their common assumptions and social ties. Rather than the working classes simply aspiring to and adopting middle-class social and cultural practices, influence went both ways. When they joined previously middle-class clubs, working-class men and women were not only fitting into new social milieux but were also changing the cultures of the clubs into which they were integrating.

The class divide in associational life

That class was often more fundamental to associational membership than the division between 'local' and 'incomer' is suggested by the fact that incomers with the right class backgrounds were welcomed into particular clubs that did not welcome locals with the wrong class backgrounds. The Lions and the Rotary Clubs welcomed incoming male professionals or businessmen (interviews: Ben Curry 19 April 2010; Evelyn Frith 10 February 2010). Working-class men and women moving into Beverley could make friends by joining sports teams, working men's clubs, churches, other voluntary associations or simply by visiting the local pub (Beverley Labour Party Minutes 1 April 1948; interviews: John Whittles 27 April 2010; Jerry Young 18 May 2010). Jean Benson's husband was from Liverpool and integrated into local society by playing for Barker and Lee Smith's football team (Jean Benson, interview, 14 January 2010). Working-class women moving into the town seem to have been easily accepted into church groups, neighbourhood informal women's clubs, or voluntary groups such as Red Cross or Scouts' parents' associations (interviews: Dorothy Jackson 10 February 2010; Lynne Norton 9 November 2009; Gerald Ibbotson 7 July 2010). The corollary of this inclusion was the exclusion of those who did not fit with the social milieu of a particular club. Les White (interview, 29 October 2010) born and bred in Beverley, played rugby for a team in Hull in the 1960s but would have nothing to do with the Beverley Rugby Club, whose members he described as: 'bigheads ... [who] don't want to know the likes of me.' Dick Gibson (interview, 11 March 2010) and his wife Joan played golf since the 1980s, but joined a club in Brandesburton rather than the Beverley club that Joan described as 'snooty'. Some clubs remained exclusively middle-class, such as the Lions and Rotary Clubs (interviews: Ben Curry 19 April 2010; Neil Cooper 14 April 2010).

Class codes implicit in associational life in the earlier part of the period were illustrated in a *Beverley Guardian* report of an occasion when Mayor James Smedley, a manual worker at Hodgson's, invited fellow councillors to the firm's social club to play the club committee at dominoes and snooker. On Smedley's election to the mayoral office, another councillor had suggested that there was 'no disgrace in him being a working man' (*Beverley Guardian*, 15 November 1947). The trip to the Hodgson's club was reported in a way that suggested councillors were crossing a divide by entering a working-class environment. A return match was organised but this would be in a setting understood tacitly as being the councillors' home turf – Beverley Golf Club (*Beverley Guardian*, 17 January 1948). So, while involvement in associational life did link individuals from different classes, their interactions were deeply inscribed with class distinction.

Furthermore, there were class hierarchies within groups. In youth groups, working-class volunteers worked with the children but middle-class men and women were involved in the higher organisational echelons. In 1963 Lord Hotham was elected president of the Beverley and District Scouts, with Neville Hobson (a local solicitor), Dr C. Cameron and Dr Paul Pearson among the vice presidents, Alderman Bielby, was re-elected chairman and Superintendent Maidment was vice chairman (*Beverley Guardian*, 17 May 1963). Tannery director George Odey was a sometime chairman of the District Scouting association (Ken Ingleton, interview, 20 April 2010). Clubs and societies sought presidents who had status within civil society, often the mayor, although local dignitaries such as Neville Hobson were also chosen (Beverley and District Sea Angling club minutes: 21 March 1967; *Beverley Guardian*, 17 May 1963). In the political sphere, those with higher status such as George Odey became county councillors; borough councillors were usually shopkeepers, smaller business owners and the skilled working classes (*Beverley Guardian*, 20 January 1977; interviews: Ed Byrne 24 May 2010; Tom Potter 24 October 2008).

However, there was some evidence that, as Stacey *et al.* (1975: 120–121) found in Banbury, class demarcations in associational life were shifting during the 1960s. Not only were the working classes joining previously middle-class clubs in the decades after the Second World War, but they were also socialising with middle-class members of these clubs. Golf was described by McKibbin (1998: 359–62) as a solidly middle-class pursuit in the 1920s and 1930s. However, the sport became popular amongst more affluent manual workers after the Second World War, with numbers of golfers doubling in the 1950s (Holt 2005: 110–26); in Beverley too, there was a widening of the sport's social base in the post-war decades (Ward 1990: 61). David Hughes (interview, 24 June 2010) worked as barman at the Beverley golf club in the 1960s and recalled that the membership at that time included butchers, shopkeepers, and workers from Hodgson's tannery and from the aircraft factory at Brough (12 miles to the south-west). John Day (interview, 10 November 2009), son of a Beverley shipyard caulker, joined the golf club whilst himself working as an apprentice caulker in the 1950s. He remembered that several other shipyard workers were also members and that working-class men were an increasing proportion of the clubs' membership at this time. Initially John joined the 'Artisans' club, a subsidiary golf club set up to provide cheap sport for working men, but was soon taken under the wing of existing members who introduced him to the main club where he had no problems being accepted – he put this down to his good manners (John and Margaret Day, interview, 8 December 2009). John and his wife spent much of their social leisure with other members of the golf club during the 1960s. The couple often invited friends back for drinks at their semi-detached house after discos held at the club. Dave Ireland (interview, 15 July 2010) grew up in a working-class family, attended Beverley grammar school and obtained a white-collar job in the council offices. He joined the golf club in the 1950s following the suggestion of friends at work, where he met and played regularly with John Day. Like John, Dave participated in the social life connected with the golf club, and thought that golf had moved from being a sport in which 'it was all shopkeepers and bankers and top bank managers' to something that 'everybody plays'.

It was not only the golf club that appeared to become more open to working-class membership as the post-war decades progressed. Neil Cooper (interview, 14 April 2010) was the son of a foreman toolmaker at Deans and Lightalloys and himself worked much of his life as an electrician at Armstrong's. He was a self-confessed 'sportaholic', and by the 1960s had joined the Beverley Town Cricket and Recreation Club at Norwood (cricket, tennis and bowls), the golf club and later a more exclusive tennis club at Seven Corners Lane. Neil recalled the sociability that membership of these clubs brought, and he himself organised social evenings including bingo nights at the Norwood clubhouse. McKibbin (1998: 352) suggested that rugby union had been more of a middle-class sport earlier in the century, but in Beverley it seemed to have been a sport with broad-based class appeal after the war. George Little, an electrician at Armstrong's, set up the Beverley Rugby Club (a rugby union club) with friends in 1959. Like the golf club, the rugby club included a significant social element (Hilda Little, interview, 19 March 2010).

The mixing of small businessmen, white collar workers and manual workers in the rugby, golf and cricket clubs was eased by the fact that in practice they often shared similar social backgrounds and cultural assumptions. It was fairly common for interviewees to have moved between socio-economic classes through their lives. Some shopkeepers and businessmen had once been shipyard workers, or had grown up in working-class families (interviews: Mick Underwood 21 July 2010; Marianne Woolly 22 February 2010; James and Peggy Alexander 18 February 2010). Grammar school was a way for people from a solidly working-class background to achieve middle-class jobs, including clerical positions in the offices of the borough council, county council or local factories (interviews: Eric and Helen Ross 16 February 2010; Dave and June Ireland 15 July 2010; Peter Cooper, ERYMS interview, 2005). That this kind of mobility could take place without people leaving the town meant that links with working-class background, family and values could be maintained. This combination of social mobility with geographic immobility meant that there was a certain overlap in terms of the personnel of the classes, with particular close links between the skilled working classes and lower middle classes. The culture of male sociability that dominated the solidly working-class associations such as bird and rabbit clubs, football and darts teams was not so different to the types of sociability that obtained in the more middle-class golf, tennis, cricket and rugby union clubs. This was a culture of male camaraderie consisting of competition, sporting enjoyment and, often, drinking. Therefore, once wages allowed working-class men to pay club fees and buy the requisite equipment, membership of these clubs did not necessarily involve a readjustment of social expectations.

The workers who were becoming involved in what were previously more middle-class clubs were those who were gaining ground materially in the age of affluence, and who were able to purchase their own houses and cars. It is possible that some did consider that they were advancing socially by joining golf or tennis clubs. David Hughes (interview, 24 June 2010), barman at the golf clubhouse in the 1960s, recalled the social pretensions of many club members, who often treated him in a patronising manner despite being 'working men' themselves. However, interviewees who had themselves joined these clubs preferred to describe the sport as the principal motivation. Neil Cooper (interview, 14 April 2010), a sports enthusiast, was prepared to tolerate some social discomfort to join sport clubs perceived as elitist but that had facilities he wished to use. He recalled that he had tried to conceal his council estate address from fellow members of his tennis club, a sport he described as 'snobbish', and he had to draw on personal networks to gain membership of the golf club. Neil told how he had an interview in a big house at the 'posh end of Beverley' in order to move from Norwood to Seven Lanes tennis club:

> I sat there, looking round this blooming great house, Tommy Ward they called him, he was an ex colonel or something like … [asked] 'Why do you want to leave them to come to us?' because it was unknown, anyone leaving Norwood … and I said, 'Yours is a better club, better tennis,' I think they had teaching there … ours didn't want to progress at Norwood.

Some 'affluent workers' who joined what had previously been more middle-class clubs had an ambivalent relationship to class; they expressed an awareness of class alongside a denial it was important socially. John Day (interview, 10 November 2009), describing the golf club of the 1950s, mimicked the middle-class accents of some of the members whilst also insisting that he never felt out of place in the club because of his class. Dave and June Ireland (interview, 15 July 2010) disagreed about the extent to which class mattered in the golf club, and indeed, more generally. June claimed that class was no longer important whereas Dave was less certain and thought some class distinctions still operated amongst club golfers. Interviewees' reactions to the subject of class in club life thus appeared to corroborate Jeffrey Hill's observation regarding class and sport during this period: sports clubs were places in which different classes could mix at this time, so long as all members submitted to unwritten codes of behaviour emphasising the principles of good humour, fellowship, sportsmanship and avoidance of controversial subjects such as class (Hill 2002: 140).

Affluence and social mobility lifted some material restrictions on leisure. Interviewees perceived themselves as having had more leisure choices than their parents, who had grown up between the wars (for example, John and Margaret Day, interview, 8 December 2009). Nevertheless, interviewees' cultural tastes continued to be influenced by their working-class background, and they took this influence with them into the clubs they shared with the middle classes. For example, John Day (interview, 10 November 2009) described how the habit of drinking pints rather than half pints of beer became normal at the golf club as a result of a growing working-class membership. Those who attained middle-class status or jobs could often retain an interest in sports and associations that were more working class. For example, Eric Ross, although playing tennis along with other staff members at Hodgson's, also played in the factory's working-class football teams (Eric and Helen Ross, interview, 16 February 2010). Similarly, June and Dave Ireland (interview, 15 July 2010) regularly socialised at golf club events in the 1960s but also spent evenings at Armstrong's club and at the British Legion with June's parents. Tom Potter (interview, 24 October 2008) described how the Grosvenor working men's club, with which he had been involved since the 1960s, had previously been solidly working-class but was increasingly frequented by middle-class men including lawyers and accountants as well as working-class men. Rather than the working classes simply aspiring to and adopting middle-class culture, as suggested by the *embourgeoisement* thesis, a 'pick and mix' approach led to a process of negotiation and mutual accommodation between different class cultures in the social spaces of associational life.

Furthermore, amidst cultural change of the 1960s and 1970s, the old, hierarchical conservative hegemony was beginning to seem anachronistic. Cub leader Ken Ingleton (interview, 20 April 2010) remembered:

> Everybody was, sort of flower power then. I mean, they used to come in fluorescent socks, you'd heck of a job trying to keep them into some sort of a uniform ... . It was the spell when Harold Wilson was in again, all the teachers were trendy liberals at the time, weren't they? Don't call me sir, call me Fred.

Ken was himself phlegmatic about these changes: 'I got rid of berets ... you can't really wear a beret with shoulder length hair,' but those higher up insisted upon conformity: 'some D.C.s [District Commissioners] wanted you to, it became a bit of a power struggle'. It appeared that young people became self-conscious about involvement in parades – Ken explained that in recent times Cub Scouts were embarrassed to march in public because their friends 'take the mickey'. The former requirement for Scout and Cub troops to attend church was loosened. The Church Lads' Brigade also responded to cultural change. The Beverley branch allowed girls to join when the national organisation became the Church Lads' and Church Girls' Brigade in 1978 (*Beverley Guardian*, 12 October 1978). The CLB's regimental atmosphere was relaxed in favour of craft activities (George Little, interviews, 24 October 2008, 12 March 2010). Similarly, Freeman (2013) noted that many of the hierarchical messages conveyed in town historic pageants were dropped during the 1960s as they became less palatable to modern audiences.

Conclusion

The evidence outlined in this chapter is important to the overall arguments advanced in the book. It points to the involvement of working-class people in the associational life of their towns across the age of affluence. This involvement – which included playing in sports clubs, debating in local politics, running and participating in youth associations – has been overlooked by those sociologists and historians who have conceptualised working-class community primarily as neighbourhood-and-kinship sociability (Young and Willmott 1962/1957; Klein 1965; Roberts 1995: 199–231; Bourke 1994: 136–169; Jones 2012: 120–54). Much of the community we witnessed in this chapter was not purely *working class* – in a small town like Beverley, there were kinship and social links between those whose education and economic trajectories placed them in different socio-economic classes; there was also cooperation and interaction between the classes in the town's associational life and civil society. But it is unlikely that the British working-class life was ever quite so self-contained as some authors have claimed (Meacham 1977: 58–9; Hobsbawm 1984). Colls (1995), for example, pointed out that working-class and 'bourgeois civic' associational life overlapped in the coal-mining and shipbuilding towns of North East England: the middle classes contributed capital for infrastructure such as the public parks in which working-class people took their open-air leisure; the middle and working classes engaged each other socially in associations such as the Wesleyan Methodists. The story of associational life in Beverley during the age of affluence reminds us that 'community-of-place' included local allegiances that were not simply reducible to class.

References

Abrams, Mark, Richard Rose and Rita Hinden (1960) *Must Labour Lose?* Harmondsworth: Penguin.

Andersen, Robert, James Curtis and Edward Grabb (2006) 'Trends in Civic Association Activity in Four Democracies: The Special Case of Women in the United States', *American Sociological Review*, 71, 376–400.

Bedarida, Francois (1991) *A Social History of England 1851–1990*, 2nd edition, London: Routledge.

Bernstein, George L. (2004) *The Myth of Decline: The Rise of Britain Since 1945*, London: Pimlico.

Birch, A.H. (1959) *Small Town Politics: A Study of Political Life in Glossop*, Oxford: Oxford University Press.

Bourke, Joanna (1994) *Working Class Cultures in Britain 1890–1960: Gender, Class, and Ethnicity*, London: Routledge.

Castells, Manuel (2004) *The Power of Identity*, 2nd edition, Oxford: Blackwell.

Cherrington, Ruth Louise (2009) 'The Development of Working Men's Clubs: A Case Study of Implicit Cultural Policy', *International Journal of Cultural Policy*, 15:2, 187–199.

Clapson, Mark (2012) *Working-Class Suburb: Social Change on an English Council Estate, 1930–2010*, Manchester: Manchester University Press.

154 *Civil society and associational life*

Colls, Robert (1995) 'Save Our Pits and Communities', *Labour History Review*, 60:2, 55–66.

Colls, Robert (2004) 'When We Lived in Communities. Working-class Culture and its Critics', in Robert Colls and Richard Rodger (eds), *Cities of Ideas. Governance and Citizenship in Urban Britain 1800–2000*, Aldershot: Ashgate, 283–307.

Dennis, Norman, Fernando Henriques and Clifford Slaughter (1969) *Coal is Our Life: An Analysis of a Yorkshire Mining Community*, 2nd edition, London: Tavistock.

Eckstein, Susan (2001) 'Community as Gift-Giving: Collectivist Roots of Volunteerism', *American Sociological Review*, 66:6, 829–851.

Freeman, Mark (2013) '"Splendid Display; Pompous Spectacle": Historical Pageants in Twentieth-century Britain', *Social History*, 38:4, 423–455.

Gans, Herbert J. (1962) *The Urban Villagers. Group and Class in the Life of Italian-Americans*, New York: Macmillan.

Goldthorpe, John Harry, David Lockwood, Frank Bechhofer and Jennifer Platt (1969) *The Affluent Worker in the Class Structure*, London: Cambridge University Press.

Granovetter, Mark S. (1973) 'The Strength of Weak Ties', *The American Journal of Sociology*, 78:6, 1360–1380.

Hill, Jeffrey (2002) *Sport, Leisure and Culture in Twentieth-Century Britain*, Basingstoke: Palgrave.

HMSO (1966) *Census 1961. England and Wales. Occupation, Industry and Socio-Economic groups. Yorkshire, East Riding*, London: HMSO.

Hobsbawm, Eric (1984) 'The Formation of British Working-Class Culture', in Eric Hobsbawm, *Worlds of Labour*, London: Weidenfeld & Nicolson, 176–193.

Holt, Richard (2005) 'Sport and Recreation', in Paul Addison and Harriet Jones (eds), *A Companion to Contemporary Britain 1939–2000*, Malden: Blackwell, 110–126.

Jackson, Brian and Dennis Marsden (1966) *Education and the Working Class*, Harmondsworth: Penguin.

Johnes, Martin (2007) 'Pigeon Racing and Working-Class Culture in Britain, c. 1870–1950', *Cultural and Social History*, 4, 361–383.

Jones, Ben (2012) *The Working Class in Mid Twentieth-Century England: Community, Identity and Social Memory*, Manchester: Manchester University Press.

Klein, Josephine (1965) *Samples from English Cultures (Volume 1)*, London: Routledge & Kegan Paul.

Lockwood, David (1994) 'Sources of Variation in Working-class Images of Society', in Martin Bulmer (ed.), *Working-class Images of Society*, London: Routledge, 16–31.

Marwick, Arthur (1990) *British Society Since 1945*, 2nd edition, London: Penguin.

McKibbin, Ross (1984) 'Why was there no Marxism in Great Britain?', *English Historical Review*, 99:391, 297–331.

McKibbin, Ross (1998) *Classes and Cultures: England, 1918–1951*, Oxford: Oxford University Press.

Meacham, Standish (1977) *A Life Apart. The English Working Class 1890–1914*, London: Thames and Hudson.

Mogey, John Macfarlane (1956) *Family and Neighbourhood. Two Studies in Oxford*, London: Oxford University Press.

Morgan, Kenneth O. (1990) *The Peoples' Peace: British History 1945–1989*, New York: Oxford University Press.

Neave, David (1990) *Mutual Aid in the Victorian Countryside: Friendly Societies in the Rural East Riding 1830–1912*, Hull: Hull University Press.

Putnam, Robert D. (2000) *Bowling Alone: The Collapse and Revival of American Community*, New York: Simon & Schuster.

Reid, Douglas A. (2000) 'Playing and Praying', in Martin Daunton (ed.), *The Cambridge Urban History of Britain. Volume III. 1840–1950*, Cambridge: Cambridge University Press, 745–807.

Roberts, Elizabeth (1995) *Women and Families: An Oral History, 1940–1970*, Oxford: Blackwell.

Seabrook, Jeremy (1984) *The Idea of Neighbourhood: What Local Politics Should be About*, London: Pluto Press.

Stacey, Margaret (1960) *Tradition and Change. A Study of Banbury*, Oxford: Oxford University Press.

Stacey, Margaret, Eric Batstone, Colin Bell and Anne Murcott (1975) *Power, Persistence and Change. A Second Study of Banbury*, London: Routledge & Kegan Paul.

Ward, J. G. M. (1990) *One Hundred Years of Golf on Westwood*, Beverley: Coxon.

Williams, Bill (1982) *Class, Culture and Community. A Biographical Study of Social Change in Mining*, London: Routledge & Kegan Paul.

Young, Michael and Peter Willmott (1962/1957) *Family and Kinship in East London*, Harmondsworth: Pelican.

Primary sources

Beverley and District Sea Angling Club minutes, ERALS: DDX 1150/1; 1150/2.

Beverley Borough Council file on 'Boots for Bairns' 1928-1959, ERALS: BOBE 2/15/1/198.

Beverley Borough Council file on St John of Beverley Day, 4 May 1958, ERALS, BOBE 2/15/1/191.

Beverley Guardian, 6 January, 21 January, 17 March, 26 May, 9 June 1945; 15 November 1947; 3 January, 17 January, 16 October, 30 October 1948; 15 January, 19 March, 7 May, 14 May 1955; 6 April 1957; 12 April, 17 May 1963; 7 May 1965; 20 January, 10 March, 17 March, 21 April 1977; 21 September, 12 October 1978.

Beverley Labour Party Minutes, 1947–1960, 1964–1970 (private collection).

Beverley Town Council records, correspondence to and from Councillor Meadley 1954–1973, ERALS, DDX 1463/2/1.

Derek Mitchell, ERYMS interview.

Ernest Symmons 'Picture Playhouse News 1942' film collection, ERALS, DDX 1369/5/15.

Green's Almanack 1955 and 1958, Beverley: Green and Son, ERALS, Y/914–274/Bev.

John Cooper, ERYMS interview 2.

Peter Cooper, ERYMS interview September 2005.

Peter Cooper, ERYMS interview 2a.

St Nicholas Church Magazine, January 1952, ERALS, PE 193/T54.

7   Identity and place

Mr Harold Ewen, aged 79, had lived on St Andrew's Street for 40 years when he heard that the council were planning to demolish his home. Harold told the *Yorkshire Post* (8 May 1981): 'I don't want to move and start paying rent at my age. I have about an acre of land which I rent and I have cultivated for many years, and I need to live nearby.' The kind of attachment that Harold conveyed, a consequence both of practical considerations and rootedness in place, was frequently expressed in the interviews. Mike Savage (2008: 151–2, 156–8, 161) has suggested that this kind of 'functional' attachment was the main component of working-class identification with community-of-place in the mid-century. Savage analysed qualitative data from several 1960s community studies, arguing that a 'functional orientation to locale' predominated: attachment to place amongst 'born and bred', working-class locals was not expressed through reference to 'an elaborated comparative frame of reference' and did not include an 'aesthetic sense regarding the quality or aura of place'. It was instead defined by 'family affiliations' and the convenience of local amenities. Savage contrasted working-class 'functional' belonging with the 'elective' belonging he found in mobile middle classes in the 1990s, who 'waxed lyrical about where they lived', emphasising 'identity, meaning and "aura"' of places in order to claim affiliation. Savage is not the only author to describe working-class identification with place in these terms. Graham Martin (2005), though for a later time period, drew on Pierre Bourdieu's (1984: 177–8) notion that working-class people develop a 'taste for the necessary' to depict working-class Londoners' attachment to their borough as rooted in material and functional rather than aesthetic or emotional considerations. There was certainly evidence in the Beverley study of working-class 'functional' attitudes to place during the post-war decades. However, the Beverley evidence suggests that there was more to local identity in the post-war era than 'functional attachment' allows.

British social investigators of the 1950s and 1960s often described working-class localism, but gave little space to its analysis (Hoggart 1957: 51–61; Young and Willmott 1962/1957: 113; Dennis, Henriques and Slaughter 1969/ 1956: 156–158). Josephine Klein (1965), synthesising 1950s and 1960s British community studies, used evidence about working-class localism to make points about the density of local networks rather than exploring local attachment in itself (Klein 1965: 76, 126, 129). But authors since the 1970s have argued that discussions of community should include fuller consideration of how people attribute social meaning to spaces and places, and have sometimes prioritised this over patterns of sociability (Suttles 1972; Relph 1976; Cohen 1985; Edwards 2000; Rogaly and Taylor 2009). The current chapter explores ways in which identities were linked to place in Beverley in the post-war decades, and shows that place- and class-based identity could both overlap and clash. The chapter will first discuss different ways in which identity as a 'Beverlonian' was understood and symbolised, including commonalities and divergences between middle- and working-class identification with the town. It will then explore how Beverley identity was cross-cut with class distinctions that mapped onto residential areas. Finally, the limits to place-based identity are considered.

The construction of an 'ancient borough'

For Edward Relph (1976: 57), among the most influential theorists of place identity, belonging or identification *with* place was intimately connected with the identity, or 'image' *of* place. We have to have a conception of what a place's identity is if we are to identify with it. He suggested that an individual's images of place are usually not independent: 'individual images have been and are being constantly socialised through the use of common languages, symbols, and experiences.' Furthermore, images of place vary across different groups within communities: 'through interest groups … communities can develop and an image be projected in which the identities of places of significance to that group are a reflection of group interests and biases.' As we have seen in the previous chapter, and as Margaret Stacey (1960; Stacey *et al.* 1975) also noted in her studies of Banbury, middle-class locals could find considerable common ground socially with middle-class incomers, living in the same parts of town and joining the same associations. Robert Colls (1995) termed this stratum of civil society the 'civic bourgeois', and Beverley's civic bourgeois groups collaborated in the construction of a shared image of the town that emphasised the historic and the picturesque.

Anthony Cohen (1985: 92–97, 99, 103) observed that the past is often used as a resource for community construction, documenting examples from a variety of contexts including Mongolia and the Scottish island of Whalsay. The use of history for the discursive construction of local community has a long history in Britain. Robin Pearson (1993) documented how civic elites used the past as an imaginative resource for the symbolic construction of community in a nineteenth-century suburb of Leeds; Mark Freeman (2013) points to the organisation of historical pageants in towns and cities across England between 1905 and the 1960s as a means of mobilising wide swathes of the community to celebrate local and national histories. Beverley has a rich history – founded in the early medieval period around a monastery reputed to be the home of a popular saint, the town became a pilgrimage site and grew to be an important centre for the Yorkshire wool trade. Though it declined in the later middle ages, Beverley enjoyed a Georgian-era renaissance as the county town of the East Riding, with town houses and fashionable entertainment for East Riding gentry and growing middle classes (Neave 1989). This history has bequeathed a wealth of architectural remains, as well as a medieval street plan that gives the town an attractive and historic atmosphere. Medieval and Georgian history and architectural heritage were emphasised as keystones of local identity by the civic elite in the twentieth century; concern to protect and project this vision of the town arguably intensified in the post-war decades.

Though civic conservationism can be dated back to the nineteenth century at least (Hewitt 2012), concern with rescuing towns' and cities' architectural antiquities from destruction became more urgent in the context of post-war urban reconstruction (Walsh 1992: 70–4). In 1961, members of Beverley Rotary Club, prompted by the imminent demolition of one of the town's historic streets, formed a Civic Society, and conservation was henceforth an evergreen issue in the town (Joan Walsh, interview, 21 November 2014). Members acknowledge that the Civic Society was and remains a largely middle-class association until the present day; this is also suggested by the addresses on a list of committee members from the period (Beverley Civic Society records; interviews: Joan Walsh 21 November 2014; Anna Nicholl 22 February 2010). The Civic Society was informed by, and helped to perpetuate, an image of Beverley as historic and picturesque. They celebrated the town's unique and valuable monuments: Beverley Minster (a gothic church renowned across Europe); the Tudor splendour of St Mary's Church; the North Bar (a medieval gatehouse); the medieval street plan; the Georgian civic and domestic architectural heritage. The Civic Society considered Beverley:

> An exceptional example of coherent unity. It still possesses qualities of character, both visible and intangible, which are rare and irreplaceable.
>
> (*Beverley Guardian*, 22 January 1965)

It appeared to be almost mandatory across the three post-war decades that public statements of local patriotism include reference to the town's ancient heritage. For example, in 1945 Ernest Symmons, a businessman who ran the town's 'Picture Playhouse' cinema, wrote in praise of new street lighting: 'Old Beverley is picturesque in any sort of light, its quaint old streets and houses possess an individuality all of their own' (*Beverley Guardian*, 28 July 1945). Hodgson's director George Odey wrote in 1955 of 'this ancient borough', where the casual visitor would notice 'the Minster and St Mary's and the ancient red-roofed houses interspersed with trees' (*Green's Household Almanack* 1955). Even left-wing locals paid homage to the town's antiquity, with JP Mr Millett announcing at a Labour adoption meeting in 1945 that the time 'had come when they should have representation on our ancient council' (*Beverley Guardian*, 27 October 1945). The medieval Minster church that dominated the town was the most potent symbol of historic Beverley.

Following an appearance of the Minster on national television in 1957, the *Beverley Guardian* columnist 'Onlooker' wrote that a 'friend' had seen this and despite being only 'Beverlonian by adoption', was 'immensely proud of our glorious minster' and hoped other people saw it around the country (*Beverley Guardian*, 12 January 1957).

The conservation movement was clearly motivated by a need to protect Beverley's architectural heritage from some dramatic town planning proposals, prompted by increasing road traffic (Brown 1989). But there was also a sense in which the historic character of the town was emphasised in contradistinction to the nearby city of Hull. A local architect speaking at a Beverley Civic Society meeting in 1965 observed, perhaps playing to his audience: 'Everybody loves Beverley ... . Not everybody loves Hull, it is so hard [to pursue conservation measures] in a place that people don't care about' (*Beverley Guardian*, 8 October 1965). There was some anxiety about the potential for Beverley to be subsumed, politically and physically, by its larger neighbour, which perhaps amplified the tendency for residents to emphasise the distinction. Hull was close to Beverley, and in practice entwined in everyday life. Residents of both Hull and Beverley might travel to the other place for work, leisure and sociability with friends and relatives. Hull was a relatively large city with a population of 303,000 in 1961 (compared with Beverley's 16,000) (Allison, 1969). The city spread outwards in the post-war years, with large sub-urban council estates encroaching on the countryside between the two settlements (Brown 1989). Anxiety about the threat to Beverley's integrity was expressed by a woman who described herself as 'exiled from the ancient borough': 'I hope Hull never, never really attach themselves to the ancient borough for there was a Beverley long before there was Hull' (*Beverley Guardian*, 9 January 1960). Local concern for the independence of the town in relation to Hull was noted by a letter-writer in 1963:

> Beverley, despite its proximity to Hull, is very much Beverley. It is a proud, old-fashioned and somewhat insular type of community ... . It is certainly not Beverley, near Hull. Even the appendage of East Yorkshire to its name is resented by a true Beverlonian ... that is how I, even as an interloper, would have it continue.
>
> (*Beverley Guardian*, 11 January 1963)

Prickliness about Hull was also evident in a 1977 letter regarding an enquiry into the ownership of common land in Beverley: 'Why is the inquiry to take place in Hull – it does not concern the people of Hull' (*Beverley Guardian*, 10 March 1977).

In creating and reinforcing of the image of Beverley as an historic town, the discourse of antiquity and the enthusiasm for conservation were joined by public ritual as means for conveying history and tradition. Eric Hobsbawm and Terence Ranger (1983) described the centrality of appeals to tradition and antiquity in such rituals. An 'invented tradition' of public civic ceremonial,

St John of Beverley Day, was initiated in 1949 (*Beverley Guardian*, 9 May 1953). This annual celebration (still undertaken at the time of writing) involved the mayor and civic leaders progressing through the town on the nearest Sunday to 7 May, at the head of a parade of mayors and macebearers from other Yorkshire towns. Beverley notables such as George Odey were in prominent attendance (*Beverley Guardian*, 14 May 1955). In 1973, 25 mayors from across Yorkshire attended the ceremony (*Beverley Guardian*, 11 May 1973). The town's civic elites had organised a historical pageant in 1937 ('Beverley through the Ages'; see Freeman 2013 and Hulme 2016 for the history of such local displays in the twentieth century). This was repeated in 1973 for the 400-year anniversary of Beverley's charter of incorporation, with a procession of local people dressed as characters from Beverley's past, and a display of the town's medieval charters in the library (*Beverley Guardian*, 4 May 1973).

At least some of this concern with local history and tradition can be identified with a conservative nostalgia for a cohesive, stable and deferential community imagined in the past. Such a conservative world-view informed portrayals in the *Beverley Guardian* of working-class Beverlonians as insular, deferential and hard-working. The paper reported milestone birthdays, wedding celebrations and retirements of locals, preferably 'born and bred Beverlonians' with lengthy service in a particular local industry (for example, *Beverley Guardian*, 7 May 1955, 11 January 1963, 9 April 1965). The self-confessed 'interloper' cited earlier worried about the potential closure of the town's shipyard in 1963, not in terms of the suffering of those made redundant, but because the artisans who worked at the shipyard would have to go elsewhere, hence diminishing the character of the town (*Beverley Guardian*, 11 January 1963). In the 1940s through to the 1960s, though toned down somewhat thereafter, local journalists conveyed the conservative view that working-class people should know their place. One column, 'Sportsman's Notebook', which often reported dialect speech and portrayed the quaint ways of country folk, lamented: 'We live in an age when Jack is as good as his master and any outward acknowledgement of superior position … is judged a weakness' (*Beverley Guardian*, 13 January 1945). 'Sportsman's Notebook' continued to appear until the 1970s, helping to define the general conservative tone of the paper.

These expressions of a conservative world-view in post-war Beverley were formed in reaction to wider social and political change. The post-war rise of Labour had some impact locally, with a surge in the party's Beverley constituency vote in 1945; Labour councillors, a rarity previously, were a constant presence in the borough council from 1952 (Beverley Labour Branch Minutes, 14 May 1952). The introduction of Labour into local politics was resisted through assertions that national party politics, with their class overtones, ought to have no place locally – post-war local councillors were almost all listed as 'Independent' until 1952, and a Labour candidate in 1949 claimed: 'The old cry has been raised that there should be no politics in Local Government, yet the majority of Beverley Councillors are prominent members of the Conservative and Liberal Parties' (*Beverley Guardian*, 25 April 1953, 7 May

1949). Strikes were reported as essentially 'un-Beverlonian' behaviour in the *Beverley Guardian*, which took a noticeably pro-management stance. During a shipyard strike in 1955 a reporter claimed to have 'spoken to many shipyard workers in the town this week, and I have yet to meet one who is in favour of the strike'. The clear implication was that the strike was nationally imposed (*Beverley Guardian*, 23 March 1955). In 1965 another shipyard strike was reported: 'Is all this effort [of management staff to secure orders] going to come to nothing through petty disagreements and grumbles which could sound the death-knell for Beverley's centuries old shipbuilding industry?' (*Beverley Guardian*, 22 January 1965). Here the conservative appeal to a conception of an historic and traditional Beverley, as opposed to modern and conflictual class politics, was overt.

So, Beverley's post-war identity as historic and picturesque market town was largely a middle-class cultural construction. But we will see below that working-class residents also conceived of themselves as 'Beverlonian', and expressed local patriotism.

Working-class Beverlonians

Authors have argued that construction of an 'historic' identity for places is one of the ways through which elites elicit popular support for consensual images of community, diverting attention from political, economic and social inequality. This can happen at a national or local level: Ranger and Hobsbawm (1983) described the invented traditions through which numerous European states sought to renew enthusiasm for their flagging institutions during the late nineteenth century; Pearson (1993) argued that middle-class elites in fast-changing Leeds suburbs during the mid-nineteenth century revived local customs as a means of projecting harmonious images of community that justified their own right to leadership positions. The resort to history and tradition of the kind witnessed in St John parades and *Beverley Guardian* editorials could be seen, therefore, as laden with 'social messages intended to support the preservation of social and political hierarchies' (Freeman 2013: 426). Certainly, there appears to have been post-war motivation for local elites in Beverley to appeal to history for consensual versions of local community, given the challenge presented by the interjection of more overtly class-based politics into the local arena.

But as Freeman (2013) and Tom Hulme (2016) point out, even the most traditional-looking parades were often mass-participation events, and the idea that all working-class participants uncritically swallowed messages of obedience, hierarchy and civic pride seems unlikely. Authors including Richard Hoggart (1957: 58–68), Hobsbawm (1984), Keith Snell (2006) and Joanna Bourke (1994: 165–8) point to deeply held local patriotism, and its converse, local xenophobia, on the part of the working classes from the nineteenth to the mid-twentieth centuries; as Dave Russell (2004: 281) argued, there is no reason to see such place identities as 'a form of false consciousness imposed upon a pliant working class'. In Beverley during the age of affluence, it appears that many amongst the working classes had attachment to their home town that was heartfelt, rooted in their own life experience rather than drawing on elite discourse about the identity of a historic town. We might relate this kind of identity to Relph's (1976: 55) category of 'existential insideness ... the most fundamental form of insideness ... in which a place is experienced without deliberate and self-conscious reflection yet is full of significances'. Relph considered that this as a feeling of being at home that is usually the result of being born and living in a place for many years.

Their home town had a pull for many interviewees who had left and returned. Iris Brown left Beverley for extended periods, first as a member of the armed forces, and then as an army wife in the 1970s. She said that she had always felt that she would one day return to Beverley, the town she thought of as her home (Iris Brown, interview, 21 May 2010). Similarly, when Jean Benson (interview, 14 January 2010) moved to Liverpool with her husband in the 1950s, she soon found that she wanted to return, claiming that it was easier to get to know people in Beverley than in the city. George Little (interview, 24 October 2008) described how, when he was sent away to work in Wales, he had never felt comfortable and always looked forward to the familiarity of his home town. For Margaret Day (interview, 23 November 2009), the question of whether she had ever thought of moving elsewhere prompted a statement of close identification with her home town: 'If I bought another house it would have to be in Beverley I think ... I couldn't settle anywhere ... there's nothing more warming than when you've been away and come back and see minster towers. Well it's just home, Beverley's me.' Margaret's statement of local identification appears to closely mirror Relph's (1976: 55) description of 'existential insideness': 'someone who does experience a place from the attitude of existential insideness is part of that place and it is part of him'.

Whilst this kind of identification *could* be interpreted as 'functional', it seems reductionist to deny the emotional aspects of belonging. Unlike the aesthetic appreciation of the town's historic landscape on the part of middle-class incomers who joined the Civic Society, working-class (and middle-class) locals saw historic architecture through the prism of their own lives and experiences:

> When we bought the other bungalow and it looked across to the Minster I sort of gained some satisfaction from that in some strange way. Which I can't really explain. But I, don't know whether, I've always been interested in history, whether it was the history of it, or the beauty of it, or whatever it was. I don't really know. It's connected to where I lived. It was like ... almost part of the furniture ... because I went to school in the shadow of it, I lived in the shadow of it, and it was accessible, you could go in and you were trusted ... . And you used to do the nativity play inside the church itself.
>
> (Ivy Shipton, interview, 17 May 2010)

It could be argued that some of these statements of belonging capture present attitudes and emotions rather than those held during the age of affluence. The emotional dimensions of place-attachment are difficult to capture in retrospect, but the evidence suggests that working-class belonging and town pride were not only contemporary with the interviews. Mick Underwood (interview, 16 June 2010) visited Ibiza annually since the 1970s and recalled telling friends from the island who had asked him why he wouldn't move to the island: 'I live in one of the finest towns in the world.' Similarly, categories such as 'Beverley people', 'Beverlonian', 'native' and 'born and bred' were all used in the period of the study as well as today, and are suggestive of identification with place. Jack Binnington (interview, 26 October 2010) defined the category of a 'Beverley person': 'People like myself, who'd been born and bred in Beverley, that had a great feel for the town.' Hilda Little (interview, 24 October 2008) thought her husband's attachment to Beverley was result of his having been 'born and bred' there. Dick Gibson (interview, 11 March 2010) noted that Beverlonians were the best local politicians:

> One of the finest local politicians in Beverley was ... Harold Godbold ... he did a lot for Beverley did that man. He's a bit like Katy Gray is now ... . She's a proper Beverlonian and she goes for the things that are right for us. And Harold Godbold was like that.

Conversely, non-Beverlonians were seen to lack this sense of investment in the town and might behave irresponsibly as a result, both in local government and more generally. Derek Saltmer (interview, 25 January 2010) complained that the influx of non-Beverlonians was behind violence in the town centre pubs – he preferred to go to pubs where he could drink with Beverlonians. The confluence between interviewees' uses of these terms and their frequent occurrence in the *Beverley Guardian* during the period suggests that interviewees' usage of such categories was not a recent innovation.

Indeed, in the 1940s and 1950s, the category of 'Beverlonian' was often contrasted with that of 'foreigner', a term used to designate incomers:

> Beverley was a close knit community in them days [1940s and 1950s]. If you didn't come from Beverley you was a 'foreigner'. As far as Judy's dad [a Beckside coal merchant] was concerned, anybody out of Beverley was 'foreigners'.
>
> (John Whittles, interview, 27 April 2010)

This hints at the 'local xenophobia' that Snell (2006) considered to be a persistent feature of parish belonging in English settings across the nineteenth and the first half of the twentieth century. Beverley people were considered to have a greater right to local resources than 'foreigners'. A letter writer to the *Beverley Guardian* (23 November 1946) compared the case of a family who had moved to Beverley to escape the bombing of Hull and were subsequently granted council housing with the plight of a 'native' family whom the council were evicting: 'No one can deny the right of anyone to settle where they please, yet in the face of this incident, are the Housing Committee justified in evicting a native of the town from what has always been considered his home?' Les White (interview, 29 October 2010) made a similar complaint at the time of the interview, contending that in the past Beverley people had priority in the allocation of local housing, which was now being taken up by 'foreigners'. Bernard Walling (ERYMS interview) felt that Labour Exchange staff had been less than enthusiastic in helping him to find a job when he moved to Beverley from London in the 1960s until he told them that he was married to a born and bred Beverley girl. At times the distinction between Beverlonians and foreigners could result in open antagonism. Bob Garbutt (interview, 25 June 2010) recalled fights in the later 1940s between local shipyard workers and workers who had moved down from the North East of England, brawls that he thought were fuelled by the belief that the incomers were taking work that rightfully belonged to locals. Fighting between local lads and locally stationed soldiers was common in the 1970s. Indeed, a special police squad was formed to look after the interests of young soldiers in 1978; a Beverley man charged with threatening behaviour towards soldiers told magistrates: 'They deserve it. They come into town and take our girlfriends' (*Beverley Guardian*, 21 September 1978).

In Beverley, working-class 'local xenophobia' frequently found expression in relation to people from Hull. The use of Hull as symbolic 'other' against which to express local belonging was a motif shared with the middle-class Beverlonian identity described above. However, working-class 'othering' of Hull residents had distinctive notes, connected to the perceived respectability of Beverley working classes in contrast with those from Hull. Doris Daniels (interview, 16 December 2009) told how her mother and father had been the victims of local xenophobia when they moved to Beverley to escape the bombing of Hull in the Second World War:

> The Beverley people did treat them a bit rough. They always thought them a bit dirty cause they'd come from Hull and been bombed out … they was a little bit nasty … . This lady, I think I'd got into some kind of argument with her daughter, and of course we was having a go. And Mam come to door, and her mam said to my mam 'you want to get back to Hull, Hull Bulldog.'

Doris' sister, Lynne Norton (interview, 9 November 2009), told a similar family story about the anti-Hull feeling they had encountered when they moved to the town to escape the Blitz:

> Hull people had a bad name. I don't know why but they got a bad name with Beverley people. And once my dad pulled a chap up … and this chap referred to them from Hull as 'mucky buggers'. And my dad pulled

him up, he said 'have you ever been under them bombs?' ... 'Well shut up then 'cause you don't know what you're talking about.' ... They always seemed to have a down on Hull people here.

So, class and status perceptions were implicated in the distinctions Beverley's working classes made between themselves and those from Hull. Jack Blakeston (interview, 10 August 2010) recalled: 'What me mum always said, after the war they built all these council houses and lots and lots of people flocked in from Hull, and she always said it sort of lowered the tone.' George and Hilda Little (interview, 24 October 2008) captured some of the ways in which Beverley people (and, it seems, those from other small towns around Hull) talked about people from the larger city:

> George: There was a chap actually came in from Hessle to work at Armstrong's, and he used to say to me, he said, 'Well if I'm working-class, some of them lot out there', that came from Hull, he said, 'they must be lower working-class' ... cause heck, was there a distinction ... . The women on the shop floor at Armstrong's, they used to come in a train, and they, you used to think that the men swore, but if you got some of them women swearing, they used words you'd never heard of ... .
>
> Hilda: Hull people have a disadvantage: they don't sound educated ... if they were describing what they did last weekend, 'and I goes upstairs, and I puts me frock on, and I comes downstairs, and I gets out and I goes to the taxi.' All their verbs are the wrong tense.

Some interviewees described the differences between Hull and Beverley people as the product of different social environments. Beverley as a market town was contrasted with Hull as a city:

> High School to me meant Beverley High School, Beverley Grammar School ... you'd passed your eleven plus to go there. And we got to this [Hull] Maybury High School [to play rugby], and they were a set of thugs, and the teachers didn't seem like they had any control over them ... you felt they were a totally different group all together. A city environment to being a market town environment ... there was certainly a distinction.
>
> (George and Hilda Little, interview, 24 October 2008)

Bill Andrews (20 January 2010) thought friendliness inversely proportionate to settlement size:

> Hull's never been a place for me really, 'cept when I worked there ... .
> Nothing there for me, nothing there what appeals to me really in Hull, it's just, I don't like big places anyway ... I like small places. Beverley's big enough ... the bigger you get, the less friendly a place gets I think.

Les White (29 October 2010) evoked the rural/urban division as explanation for his gang's territorial behaviour during the 1970s:

> You didn't go into Hull and start any bother there, 'cause you got kicked to fuck ... city people are different from town people, they're a bit wiser aren't they? A lot wiser anyway ... and then when you get into country you're wiser than they are, or you think you are.

Whilst identity could be understood and symbolically constructed through reference to 'others', there was also significant working-class involvement in more positive creations of a sense of town togetherness. Working-class men formed, or were involved in forming, sports clubs that carried the town name such as the Beverley Rugby Union Club in 1959 and the Beverley and District Sea Angling Club in 1967 (Beverley and District Sea Angling Club minutes 1967; interviews: George Little 12 March 2010; Dick Gibson 11 March 2010). Working-class people represented the town in cricket and rugby teams and watched their town teams play (interviews: George Little 12 March 2010; Mick Underwood 16 June 2010; Keith Barrett 2 September 2010). In 1969, working-class men and women helped form, run and play in a Beverley Brass Band that competed nationally, performed at town events and during the 1970s visited Germany several times with the Town Twinning Society (Ellen and Harry Malster, interview, 21 May 2010). Working-class men (and occasionally, women) served as local councillors and thus took leadership roles in civic ceremonies. Working-class children certainly participated in the parades and civic ceremonies that helped symbolise town unity. Many interviewees had been members of Scouts, Guides, and Church Lads' Brigade as children and thus marched through the town on Armistice Day, the Mayor's Parade and St George's Day (interviews: Iris Brown 21 May 2010: Evelyn Frith 10 February 2010). Those who didn't take part directly often witnessed such civic events, as large crowds were reported – and appear on photographic and filmic evidence (Ernest Symmons films, 'Picture Playhouse News'). Children's groups such as the Church Lads' Brigade competed with others nationally in drill and athletics competitions (Beverley Church Lads' and Church Girls' Brigade Records). As Freeman (2013) noted, those who organised local historic pageants hoped to foster community spirit not only by symbolising the unique history of places, but also through securing the participation of a diverse sections of the local population in what was hoped to be community-building activity. Beverley's Town Charter anniversary celebrations of 1973 included a historic pageant in which working-class members took part dressed in historic costume; one interviewee recalled dressing as a monk and carrying a representation of the town's ancient shrine of St John (Ellen and Harry Malster, interview, 21 May 2010).

Those who held different types of attachment to place could come into conflict. Aesthetic emphases on Beverley's tradition and architectural heritage were contested when these conflicted with more personal or practical attachments to place. A shipyard worker wrote to the *Beverley Guardian* in 1965 to protest against the paper's version of the shipyard strike as corrosive of Beverley's traditional shipbuilding industry; he appealed instead to a different kind of connection with the town and its past. He argued that the paper was cavalier in attaching little import to the loss of 400 jobs so long as the ancient tradition of shipbuilding continued and in ignoring the plight of those who would now have to uproot from the town to look for work. 'Most of our fathers were also shipbuilders', he wrote, 'who were from time to time made redundant, and workers would be letting them down if they did not fight for good wages' (*Beverley Guardian*, 29 January 1965). Opposing versions of belonging and identification were also suggested by conflict over a redevelopment project in the late 1970s. The borough council sought to demolish St Andrew's Street, a dilapidated street of working-class terraced houses sheltering in the shadow of the Minster. Residents, some of whom had lived in the street for many years, and had other relatives living in the same street, sought to resist this demolition. In 1977, on the advice of a group of architects, the residents formed a cooperative that later purchased the houses. The cooperative planned to refurbish those homes that could be saved and replace those that had to be demolished with new buildings on adjacent land. However, the proposed building scheme was contested by members of the Civic Society who claimed that the new homes would obstruct views of the Minster from the south. Three individuals put considerable amounts of their own money into fighting the planning proposal in a High Court case that they lost (Birchall 1988: 135–40).

Middle-class conservationism could also clash with working-class interests by obstructing local industry. In the 1960s and 1970s there was ongoing debate about the town's medieval friary, encircled by the Armstrong's factory. Armstrong's applied to demolish the building in 1962. Opposition from con-servation-minded residents secured a preservation order for the friary and Armstrong's was forced instead to expand on a new site to the east of Beverley. The long-term fate of the building remained uncertain across the period (it was later restored and turned into a youth hostel) (Brown 1989). A 'Beverley Friary Preservation Trust', headed in 1978 by the now-retired George Odey, proposed the removal of the Armstrong's site altogether because it was unsightly in the environs of the historic Minster and Friary. Odey suggested that the Armstrong's factory would be better situated to the east of railway on a disused part of the Hodgson's tannery site. Even were this not possible, he argued, and the company withdrew its operations from Beverley, this would only result in the loss of around 200 jobs; these would be replaced by jobs in a stimulated tourism sector. Odey's suggestion prompted debate in the *Beverley Guardian*, inflected with assumptions about insiders and outsiders, and their respective rights to make decisions about the town. Those who wished to keep the factory in its present site stressed the need to safeguard Armstrong's jobs and criticised the preservationists for attempting to saddle ratepayers with the expense of saving dilapidated buildings. A letter writer with an east Beverley address (Grovehill Road) wrote: 'the question may be put as to whether some of those people who want to hack about with our town [by moving Armstrong's factory] actually live in it themselves' (*Beverley Guardian*, 3, 17, 24 August 1978). In the event, Armstrong's withdrew completely from their town-centre site in 1981 (Brown 1989).

These debates suggest a distinction made by Savage (2010), though for a later period, between belonging that arises from 'dwelling' in a place, and belonging that is 'elective'. 'Dwelling' implies the priorities and bonds that arise when one's whole life has been lived in a particular place, often practical though emotional in a way that does is not always amenable to description. 'Elective' belonging is that entered into by middle-class residents who may have moved around before settling in a particular place, and set about discursively investing that place with an aestheticised aura in order to rationalise their choice and establish a claim to belong. When those who valued a place for its aesthetic qualities came into conflict with those whose belonging was predicated on 'dwelling' the clash might be unequal, as Savage (2010: 132) suggests: 'different forms of belonging convey different political resources. Middle class "elective belonging" is readily able to tap planning issues regarding conservation through the awareness of historical referents, whereas dwelling perspectives operate differently, through concerns with how the house can accommodate family concerns' (for 'house' we might read also street, neighbourhood and town more generally).

The 'Berlin Wall', 'Becksiders' and 'Shanghai Shetrivers'

If local, born-and-bred townspeople shared an identity as 'Beverlonian', this was compromised by considerations of class. Stacey (1960: 171) found in her studies of the midlands town of Banbury that class was a more important factor in the social divisions of the town than status as 'traditional' (i.e. local) or 'non-traditional' (i.e. incomer). In Beverley, as with most towns and cities before and since, different residential areas had class characteristics that were all too evident to residents; the identity that residents felt with these neighbourhoods could not help but be bound up with understandings of class. Interviewees frequently described how they had identified with, and felt comfortable living in, distinct parts of town, and ascribed alternate social identities to those living in other parts of the town. Gerald Suttles (1972: 28–32, 52) described this process as 'cognitive mapping', a means by which people symbolically subdivide the complexity of urban space. For Suttles, such cognitive maps relied on widely accepted understandings about the identities of particular neighbourhoods. In Beverley, as elsewhere (Rogaly and Taylor 2009: 6–11; Jones 2012: 120–54), it was clear that such processes could result in stigmatising the populations of some areas, who then had to accommodate or resist such stigma in their own identity construction.

Many residents recognised the simple division of Beverley by the railway line that split the town into east and west. Predominantly working-class residential areas were situated to the east, with wealthier neighbourhoods lying to the west of the railway. Topographical facts (the situation of waterways, the direction of prevailing winds) encouraged the situation of factories in nineteenth-century Beverley to the east, and these factory sites continued to be the principal industrial employers in the twentieth century. Much of the new working-class housing built from the later nineteenth century was therefore situated east of the railway, adjoining the older working-class area of Beckside, which had been associated with industry since the Middle Ages. So, although it was not an absolute dividing line (there was also working-class housing in the western part of the town) the railway was a potent symbolic boundary between areas understood to have different class characteristics. Railway lines as a marker of social space are a commonplace of popular imagination, enshrined prover-bially in terms such as 'the wrong side of the tracks'. Suttles (1972: 235) noted that such physical markers could become 'a point beyond which the gradation in what people are like is said to make a qualitative change'. As Cristina Purcar (2010: 89) has observed, the routing of railways through towns could provide a convenient boundary marker for subsequent town development, with lower status housing and industrial works becoming concentrated on one side of the rails.

The symbolic marker of the railway remained significant across the period. 'I came to know something about men of the working class', recalled the Congregationalist Herbert Abba, of his 45 years' ministry in industrial east Beverley (Abba 1958: 42). George Wigton (interview, 15 February 2010) grew up in this area in the 1920s and 1930s and remembered:

> They always used to say, well they still say, it just depends, which side of the railway lines you are. If you were at the shipyard side, well you were working, you were a cloth cap man, if you were at the other side, you weren't, you were academic or something.

Les White (interview, 29 October 2010) articulated a similar sense of us and them: 'They always reckon you live at one side of the lines you're not wanted at the other side of the lines, cause at the other side of the lines, when you think about it, all the poshies live.' The class divide was obvious to a policeman who moved to the town in the 1960s:

> In those days if people were going on holiday from the posh end of the town … you'd keep an eye on their house … . You had a big east west split in those days.
>
> (Ben Curry, interview, 19 April 2010)

Tom Potter (interview, 24 October 2008) grew up on the Cherry Tree council estate in east Beverley; his father was a shipyard worker and Labour sup-porter but Tom became a businessman and a Conservative councillor. Tom discussed how local politics in the 1950s and 1960s were divided in class terms and how, for him, the railway lines symbolised this class and political dividing line:

> People from my end of the town, they used to call it, he lives on the other side of the lines, which is the crossing, the railway line ... that was a stigma in itself, that people who lived on that side were lowlife. So it was clearly defined. I went to the other side [the Conservative Party] ... when you stood as a candidate in the 1970s you were welcome. You wouldn't have been welcome in 1940s and '50s, you were from the other side of the lines. If you worked at Shipyard or Hodgson's or Armstrong's you were expected to stand as a socialist ... a clear, defined line.

The railway line retained significance across the period and subsequently. In 1977 the Reverend Bruce Hannah of St Nicholas Church asked if the annual Lions Carnival procession could visit 'the Cinderella part of the town', since, 'we who live on the other side of the tracks are totally forgotten in the carnival processions' (*Beverley Guardian*, 20 June 1977). In 2008 the website of the Beverley Civic Society described the railway as a 'Berlin Wall', demonstrating the persistence of this symbolic boundary line (Beverley Civic Society website).

   In fact, this division of the town was consolidated after the Second World War by the building of large council estates to the east, replacing old slum housing across the town. Between 1945 and 1965 the borough council built 1,000 houses, enlarging the pre-war Cherry Tree and Grovehill estates and linking them with the new Riding Fields and Swinemoor estates (*Beverley Guardian*, 20 August 1965). Together these formed a single large conglomeration of council housing, known to many residents simply as 'the council estate'. The inhabitants of council estate housing in this period were undeniably working-class (interviews: William Vincent 25 May 2010; Patrick Mateer 13 January 2010; George Hunter 14 January 2010; Eva White 18 June 2010). There was therefore a growth in the proportion of the working-class population of the town living east of the railway lines, exaggerating the sense of a town divided by class and geography (*Beverley Guardian*, 1 June 1945; interviews: Bill Andrews 20 January 2010; Les White 21 October 2010; Ken Ingleton 23 March 2010).

   Alongside understandings of Beverley as fundamentally divided by the railway, there were micro-geographical divisions, often expressed in terms of status. Working-class residents in the older terraced housing to the east of the lines had, since the early part of our period, observed finer spatial distinctions. Judy Whittles grew up on Beckside in the 1940s and identified a neighbouring street as having been 'posh' (John and Judy Whittles, interview, 10 May 2010). Both Jack Binnington (who lived on Beckside) and Richard Webb (who lived on the adjacent street of Holme Church Lane) agreed that in the 1940s and 1950s, Holme Church Lane was seen as socially superior (Jack Binnington, interview, 3 August 2010; Richard Webb, ERYMS interview). Albert Newby (interview, 12 January 2010) claimed that when his aunt moved a few yards from a terraced house in a back street to a slightly grander house facing onto Grovehill Road in the 1930s, the doctor charged her more as she had moved up in the world. The veracity of this story is less important than the perception of micro-degrees of socio-spatial differentiation.

Whilst the concentration of post-war council housing in the east helped consolidate east/west class divisions, it also contributed to the status distinctions within the working classes. Evidence of a stigmatisation of some rougher council estate streets could be seen as early as 1945 in letters to the *Beverley Guardian*. One letter-writer congratulated the council on appointing a housing manager, 'having regard to conditions obtaining on at least one of the corporation's estates'; another commented on the problems of moving people from 'the slums' into estates without making social facilities available: 'Where this is not done it is unfair for anyone to speak disparagingly of corporation house tenants' (*Beverley Guardian*, 9 June 1945). All across the period, terms such as 'Corned Beef Island' and 'Shanghai' were used for those streets within the council estates that were deemed particularly rough (interviews: Bob Miles 11 February 2010; Keith Barrett 2 September 2010).

It was clear that council housing was regarded as a desirable option for many, including the skilled working classes, during the immediate post-war years of housing shortages, and there were long waiting lists (interviews: Fred Reid 26 January 2010; Gwen Harris 30 July 2010). But by the 1960s, the affordability of home ownership meant that council housing began to be seen as lower-status by some. Janet Thompson (interview, 23 November 2009) was born in 1948 and grew up on the Swinemoor council estate, but by the 1960s her parents wanted to move out, and did so in the early 1970s:

> I think because you got a stigma with it … you were seen to be a lower class of people if you were in a council house. I don't know why but that's how it appeared to be … in the sixties … . And the amount of people round about us that did the same thing … moved out.

Residents of neighbourhoods designated rough by those around them could use stigmatising labels as positive symbols of their own – Anthony Cohen (1985: 60) termed this 'honouring' a stigma. At least in retrospect, interviewees took a certain pride in coming from the rougher neighbourhoods. For example, some of those who grew up in the part of the estate termed 'Shanghai' appeared to have accepted the label 'Shanghai Shetrivers' with good humour (interviews: Les White 21 October 2010; Bob Miles 11 February 2010; Patrick Mateer 13 January 2010). Residents could also use poverty as a positive symbol of their social homogeneity, and therefore togetherness, as in the remark: 'Everybody was in the same boat 'cause nobody had nowt' (Patrick Mateer, interview, 13 January 2010). However, this does not mean that many residents did not experience hurt as a result of stigmatisation. George Hunter (interview, 14 January 2010) recalled that the rough reputation his neighbourhood enjoyed in the 1940s was 'far-fetched'; his mother had thought that the popular label of 'Corned Beef Island' used for their neighbourhood was 'ridiculous'. Pete Daniels (interview, 28 July 2010) grew up on the Swinemoor council estate in the 1960s and rejected implicit connotations of social superiority and inferiority in what he described as the 'myth' of an east/west split in the town: 'I went to school up there [west Beverley], and [know] a lot, a lot of people from that area, and even then I didn't see them as any better than myself or a lot of people from this side.' Neil Cooper (interview, 14 April 2010), an electrician who joined a 'posh tennis club' in the 1970s, did not like to reveal that he lived on the Swinemoor council estate: 'I used to get picked up for matches ... I used to cut through and wait on Swinemoor Lane so they didn't know where I lived.'

In addition to defining their own neighbourhoods in contradistinction to others, residents often found that their own residential areas provided the most comfortable and familiar social milieux. Some had a strong preference for certain parts of the town when it came to choosing a place to set up home. Fred Reid (interview, 26 January 2010) and his wife, Anne, bought their first house on Cherry Tree Lane (to the east of the railway lines) in 1954. Fred's preference was for the part of town in which he had grown up:

> Anne: He didn't want to come up to this end of the town, did you? He wanted to stop Beckside end.
> Stefan: Why was that?
> Fred: I don't know ... I like Beck end and Flemingate way ... .
> Stefan: What did you like about Beckside area?
> Anne: He didn't want to leave his mother.
> Fred: I didn't want to leave my roots ... . It's just the area. I knew quite a lot of people.

Janet Thompson (interview, 23 November 2009) grew up on the Swinemoor council estate and several members of her family had lived nearby on the eastern side of the tracks. In the 1970s, following four years of married life living around half a mile away in a privately owned house on the western side of the tracks, Janet and her husband moved back to a house next door to her grandmother in a street close to where she had grown up:

> I settled reasonably ok when we were four years the other way, but I must admit I was happy to come back again ... I've not really known anything else.

Although residents identified with familiar neighbourhoods, the more positive creation of identification with place through myth and ritual that Cohen (1985) described was largely absent at a neighbourhood level in Beverley. The only neighbourhood in which there was a suggestion of this kind of positive community construction was Beckside in the 1940s and 1950s. Beckside had a long association with the barge trade, and had something of an occupational community, with several generations of 'bargee' families having lived in the area. The neighbourhood contained shops and industry and was positioned some distance from the centre of Beverley, all of which gave it a distinct atmosphere as a separate neighbourhood; indeed, it was claimed in a public enquiry into a planning decision in 1973 that: 'Beckside was regarded as a "little town on its own and cut off from the rest of Beverley"' (*Beverley Guardian*, 5 January 1973). Until the outbreak of the Second World War, Beckside's bargees celebrated their community through an annual water sports day (interviews: George Wigton 15 February 2010; Fred Reid 26 January 2010). There was also some suggestion of a symbolic construction of difference through slight dialectic variations and through storytelling amongst residents, as a former Becksider wrote of the 1940s and 1950s:

> Becksiders had their own dialect words which seemed to be quite different to the surrounding area. The descriptive word 'sleastering' meant a furtive/ sinister/up to no good way of walking ('he came sleastering round the corner'). There were some interesting pronunciations of words such as 'strength' – the 'st' took on a 'th' sound … . Folkloric tales were many – told to amuse around firesides or sitting on the bench at Low Brigg. Unfortunately I cannot remember much of the oft-longwinded detail of these. There was a woman known as 'Seagull Sarah' who lived by the beck. I remember her name was due to her pet seagull which came in to eat off the kitchen table. Also there was the tale of mariners in sloops and barges running aground on 'Tea-Leaf Island'.
>
> (Richard Malton, written reminiscence, ERYMS)

The term 'Becksiders' was commonly used, and symbolised some sense of belonging to a place with its own identity; Becksiders were often claimed to have embodied working-class virtues of hard work, toughness, helpfulness and humour (interviews: Jack Binnington 22 June 2010; Fred Reid 26 January 2010; John and Judy Whittles 10 May 2010).

The limits of identification with place

Identities are not fixed and constant; people claim different identities at different times. Though identity can relate to a wide range of categories, including gender and ethnicity, for present purposes I will concentrate on class- and place-based identities. Beverley interviewees expressed place-based affiliation at a variety of scales, from nation and region down to town and street. For some purposes, class and status were seen as more salient than place in defining the boundaries between 'us' and 'them'. Class and place-based identities also intertwined in various and complex ways. Class could *cut across* place-based identity – for example, most interviewees recognised that there were significant class differences between 'Beverlonians'. Class could also *align* with place-based identities – one's own neighbourhood could be seen to contain people who were similar in class terms, whereas other streets were 'rough', or 'posh'. Writers have advanced the concept of 'relational' identity to capture the multiplicity and fluidity of identifications: identities are always produced through social interaction; thus they are conditional on social contexts, implied 'others', and the communicative purposes of those asserting them (Cohen 1985:12; Edwards 2000: 21; Rogaly 2009: 6; Jenkins 1996: 23–4).

Mick Underwood 's testimony illustrates the different scales at which place-based identity could be expressed, as well as some nuances in the relationship between class and place-based identities. Mick considered that 'there is a defining difference between a Hullite and a Beverlonian', identifying Hullites' 'awful dialect' and fickle support for their sports teams as distinguishing factors (Mick Underwood, interview, 21 July 2010). Within his identification as Beverlonian, Mick had a particular affinity with the eastern half of the town, where he had spent his entire life:

> I grew up in this estate, this side of Beverley, if you know what I mean, not the other side of the track … . Even a lottery win wouldn't knock me loose.

But Mick also sought to distinguish himself from others within that geographical area using ideas of class or status:

> Everybody knows me. But everybody that I want to know, the nice people of Beverley, the decent people of Beverley, the funny people of Beverley, I know. There's some right bags of shite mate, I'll tell you, in this town, there really is, unfortunately … . On there, Cherry Tree estate. It's running with them … guys, kids, females as well as males but mostly males … I mean, I can spot them mate, I've got used to it because I lived on there didn't I.

Although the distinctions reported here were made in the present tense, Mick also pointed out that there were rough people with whom he disassociated himself in his youth during the 1940s and 1950s. He described these rough individuals as:

> People who didn't want to work. People who are, were violent … Riding Fields Square housed most of them. Don't get me wrong there was lots and lots of guys on Cherry Tree that I see today that were good guys.

When stressing Hull's difference to Beverley, Mick temporarily screened out Beverley's internal differentiation; when claiming a working-class east Beverley identity, the status divisions between the respectable and the rough within these neighbourhoods were forgotten. Jack Binnington (interview, 13 July 2010) also alternated between a variety of class- and place-based assertions of identity. Jack claimed he had a particular 'feeling' for Beverley having been 'born and bred' in the town. He also felt an intense local patriotism for his particular part of Beverley: 'I was born and bred down Beckside, and if I could have lived down Beckside, I would have lived down Beckside, 'cause I've never moved far away from it.' Jack was intensely conscious of social divisions within the town and beyond. His sense of class injustice drove him to a deepening involvement with trade union organisation and Labour party activism from the 1960s onwards, a political life that involved meetings outside the town and concern with broader class struggle.

Neither did localism act as a limit on sociability. Though interviewees claimed to have felt comfortable living in a certain part of town, neighbourhoods rarely contained the entirety of their social lives; sociability was organised at the level of the town and often more widely. Friendship groups and workmates, as well as workplaces, were spread across the town and beyond. Identity as a proud Beverlonian did not preclude membership of sports and interest groups were organised at a regional level or located in a different town. Bill Andrews (interview, 20 January 2010) remembered joining the Beverley and District Motor Club during the 1950s:

> They were all working people, joiners, brickies, people off the fish docks ... . There was a lot of Hull people, more than Beverley people.

Similarly, although Mick Underwood (interviews, 21 July 2010, 16 June 2010) stressed differences between 'Hullites' and Beverlonians, he had also enjoyed extensive sociability with people from Hull across his life – his wife was from Hull, and during the seventies he regularly socialised in the city with a group of Hull friends; he spent happy years playing cricket for a Hull team, was a lifelong Hull City fan and currently met a regular crowd of Hull men at a sauna in one of the city's sports centres. Therefore, whilst sometimes stressing a distinction between people from Beverley and Hull, Mick also answered a question about whether there was a difference between residents of the two towns: 'I don't think there is actually.'

Just as place-based identities could be less important in some social contexts, the strength of attachment to place inevitably varied from individual to individual. Peter Cooper described how he broke his social ties to Beckside when his family moved away in the 1950s, whereas his brother did not (Peter Cooper, ERYMS interview 2a). Positive memories of childhood created associations that helped produce stronger attachment to place amongst some. George Little and his wife Hilda (24 October 2008) had different views on Beverley. George was 'born and bred', and had many layers of positive memories associated with the town. He had warm memories of his parents, and his father was also a born and bred Beverlonian. George had been an enthusiastic member of the Beverley Church Lads' Brigade, remaining involved in their Old Boys' group as an adult. He helped set up the local rugby union club in 1959, and he had always worked in Beverley factories. Overall, George identified strongly with the town and had never wanted to live anywhere else. Hilda on the other hand moved to Beverley at the age of 12, attended Bridlington Grammar School, an experience she had not enjoyed and that had prevented her from making many friends locally as a girl. Throughout her life Hilda had had a smaller circle of friends than her husband – the friends with whom she remained especially close had moved away from the town in the 1950s. For Hilda, her husband's involvement in the rugby club had brought unhappiness – she disliked her support role, washing kits and helping with the catering at events. Though we have seen that Hilda considered Beverley residents to be less rough than those from Hull, her appraisal of her home town was downbeat – she claimed there had been nothing to do there for young girls, and that she would have happily moved away.

Because this study was conducted in a single place, the majority of people interviewed were those who had chosen to remain living in Beverley. However, many could talk about brothers, sisters and friends who had left, both for 'push' and 'pull' reasons. Several moved away settle down with husbands or wives met whilst in the forces or whilst the future spouse was stationed in Beverley (which was a garrison town during the war and for years afterwards) (interviews: Derek Saltmer 25 January 2010; Bill Andrews 20 January 2010; Ivy Shipton 17 May 2010). Some left for work reasons, particularly those with specific skills who could no longer find employment when local industries contracted or closed (as, for example, when the shipyard shed hundreds of jobs in the early 1960s and then again in the late 1970s) (Bob Garbutt, interview, 28 June 2010; John Cooper, ERYMS interview). Some interviewees currently resident in Beverley described how they had followed their youthful urge to leave the town. Betty Carr (interview, 19 March 2010) left Beverley as a young woman because she met a serviceman; she went eagerly because she had always had a difficult relationship with her mother, and enjoyed her new life in her husband's West Yorkshire village. Anna Mason (interview, 12 July 2010) always thought she would leave Beverley and did so with her RAF husband in the 1957.

Those who lived in Beverley most of their lives did not always express positive feelings about place and community. Some continued to live in Beverley for practical reasons or the lack of an imagined alternative. Peter Lawson (interview, 4 May 2010), for example, was made redundant from the shipyard in 1978, and subsequently worked on short-term contracts that took him away from his family for weeks at a time. He did not attempt to leave Beverley permanently, however:

> Peter: I don't know whether I'd have left to be quite honest with you … .
> There's nobody I knew who left, they all sort of diversified their work … a lot of lads changed jobs, postmen, and things like that … .
> They never moved, 'cause as I say you couldn't move cause there was nothing, there was nowhere to go.
> Joan (wife): Well where do you go, that's the thing?

Similarly, George Cattle, a worker made redundant from Hodgson's tannery in 1978, told the *Beverley Guardian* (1 June 1978) that he 'does not want to move away from Beverley to find work because he has lived in the town all his life'. This was suggestive of Hoggart's description of long-standing residents in Hunslet, Leeds, for whom their neighbourhoods came to exercise a 'gripping wholeness', which made it difficult to leave (Hoggart 1957: 68).

Neither should the strength of local xenophobia be overstated. 'Foreigners' were soon integrated into the town once some early tensions had been dealt with. Just as for Stacey's Banbury residents, there was seldom long-term hostility between 'born-and-bred' Beverlonians and incomers (Stacey 1960: 165). Bob Garbutt (interview, 25 June 2010) worked at the shipyard in the 1940s and 1950s, at a time when lots of shipyard workers moved to Beverley from other shipbuilding areas, particularly the North East. Initial hostility soon mellowed:

> The Geordies was a bit strange at first but they got to know them ... . They settled, you know, they're still, well there's still a few ... they didn't just come and pinch a couple of years' work, they stayed in Beverley, married Beverley lasses.

Sociability did not exclude incomers. Working-class culture of pubs, working men's clubs and team sports such as football enabled men in particular to assimilate quickly when moving to new places. Whilst some interviewees felt that a distinction between workers from Hull and Beverley was observed in factories, this perhaps depended on the viewpoint. For a skilled worker like George Little (interview, 24 October 2008) at Armstrong's, there was clearly a distinction between the tradesmen (who often lived in Beverley) and the unskilled women from Hull. These workers were often temporary and did not have the same investment in their jobs as the tradesmen, as was noted by a former female worker from Hull (Linda Roberts, interview, 29 April 2010). However, amongst women workers in the factory, who perhaps shared similar skill levels and commitment to their jobs, the distinction between those from Hull and Beverley was less obvious (interviews: Janet Hill 3 March 2010; Linda Roberts 29 April 2010).

Therefore, identification with place was not all-encompassing. It was cross-cut by other types of group identity, including those relating to class and status. Different types of identity might be highlighted or suppressed according to context and in response to different perceived 'others'. Attachment to place could spring from inertia as much as from positive feelings about locality. Common class culture and economic position could quickly overcome any local xenophobic feeling in relation to incomers.

Conclusion

At the level of identification with the town as a whole, the Beverley evidence can usefully be compared with Savage's findings about place-based identity in the 1950s and 1960s. Whilst there is much in the present study that confirms Savage's account – in particular the evidence of a strongly practical element in working-class attachment to place – I believe that he over-simplified the complexity of local identity and belonging in the past in order to highlight the late-twentieth-century novelty of 'elective belonging'. Savage ignored civic pride and celebrations of local heritage and distinctiveness, which dated back to at least the nineteenth century. There is no doubting the extent to which middle-class residents of Beverley 'waxed lyrical' about the aesthetic and historic 'particularities' of the town.

Furthermore, whilst 'functional orientation' captures the practical dimension to working-class expressions of belonging, this formulation implies a lack of emotional depth that is not justified. The failure of working-class people to articulate expansively the virtues of place in the data studied by Savage may have been a symptom of communicative style rather than lack of feeling. As Craig Calhoun (1983: 98) pointed out 'we have a certain investment in the familiar even if it is not what we might choose'. The attractions of the familiar – family, friends, acquaintances and memory – could be strong. Those who remained in Beverley did not do so only because of a lack of alternatives, and many who left were subsequently drawn back to the town. The apparent resonance of terms such as 'born and bred' and 'foreigner', as well as instances of 'local xenophobia', suggested that the town held a place in working-class residents' sense of identity that went deeper than Savage's (2008: 156, 161) portrayal of a functional concern for local amenities and 'family affiliations'. Similarly, the hypothesis of functional orientation neglects the symbolic processes by which people made places meaningful. Whereas Savage found that respondents in Brian Jackson's studies 'did not compare features of Huddersfield with other places salient to them', this could not be said of Beverley residents, many of whom conceptualised a Beverlonian identity through comparison with the city of Hull. Savage (2010) has more recently posited 'dwelling' attachment – an emotional bond with place distinct from 'functional' and 'elective' belonging. This 'dwelling' attachment, in which place is invested with meaning over a lifetime, resembles what Relph (1976) termed 'existential insideness', and more closely matches the sense of belonging that many Beverley interviewees described.

As Cohen (1985) pointed out, identification with community-of-place implies turning a conceptual blind eye to the myriad ways in which the community is divided internally. Nevertheless, those who identified as 'Beverlonian' were fully aware that the town was divided along class lines, and that different residential areas had distinct class identities. As well as their Beverlonian identity, then, interviewees identified at a more local scale with the residential neighbourhoods in which they felt comfortable socially. Though the strength of identity with particular *streets*, exemplified by the traditions and symbolic construction of distinctiveness in Beckside during the 1940s, probably waned over the period, the social meanings attached to the east/west division of the town by the railway lines remained constant. This social division was reinforced by the post-war concentration of council housing to the east of the lines.

I have tried not to over-emphasise the strength of place-belonging. As is now well established, identities are multiple and often contradictory, and therefore it is possible to claim that place was an important dimension of social identity for many during the age of affluence without claiming that it was the most important.

References

Abba, Herbert W. (1958) *To Build and to Plant. Memoirs of a Forty-Five Year's Ministry*, London: Independent Press.

Allison, K.J. (ed.) (1969) *A History of the County of York East Riding: Volume One: The City of Kingston upon Hull*, London: Oxford University Press.

Birchall, Johnston (1988) *Building Communities: The Co-Operative Way*, London: Routledge & Kegan Paul.

Bourdieu, Pierre (1984) *Distinction. A Social Critique of the Judgement of Taste*, Cambridge, MA: Harvard University Press.

Bourke, Joanna (1994) *Working Class Cultures in Britain 1890–1960: Gender, Class, and Ethnicity*, London: Routledge.

Brown, Lucy (1989) 'Modern Beverley: Economy, 1835–1918', in K.J. Allison (ed.), *A History of the County of York East Riding: Volume 6: The Borough and Liberties of Beverley*, London: Oxford University Press, 136–141.

Calhoun, Craig (1983) 'Community: Toward a Variable Conceptualization for Comparative Research', in R.S. Neale (ed.), *History and Class. Essential Readings in Theory and Interpretation*, Oxford: Basil Blackwell, 86–113.

Cohen, Anthony P. (1985) *The Symbolic Construction of Community*, London: Routledge.

Colls, Robert (1995) 'Save Our Pits and Communities', *Labour History Review*, 60:2, 55–66.

Dennis, Norman, Fernando Henriques and Clifford Slaughter (1969/1956) *Coal is Our Life: An Analysis of a Yorkshire Mining Community*, 2nd edition, London: Tavistock.

Edwards, Jeanette (2000) *Born and Bred. Idioms of Kinship and New Reproductive Technologies in England*, Oxford: Oxford University Press.

Freeman, Mark (2013) '"Splendid Display; Pompous Spectacle": Historical Pageants in Twentieth-century Britain', *Social History*, 38:4, 423–455.

Hewitt, Lucy (2012) 'Associational Culture and the Shaping of Urban Space: Civic Societies in Britain Before 1960', *Urban History*, 39, 590–606.

Hobsbawm, Eric and Terence Ranger (1983) *The Invention of Tradition*, Cambridge: Cambridge University Press.

Hobsbawm, Eric (1984) 'The Formation of British Working-Class Culture', in Eric Hobsbawm, *Worlds of Labour*, London: Weidenfeld & Nicolson, 176–193.

Hoggart, Richard (1957) *The Uses of Literacy*, London: Chatto & Windus.

Hulme, Tom (2016) '"A Nation of Town Criers": Civic Publicity and Historical Pageantry in Inter-war Britain', *Urban History*, (FirstView Article), https://www.cambridge.org/core/journals/urban-history/article/a-nation-of-town-criers-civic-publicity-and-historical-pageantry-in-inter-war-britain/9F9E92FE8E957F0B21E553DABD0168C4/core-reader (accessed 9 September 2016).

Jones, Ben (2012) *The Working Class in Mid Twentieth-Century England: Community, Identity and Social Memory*, Manchester: Manchester University Press.

Klein, Josephine (1965) *Samples from English Cultures (Volume 1)*, London: Routledge & Kegan Paul.

Martin, Graham (2005) 'Narratives Great and Small: Neighbourhood Change, Place and Identity in Notting Hill', *International Journal of Urban and Regional Research*, 29:1, 67–88.

Neave, David (1989) 'Beverley, 1700–1835: Social Life and Conditions', in K.J. Allison (ed.), *A History of the County of York East Riding: Volume 6. The Borough and Liberties of Beverley*, London: Oxford University Press, 131–135.

Pearson, Robin (1993) 'Knowing One's Place: Perceptions of Community in the Industrial Suburbs of Leeds, 1790–1890', *Journal of Social History*, 27:2, 221–244.

Purcar, Cristina (2010) 'On the Wrong Side of the Track: Railways as Urban Boundaries in the Towns of the First Transylvanian Railway', *Urban History*, 37:1, 66–89.

Relph, Edward (1976) *Place and Placelessness*, London: Pion Ltd.

Rogaly, Ben and Becky Taylor (2009) *Moving Histories of Class and Community. Identity, Place and Belonging in Contemporary England*, Basingstoke: Palgrave Macmillan.

Russell, Dave (2004) *Looking North. Northern England and the National Imagination*, Manchester: Manchester University Press.

Savage, Mike (2008) 'History, Belongings, Communities', *International Journal of Social Research Methodology*, 11:2, 151–162.

Savage, Mike (2010) 'The Politics of Elective Belonging', in Mike Savage, Chris Allen, Rowland Atkinson, Roger Burrows, María Luisa Méndez, Paul Watt, 'Focus Article', *Housing, Theory and Society*, 27:2, 115–135.

Snell, Keith, (2006) *Parish and Belonging, Community, Identity and Welfare in England and Wales, 1700–1950*, Cambridge: Cambridge University Press.

Stacey, Margaret (1960) *Tradition and Change. A Study of Banbury*, Oxford: Oxford University Press.

Stacey, Margaret, Eric Batstone, Colin Bell and Anne Murcott (1975) *Power, Persistence and Change. A Second Study of Banbury*, London: Routledge & Kegan Paul.

Suttles, Gerald (1972) *The Social Construction of Communities*, London: University of Chicago Press.

Walsh, Kevin (1992) *Representation of the Past: Museums and Heritage in the Post-Modern World*, London: Routledge.

Young, Michael and Peter Willmott (1962/1957) *Family and Kinship in East London*, Harmondsworth: Pelican.

Primary sources

Bernard Walling (ERYMS interview).

Beverley and District Sea Angling Club minutes 1967, ERALS, DDX/1150/2.

Beverley Civic Society Records, executive committee list 1974–5 (records in private ownership).

Beverley Church Lads' and Church Girls' Brigade Records, ERALS, DDX1344/4/289.

Beverley Civic Society website, http://www.beverleycivic.co.uk/planning.html [Accessed: 9 January 2008].

Beverley Guardian, 13 January, 1, 9 June, 28 July, 27 October 1945; 23 November 1946; 7 May 1949; 25 April, 9 May 1953; 23 March, 7, 14 May 1955; 12 January 1957; 9 January 1960; 11 January 1963; 22 January, 29 January, 9 April, 20 August, 8 October 1965; 5 January, 4,11 May 1973;10 March, 20 June 1977; 1 June, 3, 17, 24 August, 21 September 1978.

Beverley Labour Branch minutes, 14 May 1952 (records in private ownership).

'Beverley through the Ages', Programme for the historical pageant procession 'ERALS, DDBB/5/14.

Ernest Symmons films, 'Picture Playhouse News', ERALS, DDX 1369/5/15.

Green's Household Almanack, 1955, Beverley: Green and Son, ERALS, Y/914–274/Bev.

John Cooper, ERYMS interview

Richard Malton, written reminiscence, ERYMS.

Yorkshire Post, 8 May 1981.

8   Conclusion

> I worked in factories, Armstrong's, Hodgson's, but all that's been closed down.
> All the factories closed down, all the dance halls and cinemas, it's all been
> closed down, and all really I can see Beverley consists of now is a load of
> overcrowded shops … . Young people, I mean such as this sort of work [in a
> care home], they don't have trouble getting a job like this, but I mean mostly
> they've to go out of town to find a job and also for entertainment.
>
> (Amy Easterling, interview, 15 February 2010)

Beverley has undergone many changes since 1980, changes that coloured
interviewees' memories of the post-war age of affluence (c.1955–1975). The town's
three largest factories (Beverley Shipyard, Hodgson's tannery and Armstrong's
engineering works) closed in the later 1970s and early 1980s (Brown 1989:
159). At the same time, service sector employment increased, partly as a result
of an expanding local government sector – Humberside County Council and
an enlarged borough council were situated in Beverley from 1972 (Brown 1989:
160). The town grew rapidly in size during the 1990s, from a population of
23,110 to 30,351; this increase (36 per cent) was well above that for the East
Riding (6 per cent) and Great Britain (2 per cent) (Office for National Statistics
website [2]). Much of the expansion was due to the transformation of Beverley
into a residential town for people working elsewhere. Beverley's attractiveness
as a historic market town, its proximity to Hull and its railway connections
helped make the town into a desirable residential choice, and by 2001, well
over a half of the Beverley's economically active residents worked outside of
the borough (Milburn Trinnaman La Court 2006: 5). The town expanded
physically, as developers responded to demand by building 3,500 new homes
between 1989 and 2006, many on green-field sites skirting the historic town
(Milburn Trinnaman La Court 2006: 5).

  Beverley's social-class profile has also changed. There is a perception that
the town has attracted wealthy incomers. The growth in the percentage of
Beverley's male residents (figures for females were not available) in 'middle-class'
socio-economic groups (professional, managerial and non-manual supervisory
employment) exactly matched that of England and Wales as a whole between
1961 and 1991 – from 13.4 per cent to 24 per cent. This figure may hide the

extent of gentrification, since it does not include retirees, or middle-class residents in surrounding villages (Office for National Statistics website [2]). Certainly, Beverley town centre has a gentrified feel today: boutique shops and restaurants proliferate. In 2007, the Royal Bank of Scotland declared the town the top place in Britain for 'affordable affluence', according to indices measuring quality of life and value for money (Hooper 2007).

Many older working-class Beverlonians feel marginalised in a town that they consider was once more stable, more communal and more working-class:

> It's totally residential ... Beverley now is just overflowing with very rich people, who's come from all corners of the earth.
>
> (Jack Binnington, interview, 26 October 2010)

> Ninety-nine percent of people in Beverley must have been working-class people ... there's also lots that are management class now. Certainly, up round this area, none of the houses to the left of the bypass running up to Molescroft are in our range.
>
> (George and Hilda Little, interview, 24 October 2008)

> It was just the fact that you could walk into town and see people you knew, where now you go in and you don't know anybody, and everybody's so smart and its sort of like upmarket.
>
> (Marianne Woolly, interview, 3 October 2008)

> It's just been gradual, it's just been like a takeover. It's far too dear to live in Beverley now.
>
> (Janet Thompson, interview, 23 November 2009)

> Having a community seemed to somehow come to an end in the seventies ... Beverley lost a lot of its industry then, and that seemed to strip a lot of it out, that sort of thing.
>
> (Dave Lee, interview, 9 November 2009)

Though there were local demographic factors, the changes to their town that these working-class residents describe are linked to broader social and economic transformations, including the decline of manufacturing industry, the rise of service sector employment (Newell 2007: 41) and the marginalisation of working-class culture (Hopkins 1991: 277–8; Todd 2014: 338–59). Across diverse British contexts, researchers have observed that working-class populations look back at the age of affluence not as a period of declining social cohesiveness and rising individualism but as one of stability and strong local communities (Charlesworth 2000:10; Batty, Cole and Green 2011: 32; Savage *et al.* 2005: 117–18).

Nevertheless, academics continue to see the age of affluence as the period in which 'traditional' working-class community was replaced by more individualistic, privatized lifestyles. In his recent interpretation of working-class cultural change, Tony Blackshaw (2013) described how an 'Inbetweener' generation, coming of age just after the Second World War, experienced a breakdown in older patterns of life. They had grown up at the end of the age of 'solid modernity', in which community was real and all-embracing for working-class people. The Inbetweener generation came of age as a new era of 'liquid modernity' – globalized, fast-changing, reflexive – shattered 'true' community, which could never return. Whatever instances of community the Inbetweener and subsequent generations might find or found would be inauthentic; in 'liquid modernity', communities represent short-term investment on the part of consumerist individuals, who are only ever partially committed and can withdraw their support at short notice. Blackshaw claims not to be writing a conventional history, but his chronology and conceptualisation of an epochal shift between an age in which community was possible to one in which society was fractured by individualism, fits squarely within the 'traditional-new' conceptualisation of post-war social investigators and historians of the working classes (Klein 1965; Goldthorpe *et al.* 1969; Hobsbawm 1984; Roberts 1984, 1995; Tebbutt 1995; McKibbin 1998). Indeed, a dichotomy between an earlier epoch in which the affective bonds of community were foremost, and a current epoch characterised by individualistic, rational, and contractual relationships has been a consistent theme of social science since Ferdinand Tönnies (1955) in the nineteenth century. It is a theme that can be reworked to fit whichever social change currently preoccupies academics (urbanisation, affluence, deindustrialisation, globalisation).

I believe that it is important to critique narratives positing the age of affluence as deleterious to working-class community, for three reasons: the notion of the age of affluence as a moment of epochal change underestimates the many aspects of continuity in working-class life across the mid-century; narratives of decline in working-class community during this period rest on an overly narrow conception of 'community'; the declinist narrative valorises the 'traditional' working classes, but implicitly denigrates more contemporary working-class culture and social practices.

Continuity

The oeuvre of post-war social investigation can now be set in a broad historical context, and it is apparent that many of these works 'fetishised' a distinction between 'traditional' and new patterns of working-class life (Todd 2008; Lawrence 2013; Black and Pemberton 2004; Majima and Savage 2008). Post-war social investigators conceptualised the changes of the age of affluence by contrasting contemporary lifestyles with a stylised model of 'traditional working-class community'. In 'traditional' communities, thought to have predominated in first half of the century, the working-class nuclear family was not the separate unit it later became, but was integrated into a three-generation, extended-family group (Young and Willmott 1962/1957: 44–75); many wives spent more time with their mothers and sisters than with their husbands, who socialised mostly with mates in the pub or club (Klein 1965: 158–60). The preference of working-class people for remaining close to their families meant that the neighbourhood was the site of dense, interwoven social networks – most people knew most other people and sociability was casual and frequent in the open spaces of the street (Mogey 1956: 87). As a result, there was little need or desire to establish and maintain close intimate friendships, or to entertain in the home. Neighbouring women supported each other in the struggle to survive, providing services and material loans (Klein 1965: 131–8). Subsequent historians have elaborated on this basic conceptualisation of 'traditional working-class community' (Meacham 1977: 58–9; Hobsbawm 1984; Roberts 1984:183–201; McKibbin 1998: 106–63; Tebbutt 1995: 173–185; Colls 2004).

The evidence from the Beverley case-study suggests that the 'traditional working-class community' model should be treated with caution. Not least, the 'traditional' model tends towards an overly communal image of working-class life in the years before the age of affluence. Among the most famous and influential of the post-war investigators, Michael Young, later admitted that his portrayal of 'traditional community' painted the working classes as he had wanted them to be, emphasising the social warmth and underplaying the desire of many Bethnal Green residents to leave the district (Kynaston 2015: 19–28). Indeed, it has often been observed that individualistic competition between residents of earlier twentieth-century working-class neighbourhoods could be vicious (Roberts 1971: 4–10; Bourke 1994: 159–63). Whilst my research did uncover evidence of mutuality, friendliness and a sense of identity in some of the older and poorer neighbourhoods, significant divisions and elements of privatism were also present. It was quite possible for women, keeping home and family with little money and anxious about the status judgements of neighbours, to avoid social contact with the other residents of their supposedly close-knit working-class streets. Furthermore, the imputed chronology of 'traditional working-class community' underestimated the degree of change, including geographical and social mobility and rising living standards, in inter-war working-class localities (Baines and Johnson 1999; Lawrence 2013; Franklin 1989). Though there was apparently a significant degree of population stability in pre-affluent era Beverley, there was much that did not match the 'traditional', gender-divided model of working-class life in the period 1935–1954; for example, many interviewees suggested that their parents had socialised together and that fathers spent significant time with their children. Lastly, the 'traditional' model presumed a certain uniformity across the working-class districts of Britain, whereas in fact there was considerable diversity; working-class people living in semi-detached houses in Bristol had a very different experience of community to residents of northern mining villages (Franklin 1989); mining villages themselves could vary considerably in local social arrangements (Williamson 2009).

The establishing of an idealised model of the 'traditional working-class community' was the first necessary plank in the construction of a narrative of community decline; the second was the depiction of dramatic social change during the age of affluence. For the post-war investigators, as well as for subsequent historians, change was at its most dramatic in the post-war rehousing of hundreds of thousands of working-class families into new homes on suburban council estates. Sociology and historiography has dwelt extensively on the plight of those working-class people, ripped from the cosy intimacy and bustle of the crowded inner-city neighbourhoods and resettled in the anonymity of spacious new estates, many miles from workplaces, shops, pubs, extended family and social networks (Mogey 1956; Young and Willmott 1962/1957; Klein 1965; McKibbin 1998; Hanley 2007; Todd 2008; Rogaly and Taylor 2009; Jones 2012; Clapson 2012). However, quite apart from the fact that many such accounts concentrated on the moment of population transfer, a point when disruption was at maximum extent, the severance of 'traditional' patterns of community living was not so evident in the post-war estates of smaller towns – and in 1961, 29 per cent of the urban population of Britain lived in towns with populations of between 10,000 and 50,000 (Wood and Carter 2000: 417). In towns like Beverley, where a traditional industrial sector survived across the post-war decades, and where new council estates were not so far from the old streets, social disruption caused by resettlement was much reduced. Indeed, in Beverley it appeared that older patterns and practices of neighbourliness lasted longer on the council estates than in the older streets. Recent historical research has made similar points for the small towns of the Black Country (Singleton 2010) and the medium-sized town of Northampton (Tebbutt 2012). So, a sociological and historiographical concentration on the admittedly dramatic and important story of post-war urban reconstruction has helped create a generalised picture of change that ignores the variety of local circumstances.

Josephine Klein (1965: 220) argued that it was not that the new estates *created* privatised, individualistic lifestyles but that 'the break with tradition which a geographical move entails allow[ed] other social forces to make a relatively more forcible impact'. These forces included the individualistic ethos connected to rising living standards during the age of affluence (Klein 1965: 224; Zweig 1961; Goldthorpe *et al.* 1969). However, just as characterisation of an earlier epoch of 'traditional community' has been historicised, so also the extent and transformative power of 'affluence' is now open to question. Shinobu Majima and Mike Savage (2008) note that British sociologists of the 1960s were in the process of redefining their discipline as one concerned with change, and discursively constructed a new, 'affluent' epoch by synthesising and simplifying what were long-term, gradual and complex changes rooted in cultural and political as well as in economic developments. Defining the new epoch through the framework of 'affluence' overestimated the extent to which the working classes participated in rising living standards: areas of urban deprivation were documented in the 1960s that made the notion of an age of affluence look less convincing (Coates and Silburn 1973); for many who moved into new council housing, the cost of rent and travel to work could eat up any rises in real wages (Todd 2008); the purchase of new consumer goods that made homes more comfortable and housework less of a chore burdened many working-class people with significant debt (Rule 2001; Todd 2014: 203).

Furthermore, whilst real wages may indeed have risen for some working-class people, the fundamental routines of daily life for many living in provincial industrial towns continued more or less as they had for many decades (Offer 2008). Indeed, Mass Observation's Tom Harrison returned to Bolton in 1960 and found that in some respects little had changed since the 1930s: 'The areas of Unchange in Worktown life are indeed at times astonishing. For instance, in everyday gesture, pub behaviour, love life, kids' games, religious seasons' (Harrison 1961: 42). Rosalind Watkiss Singleton (2010: 38–9) found that the strength of traditional working-class attitudes in the small Black Country towns of Pensnett, Sedgley and Tipton meant that rising levels of affluence in the 1960s did little to affect practices of mutuality between neighbours and kin, or change working-class approaches to saving and spending. Although I have argued overall for more change than Singleton allows, the Beverley research also suggests that for many working-class residents there was considerable continuity in the community practices. Neighbours and kin continued to be important local sources of sociability for many married women, particularly those in poorer neighbourhoods where material mutuality was still required; the survival of a traditional industrial sector into the 1970s underpinned population stability and density of local social and kinship networks, as well as nourishing a sense of town identity. Many married couples conducted their sociable leisure separately in a manner that was not appreciably different to what has been described in the 'traditional', gender-divided communities.

So, community in the pre-affluent years was often less cohesive than is portrayed in some descriptions of 'traditional' working-class life; at the same time, there was considerable continuity of older practices into the affluent era. Any claims about an overall, fundamental decline in British working-class community during the 'age of affluence' are therefore called into question.

Change

But whilst accounts of epochal change during the age of affluence are overdrawn, there were of course, important economic, social and cultural shifts across these decades. Concern with the decline of a particular, narrowly conceived version of community-of-place – the 'traditional working-class community' – means that historians have been slow to consider new ways in which working-class people socialised during the post-war age of affluence. However, these new patterns of sociability often had a strong local dimension, and should be seen as reinforcing, rather than disrupting, community-of-place.

Although the 'traditional' model has been critiqued, it remains the only lens through which many historians are willing to view working-class community-of-place. Ben Jones (2012: 120–54) chooses to see community in mid-century Brighton only in terms of sociability in, and allegiance to, particular neighbourhoods. Thus, he makes judgements about declining neighbourliness on the new estates, but has little to say about forms of sociability and belonging configured at a wider local scale. For example, there is nothing in his discussion of community about a sense of 'Brightonian' identity amongst his working-class interviewees. Robert Colls (2004: 284) associates working-class community entirely with a version approximating the 'traditional' model, incorporating streets 'held' by women and a civic bourgeois culture forged by men; he claims the complete disintegration of this community in the last thirty years of the twentieth century, and implies that as a result, community no longer exists in the north-eastern region in which he grew up. Bourke dismissed the entire notion of 'working-class community' by pointing to elements of implausible romanticism within the 'traditional' model, and by highlighting evidence of disharmony within historic working-class neighbourhoods (Bourke 1994: 136–69). Though their arguments are very different, neither Jones, Colls nor Bourke give much consideration to the possibility that patterns of sociability unlike the traditional working-class model might still constitute 'community'. It seems that once the 'traditional' model has been discarded, there is no conceptual framework through which to consider the role of local sociability and identity – community-of-place – in working-class life.

Rather than working-class community being something that only existed in the 'traditional' form, my research suggests that the economic, social and cultural changes of the post-war age of affluence brought new ways to build community-of-place. Of course, as living standards rose, some of the older forms of mutuality such as exchange of foodstuffs between neighbouring women became less important; but ceasing to do something that no longer has a purpose is hardly indicative of selfish individualism. Mutual assistance took on new forms: neighbours, as well as extended family, could be important providers of child-minding for mothers going out to work; as Ian Procter (1990) also discovered in a working-class suburb of Coventry, friends, family and neighbours loaned each other tools as well as helping one another with gardening and home improvement projects. The suggestion that many couples were spending more leisure time together as homes and living standards improved is often taken as both cause and consequence of a shift from communally oriented to privatised working-class culture – but a great deal of couples' leisure time could be spent in sociability with other married couples. Any rise in nuclear-family orientation need not preclude wider sociability, since spouses and children could be accommodated into social activity. Cars, often perceived as the symbol of the new individualism, could be used for daytrips, holidays and visiting restaurants with extended family and friends. Improved standards of housing meant that homes could now be used for entertaining. Even television, usually portrayed as the harbinger of a privatised, home-centred existence, could provide a focus for sociability in the home. During this period, working-class people joined clubs to which they had been denied access in previous years. Crucially for the arguments being advanced in this book, much of this sociability took place with others who lived locally – not necessarily in the same street, but in the same town.

Historians therefore need to broaden their conceptualisation of community beyond the 'traditional' model in order to consider ways in which working-class people remade their local communities in the age of affluence and subsequently. Community in social terms can be seen as a quality of social networks that are 'dense' or 'close-knit' – that is to say, in which there is a good chance that the people who are nodes in any individual's social network will also know each other independently of that individual (Bott 1971; Granovetter 1973; Calhoun 1991). There is usually, though not always, a spatial context for such networks, for example a village, town, residential neighbourhood, or workplace (Hernes 1991). In addition, there is an element of subjectivity implied in most understandings of 'community': consciousness of belonging to a group and/or place (Relph 1976; Cohen 1985), and an understanding of the implicit rules and codes that come with this belonging (Durkheim 1984: 64; Colls 2004). The social and the subjective elements of community are tied together, since the identity and cultures of groups and places are produced in part through the meaning-making that takes place in face-to-face social interaction (Shils 1991). Community in these terms – a feeling of identity with place or group shaped through face-to-face social interaction within overlapping social networks – is not the property of any particular historical epoch, but is historically variable in extent (Calhoun 1978: 370). Indeed, the desire to belong to such groups can be seen as a basic human drive; people attempt to construct community in whatever time or place they find themselves (Dunbar 2010: 82).

It is often argued that 'place' and 'community' were less likely to overlap as communications became cheaper, more accessible and more effective in the later twentieth century (Giddens 1990: 21–9) Thus, Liz Spencer and Ray Pahl (2006) depict as 'personal communities' those constellations of significant others we construct and maintain in early twenty-first century Britain; such groupings are not part of localised communities-of-place to the extent that they might have been in the past. Nevertheless, Spencer and Pahl (2006: 194) observed that, though personal communities might be geographically scattered, most of their research participants included local sources of 'fun and sociability' in their lists of important social ties. Furthermore, the working classes remain more likely than the middle classes to live where they grew up, and their personal communities are therefore more likely to overlap with locality (Bertaux-Wiame and Thompson 1997: 154–5; Charles, Davies and Harris 2008: 164). This does not mean that the local communities need necessarily look or feel as they did fifty or one hundred years ago. It is possible that in modern, 'mass societies' with advanced welfare state provision, communities-of-place are no longer valued so much for what they provide in terms of everyday physical survival, but for their ability to satisfy members' social and emotional needs – they have become 'affective communities' (Hunter 2004). Part of my argument in this book has been that the age of affluence was a period in which there was some movement away from mutuality and neighbourliness within the area of a 'yard or a few streets' (Tebbutt 1995: 178) that had comprised the social worlds of many working-class women, and towards the importance for both men and women of sociable leisure conducted with family, friends and acquaintances spread over a broader geography. This was nevertheless still a recognisably 'local' geography – Beverley contained much of the sociability of my interviewees during the age of affluence. Many working-class people arguably valued their local communities all the more as the 'age of affluence' unlocked time and money for sociable leisure.

Implications

This book has shown how working-class people during the age of affluence could take advantage of a greater choice of homes, consumer products and leisure without discarding their local networks of support and sociability, their sense of identification with community or their willingness to commit time and energy in service of others living around them. Although many working-class people did leave Beverley for a variety of reasons, as human beings have left their localities throughout history, many others embraced rising material standards of life without abandoning community-of-place. In short, there is no suggestion in the evidence that the age of affluence led to any appreciable decline in community.

However, narratives of declining community remain pervasive in popular culture as well as in the academy – indeed, the death of community is a cultural trope with origins dating back to antiquity (Williams 1973: 35, 46–7). At least in part, this narrative should be seen as a natural emotional and moral response to social change. But there is a sense in which, when applied to the working classes, the narrative of community decline can be pernicious, since it imputes a cultural worth to the historic working classes that is denied to those in the present. The term 'community' comes imbued with positive overtones, and narratives of a decline in working-class community imply a moral judgement. According to Eric Hobsbawm (1984: 188), what was formerly a working-class 'we' culture – built around a commitment to mutuality and solidarity in poor but supportive neighbourhood communities – became an 'I' culture of isolated individuals. Hobsbawm did not hide his admiration for the working classes' communally oriented culture, which he saw as an achievement they threw away when embracing post-war affluence. Richard Hoggart (1957: 318) also preferred the older culture, writing that, alongside material advances in working-class life, 'the accompanying cultural changes are not always an improvement but in some of the more important instances are a worsening'. Jeremy Seabrook (1984: 4) wrote that community decline was part of a diminishing commitment to collective values that had previously sustained working-class movements such as Chartism, trade unionism and the Labour Party. Avner Offer (2006: 4) argued that rising affluence since the Second World War weakened the 'commitment strategies' inherent in the older communal culture and exposed the working classes to the panoply of present day social ills. Such narratives champion an earlier, communal working-class culture, in comparison to which the lifestyles of recent working classes are seen as inadequate. Historians may thus accidentally collude in the broader denigration of the contemporary working classes noted by authors such as Owen Jones (2011) and Steph Lawler (2008), implicitly casting them as lacking a culture worthy of investigation.

In response to this, I have suggested that it is far from clear that such a 'we' culture was ever foremost amongst the working classes. The present study confirmed that individualism, privatism and family-first attitudes existed alongside communal sociability and mutual assistance in the early, pre-affluent part of the period, as indeed they did later. Authors describing poor working-class neighbourhoods in the first quarter of the twentieth century attributed cultures of mutual assistance to a complex of motives and circumstances, amongst which was simple self-preservation. Those in precarious economic situations made loans to others in need because it was understood that they would themselves need help in turn (Roberts 1971; Ross 1983). Max Weber (1978: 360–3) described mutual assistance in pre-modern villages, seen by some authors as the embodiment of community, as an 'unsentimental economic brotherhood', in part motivated by self-interest; Alan Macfarlane (1978: 5, 196) argued that individualism, calculation and the profit motive were pervasive aspects of English village life dating back to the thirteenth century.

Many older forms of mutuality, the social insurance implicit in networks of exchange, were simply not needed in the age of affluence, as the welfare state, rising living standards and improved housing took many above the poverty line; it would be strange had these forms of exchange continued. Working-class people could distance themselves from the less desirable aspects of the older patterns of community – pressing need for material mutual exchange amongst neighbours, intrusiveness of neighbourhood gossip, intimate knowledge of neighbours' personal lives. But the desirable parts of community could be retained – locally available sociability, companionable exchange of services, help in emergencies, sense of identity, familiarity and 'ontological security' (Walkerdine 2010). Post-war provision of social services eased the stress of poverty, and therefore 'sweetened' relationships between members of extended families, because younger generations no longer found the burden of caring for elderly relatives so onerous (Klein 1965: 299–300). This principle can be extended to wider community relations, since as the need for mutual assistance became less urgent, relationships could be developed with an emphasis on affection, sociability and enjoyment. Family, friends and neighbours continued to help each other in ways appropriate to the new times (help with DIY and babysitting); many working-class people in Beverley were committed to the broader public good during and after the affluent decades, for example working voluntarily as leaders of youth groups and serving as borough councillors.

Indeed, the loss of some aspects of the older communities was cause for celebration rather than mourning. Hobsbawm (1984: 188) admitted that women were the 'most permanent victims of proletarian culture'. Neighbourhood gossip, intense status awareness and the limited social horizons of the old poor working-class neighbourhoods could drive women to nervous breakdown (Tebbutt 1995: 87). In addition to more social freedom for some women, the affluent era also saw both male and female working classes participate in a broader range of associational life. Cultural shifts loosened the grip of a conservative hegemony that reinforced social hierarchy and cast working-class people as deserving or undeserving of charitable hand-outs.

Some writers located the decline of working-class community of place not in the 1950s and 1960s, but in the final decades of the twentieth century, decades that encompassed the decimation of British manufacturing industry and the diffusion of Thatcherite individualistic ideology (Colls 2004: 307; Collins 2005: 149–55; Taylor 2005: 380–4; Offer 2008: 29–30). But even after these changes, community-of-place remained important for many working-class people. In recent years sociologists and geographers have begun to rediscover and rehabilitate community as a concept and community studies as a method, showing that, for many amongst the working classes, local networks remain crucial for everyday sociability and support (for example, Allan and Phillipson 2008; Charles and Crow 2012; O'Connor and Goodwin 2012). In poorer working-class areas, job insecurity and worklessness could again throw people back for material support on networks of local friends and family (Strangleman 2001; Wight 1993; Batty, Cole and Green 2011); those living in more affluent working-class towns and districts relied on their local networks for sociability, and continued to articulate identification with place (Procter 1990; Savage, Bagnall and Longhurst 2005).

Instead of identifying community-of-place solely with the particular social configurations of a vanished 'golden age', this book has suggested that we need to recognise and document how working-class people utilised and adapted local community in response to wider structural change. As we have seen, Beverley's working classes are now a less visible presence – reduced as a percentage of the population, mostly living to the east of the railway lines and no longer working in large factories in the heart of the town. However, there was evidence of working-class community at the time of the interviews. One woman who moved to Beverley in the 1990s, and whose boyfriend lived on the Swinemoor council estate, claimed the estate was: 'close-knit ... everybody knows everybody and everybody is related to everybody' (Hayley Morphitt, interview, 30 November 2009). In conducting the research I visited clubs, societies and pubs that seemingly contained no shortage of community senti-ment. Many older interviewees were surrounded by locally resident family, neighbours and friends who visited and helped them on a day-to-day basis, belying the suggestion that selfish individualism is the characteristic *modus operandi* of modern life. At a moment when the working classes are the sub-ject of a multiplicity of negative and distorting representations, it is time that historians avoided morally loaded declinist narratives and instead traced change and continuity in local patterns of local interaction and belonging, in all their complexity and ambiguity, into the more recent past and across a greater range of settings.

References

Allan, Graham and Chris Phillipson (2008) 'Community Studies Today: Urban Perspectives', *International Journal of Social Research Methodology*, 11:2, 163–173.

Baines, Dudley and Paul Johnson (1999) 'In Search of the 'Traditional' Working Class: Social Mobility and Occupational Continuity in Interwar London', *Economic History Review*, LII:4, 692–713.

Batty, Elaine, Ian Cole and Stephen Green (2011) *Low-Income Neighbourhoods in Britain. The Gap Between Policy Ideas and Residents' Realities*, York: Joseph Rowntree Foundation.

Bertaux-Wiame, Isabelle and Paul Thompson (1997) 'The Familial Meaning of Housing in Social Rootedness and Mobility: Britain and France', in Daniel Bertaux and Paul Thompson (eds), *Pathways to Social Class*, Oxford: Clarendon Press, 124–182.

Black, Lawrence and Hugh Pemberton (2004) 'Introduction – The Uses (and Abuses) of Affluence', in Lawrence Black and Hugh Pemberton (eds), *An Affluent Society? Britain's Post-War 'Golden Age' Revisited*, Aldershot: Ashgate, 1–14.

Blackshaw, Tony (2013) *Working-class Life in Northern England, 1945–2010*, Basingstoke: Palgrave Macmillan.

Bourke, Joanna (1994) *Working Class Cultures in Britain 1890–1960: Gender, Class, and Ethnicity*, London: Routledge.

Bott, Elizabeth (1971) *Family and Social Network: Roles Norms and External Relationships in Ordinary Urban Families*, 2nd edition, Thetford: Tavistock.

Brown, L. (1989) 'Modern Beverley: Beverley After 1945', in K.J. Allison (ed.), *A History of the County of York. East Riding: Volume 6: The Borough and Liberties of Beverley*, London: Oxford University Press, 136–160.

Calhoun, C.J. (1978) 'History, Anthropology and the Study of Communities: Some Problems in Macfarlane's Proposal', *Social History*, 3:3, 363–373.

Calhoun, Craig (1991) 'Indirect Relationships and Imagined Communities: Large-Scale Social Integration and the Transformation of Everyday Life', in Pierre Bourdieu and James S. Coleman (eds), *Social Theory for a Changing Society*, Oxford: Westview Press, 95–120.

Charles, Nickie, Charlotte Aull Davies and Chris Harris (2008) *Families in Transition: Social Change, Family Formation and Kin Relationships*, Bristol: Policy.

Charles, Nickie and Graham Crow (2012) 'Introduction. Community Re-studies and Social Change', *The Sociological Review*, 60, 399–404.

Charlesworth, Simon J. (2000) *A Phenomenology of Working Class Experience*, Cambridge: Cambridge University Press.

Clapson, Mark (2012) *Working-Class Suburb: Social Change on an English Council Estate, 1930–2010*, Manchester: Manchester University Press.

Coates, Ken and Richard Silburn (1970) *Poverty. The Forgotten Englishman*, Harmondsworth: Penguin.

Cohen, Anthony P. (1985) *The Symbolic Construction of Community*, London: Routledge.

Collins, Michael (2005) *The Likes of Us. A Biography of the White Working Class*, London: Granta.

Colls, Robert (2004) 'When We Lived in Communities. Working-class Culture and its Critics', in Robert Colls and Richard Rodger (eds), *Cities of Ideas. Governance and Citizenship in Urban Britain 1800–2000*, Aldershot: Ashgate, 283–307.

Dunbar, Robin (2010) *How Many Friends Does One Person Need? Dunbar's Number and Other Evolutionary Quirks*, London: Faber and Faber.

Durkheim, Émile (1984) *Division of Labour in Society*, Basingstoke: Macmillan.

Franklin, Adrian (1989) 'Working-Class Privatism: An Historical Case Study of Bedminster, Bristol', *Environment and Planning D: Society and Space*, 7, 93–113.

Giddens, Anthony (1990) *The Consequences of Modernity*, Cambridge: Polity.

Goldthorpe, John Harry, David Lockwood, Frank Bechhofer and Jennifer Platt (1969) *The Affluent Worker in the Class Structure*, London: Cambridge University Press.

Granovetter, Mark S. (1973) 'The Strength of Weak Ties', *The American Journal of Sociology*, 78:6, 1360–1380.

Hanley, Lynsey (2007) *Estates: An Intimate History*, London: Granta.

Harrison, Tom (1961) *Britain Revisited*, London: Victor Gollanz.

Hernes, Gudmund (1991) 'Comments', in Pierre Bourdieu and James S. Coleman (eds), *Social Theory for a Changing Society*, Oxford: Westview Press, 121–124.

Hobsbawm, Eric (1984) 'The Formation of British Working-Class Culture', in Eric Hobsbawm, *Worlds of Labour*, London: Weidenfeld & Nicolson, 176–193.

Hoggart, Richard (1957) *The Uses of Literacy*, London: Chatto & Windus.

Hooper, Duncan (2007) 'Top Ten British Towns for Affordable Affluence', *The Telegraph*, 3 September 2007.

Hopkins, E. (1991) *The Rise and Decline of the English Working Classes 1918–1990: A Social History*, London: Weidenfeld & Nicolson.

Hunter, Albert (2004), 'Persistence of Local Sentiments in Mass Society', in W. Allen Martin (ed.), *The Urban Community*, Upper Saddle River, NJ: Pearson Education, 72–88.

Jones, Ben (2012) *The Working Class in Mid Twentieth-Century England: Community, Identity and Social Memory*, Manchester: Manchester University Press.

Jones, Owen (2011) *Chavs: The Demonization of the Working Class*, London: Verso.

Klein, Josephine (1965) *Samples from English Cultures (Volume 1)*, London: Routledge & Kegan Paul.

Kynaston, David (2015) *Modernity Britain. 1957–1962*, London: Bloomsbury.

Lawler, Steph (2008) *Identity: Sociological Perspectives*, Cambridge: Polity.

Lawrence, Jon (2013) 'Class, "Affluence" and the Study of Everyday Life in Britain, c.1930–1964', *Cultural and Social History*, 10, 273–299.

Macfarlane, Alan (1978) *The Origins of English Individualism: The family, Property and Social Transition*, Oxford: Blackwell.

Majima, Shinobu and Mike Savage (2008) 'Contesting Affluence. An Introduction', *Contemporary British History*, 22:4, 445–455.

McKibbin, Ross (1998) *Classes and Cultures: England, 1918–1951*, Oxford: Oxford University Press.

Meacham, Standish (1977) *A Life Apart. The English Working Class 1890–1914*, London: Thames and Hudson.

Milburn Trinnaman La Court (2006) 'Facts and Figures for a Beverley Town Plan', Summary, Beverley: Beverley Town Council and Partners.

Mogey, John Macfarlane (1956) *Family and Neighbourhood. Two Studies in Oxford*, London: Oxford University Press.

Newell, Andrew (2007) 'Structural Change', in Nicholas Crafts, Ian Gazeley and Andrew Newell (eds), *Work and Pay in Twentieth Century Britain*, Oxford: Oxford University Press.

O'Connor, Henrietta and John Goodwin (2012) 'Revisiting Norbert Elias's Sociology of Community: Learning from the Leicester Re-studies', *The Sociological Review*, 60, 476–497.

Offer, Avner (2008) 'British Manual Workers: From Producers to Consumers, c. 1950–2000', *Contemporary British History*, 22:4, 538–571.

Offer, Avner (2006) *The Challenge of Affluence. Self-control and Well-being in the United States and Britain since 1950*, Oxford: Oxford University Press.

Office forNational Statistics, 'Neighbourhood Statistics' website, http://www.neigh bourhood.statistics.gov.uk [accessed 28 September 2008].

Office for National Statistics, 'Neighbourhood statistics' website [2], http://neighbour hood.statistics.gov.uk/dissemination/NeighbourhoodProfile.do?a=7&b=6275090&c= HU17+8SP&g=6380498&i=1001x1012&j=6295074&m=1&p=1&q=1&r=0&s=1472 723887523&enc=1&tab=9 [accessed 1 August 2016].

Procter, Ian (1990) 'The Privatisation of Working-Class Life – a Dissenting View', *British Journal of Sociology*, 41:2, 157–180.

Relph, Edward (1976) *Place and Placelessness*, London: Pion Ltd.

Roberts, Elizabeth (1984) *A Woman's Place: An Oral History of Working-Class Women 1890–1940*, Oxford: Basil Blackwell.

Roberts, Elizabeth (1995) *Women and Families: An Oral History, 1940–1970*, Oxford: Blackwell.

Roberts, Robert (1971) *The Classic Slum. Salford Life in the First Quarter of the Century*, Manchester: University Press.

Rogaly, Ben and Becky Taylor (2009) *Moving Histories of Class and Community. Identity, Place and Belonging in Contemporary England*, Basingstoke: Palgrave Macmillan.

Ross, Ellen (1983) 'Survival Networks: Women's Neighbourhood Sharing in London before World War One', *History Workshop*, 15, 4–27.

Rule, John (2001) 'Time, Affluence and Private Leisure: The British Working Class in the 1950s and 1960s', *Labour History Review*, 66:2, 223–242.

Savage, Mike, Gaynor Bagnall and Brian Longhurst (2005) 'Local Habitus and Working-Class Culture', in Fiona Devine, Mike Savage, John Scott and Rosemary Crompton (eds), *Rethinking Class. Culture, Identities and Lifestyle*, Basingstoke: Palgrave Macmillan, 95–122.

Seabrook, Jeremy (1984) *The Idea of Neighbourhood: What Local Politics Should be About*, London: Pluto Press.

Shils, Edward (1991) 'Comments', in Pierre Bourdieu and James S. Coleman (eds), *Social Theory for a Changing Society*, Oxford: Westview Press, 126–130.

Singleton, Rosalind Watkiss (2010) '"Old Habits Persist" Change and Continuity in Black Country Communities: Pensnett, Sedgley and Tipton, 1945–c.1970', unpublished PhD thesis, University of Wolverhampton.

Spencer, Liz and Ray Pahl (2006) *Rethinking Friendship: Hidden Solidarities Today*, Oxford: Princeton University Press.

Strangleman, Tim (2001) 'Networks, Place and Identities in Post-Industrial Mining Communities', *International Journal of Urban and Regional Research*, 25:2, 253–267.

Taylor, Robert (2005) 'The Rise and Disintegration of the Working Classes', in Paul Addison and Harriet Jones (eds), *A Companion to Contemporary Britain*, Oxford: Blackwell, 371–388.

Tebbutt, Melanie (1995) *Women's Talk? A Social History of 'Gossip' in Working-Class Neighbourhoods, 1880–1960*, Aldershot: Scolar Press.

Tebbutt, Melanie (2012) 'Imagined Families and Vanishing Communities', *History Workshop Journal*, 73, 144–169.

Todd, Selina (2008) 'Affluence, Class and Crown Street: Reinvestigating the Post-War Working Class', *Contemporary British History*, 22:4, 501–518.

Todd, Selina (2014) *The People: The Rise and Fall of the Working Class 1910–2010*, London: John Murray.

Tönnies, Ferdinand (1955) *Community and Association (Gemeinschaft und Gesellschaft)*, London: Routledge & Kegan Paul.

Walkerdine, Valerie (2010) 'Communal Beingness and Affect: An Exploration of Trauma in an Ex-industrial Community', *Body and Society*, 16:1, 91–116.

Weber, Max (1978) *Economy and Society: An Outline of Interpretive Sociology*, London: University of California Press.

Wight, Daniel (1993). *Workers Not Wasters: Masculine Respectability, Consumption and Unemployment in Central Scotland: A Community Study*, Edinburgh: Edinburgh University Press, 1993.

Williams, Raymond (1973) *The Country and the City*, London: Chatto & Windus.

Williamson, Margaret (2009) 'Gender, Leisure and Marriage in a working-class community, 1939-1960', *Labour History Review*, 74:2, 185–198.

Wood, Bruce and Jackie Carter (2000) 'Towns, Urban Change and Local Government', in A. H. Halsey and Josephine Webb (eds), *Twentieth Century British Social Trends*, Basingstoke: Macmillan, 412–433.

Young, Michael and Peter Willmott (1962/1957) *Family and Kinship in East London*, 2nd edition, Harmondsworth: Pelican.

Zweig, Ferdynand (1961) *The Worker in an Affluent Society. Family Life and Industry*, London: Heinemann.

Appendix

Only those people interviewed by the author as part of the research and mentioned in the text are included (all names are pseudonyms).

Some interviews from the collections of East Riding of Yorkshire Council Museum Service are cited in the text but are not included in this appendix.

Adams, Sally, b.1959	Worked in Melrose tannery until it closed, and then an electronics factory in Beverley.
Alexander, James, b.1936	Trained as car mechanic and had a number of businesses including a garage.
Alexander, Peggy, b.1939	Worked as telephonist then clerical work in Beverley offices; worked in businesses with husband
Andrews, Alice, b.1930	Alice met her husband whilst working in Armstrong's in 1951. Alice did not work after marrying.
Andrews, Bill, b.1929	Started work in 1943 as apprentice at Deans and Light Alloys in Beverley. Did not complete apprenticeship and worked in variety of semi-skilled jobs in the town.
Baker, Vic, b.1930	Father of Sally Adams. Worked in various unskilled jobs in Beverley, but many years in semi-skilled job in Melrose tannery.
Baker, Sarah, b. -	Wife of Vic, appears in same interview. Moved to Beverley from Hull after the couple married.
Barrett, Keith, b.1954	Various unskilled jobs, also worked on tours for famous rock bands in the 1970s.
Benson, Jean, b.1933	Sister of Bill Holland. Various jobs including shop work, barmaid, Armstrong's, in army for a few years. Lived in Liverpool briefly.
Binnington, Jack, b.1944	Apprenticed in shipyard, then worked on barges, later became a lorry driver.
Blakeston, Jack, b.1938	Brother of Joyce Sumner. Worked as a motor mechanic.

Bolton, Enid, b.1919	Worked on father's farm then ran a corner shop in Beverley. Husband was a farm labourer.
Brown, Iris, b.1943	Joined the RAF for four years after school. Married twice; both husbands in the forces and lived all over Britain and in Germany before returning to Beverley in the 1990s.
Byrne, Ed, b.1921	Working-class background. Served in WWII, then worked as administrator in hospital, becoming superintendent. Long service as borough councillor.
Carr, Betty, b.1934	Worked in a shop and then married and left Beverley, later returned.
Christopher, Louise, b.1954	Various jobs including managing shops, working as a nurse and as a recruitment consultant. Divorced. Lived on the Swinemoor council estate twice – as a child and then more recently since the 1980s.
Cooper, Neil, b.1931	Worked as electrician at Armstrong's among other places.
Curry, Ben, b.1931	Moved to Beverley in 1962 where he worked as a policeman until 1976 when he went to work for his son's haulage business.
Daniels, Doris, b.1932	Sister of Lynne Norton. Worked in shops, stopped working when married, later went back to shop work.
Daniels, Pete, b.1958	Son of Doris Daniels. Worked for a garage and then as HGV driver.
Davies, Julie, b.1965	Various jobs, including retail and clerical.
Day, John, b.1937	Worked as a caulker at the shipyard, and then as an electricity meter reader.
Day, Margaret, b.1938	Worked in Boots shop after leaving school, and returned to work there after her children went to school.
Duke, Dennis, b.1949	Worked on barges then became a lorry driver.
Easterling, Amy, b.1931	Worked in Armstrong's, Hodgson's and other Beverley factories until moving to Hull.
Fisher, Jim, b.1950	Worked in shipyard as a joiner until it closed and then for building firm.
Frith, Evelyn, b.1928	Working-class background, became a policewoman, moved away from Beverley and married a policeman. Later moved back to Beverley.
Garbutt, Bob, b.1930	Worked as plater at the shipyard, had a side-line as a bookmaker and later did this as his main job.

Gibson, Dick, b.1932	Worked as a cinema projectionist and then for the Coop shop in Beverley before becoming an insurance salesman. Lived most of adult life on Cherry Tree council estate.
Gibson, Joan, b.1934	Went to grammar school and then worked as a nurse, after having children returned to nursing.
Harris, Gwen, b.1935	Moved away from Beverley as a child, came back as a teenager, started working on shop floor at Hodgson's then Armstrong's, worked part-time after having children.
Hill, Janet, b.1926	Worked for 'WarAg' during the war. Gave up work when had children, when husband died got a clerical job in County Hall.
Holland, Bill, b.1934	Worked in unskilled jobs in the shipyard and other Beverley factories.
Holland, Jane, b.1936	Moved to Beverley in 1950s, married Bill. Worked in Deans.
Hudson, Michael, b.1968	Worked for and then took over father's glass-blowing business.
Hughes, David, b.1926	Grew up in Wales but had relatives in Beverley, came to Beverley as a teenager to work as a jockey for a racing stables. Continued with stable work on and off through life while also working in unskilled jobs in factories in Beverley.
Hunt, Bernard, b.1938	Worked for a market gardener and then as a groundsman for Hodgson's sports ground and continued working when the sports field was taken over by the local council.
Hunter, George, b.1931	Worked at Deans and later as a painter and decorator. Became a Labour councillor.
Ibbotson, Gerald, b.1948	Came to Beverley as a child, father worked for the railways. Apprenticed as a printer, became a policeman, then went back to printing.
Ingleton, Ellen, b.1936	Worked in offices in Hull until starting a family, and later returned to work in a solicitor's offices in Beverley.
Ingleton, Ken, b.1934	Skilled engineer at Armstrong's.
Ireland, Dave, b.1938	Went to grammar school. Clerical work including County Hall.
Ireland, June, b.1946	Daughter of Eva White. Went to grammar school. Worked in bank.
Jackson, Dorothy, b.1927	Worked in retail in London, then married an East Riding farmer before moving to Beverley.
Johnson, Bill, b.1928	Worked as crane operator in Hodgson's.

Lawson, Peter, b.1947
: Worked as a plumber in Beverley shipyard until this closed down in 1978 and then travelled to work in various jobs around the country.

Lee, Dave, b.1972
: Son of Lynne Norton. Worked in labouring jobs at caravan works and in greenhouses.

Little, Hilda, b.1937
: Moved to Beverley in 1944, went to grammar school in Bridlington. Worked in offices at shipyard and after having children did part-time office work.

Little, George, b.1937
: Worked as a fitter at Hodgson's and later Armstrong's.

Malster, Ellen, b.1933
: Worked in shipyard offices. After had children became a surgery receptionist.

Malster, Harry, b.1931
: Worked as a joiner at the shipyard.

Mason, Anna, b.1935
: Working-class background; moved away from Beverley when married to RAF engineer, became teacher.

Mateer, Elaine, b.1952
: Worked in shops and offices in Beverley until having children. Second husband Patrick had a building business.

Mateer, Patrick, b.1949
: Worked as a bricklayer and played in bands in the 1960s, later became self-employed and had own building business.

Matthews, Ron, b.1946
: Moved with his parents to Swinemoor council estate in Beverley when he was 16. Had various unskilled jobs in factories and shops but has more recently worked with computers.

Miles, Bob, b.1926
: Bricklayer.

Morphitt, Hayley, b.1981
: Born in Beverley but moved away with family as a baby; returned to live in the town aged 18.

Newby, Albert, b.1925
: Worked as a skilled maintenance engineer at Hodgson's for thirty years.

Newby, Brenda, b.1926
: Brenda worked in clerical positions until married, and she did not work after this.

Nicholl, Anna, b.1920
: Came to Beverley in the 190s to work as a social worker.

Norton, Lynne, b.1942
: Worked in a post office, a printing works and various other jobs including as a bar maid. Husband worked at Deans and at a caravan works.

Peters, Fred, b.1937
: Apprenticeship as a plater in the shipyard.

Peters, May, b.1938
: Clerical position in Deans until the couple had children.

Potter, Tom, b.1934
: Father was a shipyard worker. Tom has been a Conservative councillor in the Beverley Borough and East Riding councils for many years.

Reid, Fred, b.1931	Worked at Hodgson's and then became a lorry driver for Hodgson's.
Reid, Anne, b.1931	Wife of Fred; appears in the same interview.
Roberts, Linda, b.1947	Worked in factories before marrying, including a year spent commuting to work in Armstrong's in Beverley.
Ross, Eric, b.1943	Went to grammar school and was sent to college by Hodgson's, attaining a middle-class career in the firm's chemical works, which survived the closure of the rest of the factory in 1978.
Ross, Helen, b.1945	Worked in laboratory in Hodgson's.
Saltmer, Derek, b.1934	Was apprenticed at the shipyard for two years before joining the navy. After a few years in the navy returned to Beverley and worked in the fire brigade and then as a lorry driver while bringing up a family.
Shipton, Ivy, b.1943	Worked in shops in Beverley. Husband worked as unskilled boilerman at Hodgson's then a hospital.
Stephenson, Peter, b.1945	Worked in shipyard as a welder.
Stocks, Ray, b.1931	Worked most of his life as maintenance engineer, at both Hodgson's and Armstrong's.
Sumner, Joyce, b.1926	First job in market gardens. Stopped work while children young but later worked as a cleaner in a hospital.
Thompson, Janet, b.1948	Clerical work in Armstrong's offices and later County Hall.
Thompson, Pete, b.1951	Worked in the building trade.
Tyler, Andrew, b.1954	In army for many years, and worked in various unskilled jobs since.
Underwood, Mick, b.1937	Worked as shipwright at the shipyard and later in the caravan industry. Had own caravan business.
Vincent, William, b.1950	Had various unskilled jobs in Beverley before moving to Hull.
Walsh, Joan, b. -	Moved to Beverley in the 1960s and has been a member of the Civic Society ever since.
Walton, Matthew, b.1936	Apprenticed as engineer at British Aerospace in Brough, and left Beverley to pursue professional career in aeronautical engineering, later returned to area.
Watton, Ellen, b.1934	Worked in office at Armstrong's, moved to Midlands when married, later returned to Beverley.
White, Eva, b.1918	Mother of June Ireland, June and husband present in the interview. Worked in factories

	after leaving school. Made munitions in Armstrong's during war. Gave up work when husband returned from war.
White, Les, b.1943	Worked on barges.
Whittles, John, b.1933	Moved to Beverley in 1937. Worked in Hodgson's for many years as bricklayer.
Whittles, Judy, b.1937	Worked in Hodgson's before marriage.
Wigton, George, b.1923	Served as infantryman in WWII. Worked in shipyard as construction worker, and later buildings maintenance in various firms. Boys Brigade leader for many years.
Witham, Hannah, b.1932	Worked for many years on the factory floor in Hodgson's tannery.
Wood, Eliza, b.1924	Lived on Swinemoor council estate since approximately 1950, and did not work after marrying.
Woolly, Marianne, b.1929	Grew up on Grovehill council estate, worked in County Hall before marrying a policeman and moving away from Beverley. Later returned.
Young, Jerry, b.1936	Worked as academic in Hull. Lived in Beverley from early 1960s and actively involved with Beverley Labour Party from that time.

Index